Indecent Theology

Theological perversions in sex,
gender and politics

Marcella Althaus-Reid

London and New York

. . . a young camel deviating from her path; a wild she-ass accustomed to the wilderness, sniffing the wind in her lust. Who can repel her desire? . . . And you said, "No! I love strangers, the different, the unknown, the *Other* and will follow them."

(Jeremiah 2: 23–25)

. . . the words זרה ("strange") and נכריה ("unknown", "foreign" . . .) have to be explained according to their particular context; they may mean "strange" but also "different", "unknown", "foreign", "Other", and even any combination of these meanings.

(Heijerman 1994: 26)

This Book is Dedicated to Young Camels who Love the Different

First published 2000
by Routledge
2 Park Square, Milton Park, Abingdon, Oxon, OX14 4RN

Simultaneously published in the USA and Canada
by Routledge
270 Madison Ave, New York NY 10016

Routledge is an imprint of the Taylor & Francis Group

Transferred to Digital Printing 2005

© 2000 Marcella Althaus-Reid

Typeset in Times by
Exe Valley Dataset Ltd, Exeter, Devon, England

British Library Cataloguing in Publication Data
A catalogue record for this book is available
from the British Library

Library of Congress Cataloguing in Publication Data
A catalog record for this book has been requested

ISBN 0-415-23603-7 (hbk)
ISBN 0-415-23604-5 (pbk)

Indecent Theology

All theology is sexual theology.

Indecent Theology is sexier than most.

What can sexual stories from fetishism and sadomasochism tell us about our relationship with God, Jesus and Mary?

Isn't it time the Christian heterosexuals came out of their closets too?

By examining the dialectics of decency and indecency and exploring a theology of sexual stories from the margins, this book brings together for the first time Liberation Theology, Queer Theory, post-Marxism and Postcolonial analysis in an explosive mixture. *Indecent Theology* is an out-of-the-closet style of doing theology and shows how we can reflect on the Virgin Mary and on Christology from sexual stories taken from fetishism, leather lifestyles and transvestism.

The point of departure is the understanding that every theology implies a conscious or unconscious sexual or political praxis, based on reflections and actions from certain accepted social codifications. These are codifications which configure our Christian visions of life and mystical projections relating human experience to the sacred. In theology, and in revolutionary theology, it is discontinuity and not continuation which is most valuable and transformative, so the location of excluded areas in theology is crucial. For instance, poverty and sensuality as a whole has been marginalised from theology. Why does a theology from the poor need to be sexually neutral, a theology of economics which excludes their desires? And what do those desires tell us about Christ in Latin America? The gap between Liberation Theology and Postcolonial Theory is one of identity and consciousness, but the gap between a Feminist Liberation Theology and an Indecent Theology is one of sexual honesty.

Indecent Theology is based on the sexual experiences of the poor, using economic and political analysis while unveiling the sexual ideology of systematic theology. Theology is a sexual act and Indecent Theologians are called to be sexual performers of a committed praxis of social justice and transformation of the structures of economic and sexual oppression in their societies.

Marcella Althaus-Reid is Lecturer in Christian Ethics and Practical Theology at the University of Edinburgh. She is a Latin American theologian who trained during the years of political conflict in the southern cone of South America.

Contents

Introduction

The fragrance of Women's Liberation Theology: odours of sex and lemons on the streets of Buenos Aires

The police cars arrived and the policemen started to criticise me for (what I consider to be) my right to dress without using underwear.
– I am a sexy woman. What would you like me to do about it?
– This is a lack of respect to morality – said one of the policemen.
– If you say so . . . Fine, I'll promise then never to leave my house again without my pants on.

(Estrada 1996: 19)

[Ironic] Preach the Gospel! . . . How has the Gospel been preached, till now, I wonder? [Serious] As a missionary in Peru, I tell you that these (*Coya*) women were taught to pray to the saints but have not even been taught to dress themselves or behave in a moral way in the streets. They sit for a second and . . . Can you imagine? No underwear, the streets are their toilets. . . . [laughter].

(From a sermon heard in a radio programme, Radio Colonia,
Uruguay, in the 1980s, referring to the fact that Coya women do
not use underwear and perform their necessities by squatting
in the streets without even lifting their long skirts.)

Should a woman keep her pants on in the streets or not? Shall she remove them, say, at the moment of going to church, for a more intimate reminder of her sexuality in relation to God? What difference does it make if that woman is a lemon vendor and sells you lemons in the streets without using underwear? Moreover, what difference would it make if she sits down to write theology without underwear? The Argentinian woman theologian and the lemon vendors may have some things in common and others not. In common, they have centuries of patriarchal oppression, in the Latin American mixture of clericalism, militarism and the authoritarianism of decency, that is, the sexual organisation of the public and private spaces of society. However, there may be differences too. The lemon vendor sitting in the street may be able to feel her sex; her musky smell may be confused with that of her basket of lemons, in a metaphor that brings together sexuality and economics. But the Argentinian theologian may be different. She may keep her underwear on at the moment of prayer, or whilst reflecting on salvation; and maybe the smell of her sex doesn't get mixed with issues of theology and economy. Writing theology without underwear may be punishable by law, who knows. An act of gross indecency such as that of the prostitute woman described by the Mexican novelist Josefina Estrada seems to be, in the words of the policeman, an action against the moral order of the country. Yet, an Argentinian feminist theologian may want to do, precisely, that. Her task may be to deconstruct a moral order which is based on a heterosexual construction of reality, which organises not only categories of approved social and divine interactions but of economic ones too. The Argentinian theologian would like then to remove her underwear to write theology with feminist honesty, not forgetting what it is to be a woman when dealing with theological and political categories. I should call such a theologian, indecent, and her reflection, Indecent Theology. Indecent Theology is a theology which problematises and undresses the mythical layers of multiple oppression in Latin America, a theology which, finding its point of departure at the crossroads of Liberation Theology and Queer Thinking, will reflect on economic and theological oppression with passion and imprudence. An Indecent Theology will question the traditional Latin American field of decency and order as it permeates and supports the multiple (ecclesiological, theological, political and amatory) structures of life in my country, Argentina, and in my continent.

The issue of lemon vendors without underwear has never been a theological issue in Latin America, yet a whole theological story and history may be revealed through them – for instance, a criticism which ranges from the *Conquista* of Latin America to militarism and theology. But first, before coming to the discussion on theology (which needs to be on Liberation Theology and which will set the basis for our Indecent Theology), we need to reflect on aspects of the genesis of Latin American theology. We need to consider the end of the Grand Narratives in Latin America, or at least the end of the first one. Allow me to start by considering you as a prospective tourist to Buenos Aires. Allow me to advise you on that, as the *Porteña* that I am (a woman from the port of Buenos Aires).

In Buenos Aires

If you visit my city, Buenos Aires, please try to go and see the women lemon vendors who sit in the streets of some neighbourhoods. Go, for instance, to the old marketplace of Constitución, where my mother used to buy a chicken still warm, with its feathers, and apples which had not yet lost the dust of the Patagonian trees. Please go for a walk around the sunny streets of my *barrio*, San Telmo, where stray dogs sleep in the doors of abandoned buildings, and prostitutes buy their newspapers at siesta time under the intense heat of summer. There is usually a sweet smell, that mixture of street garbage at the junctions of the Avenue Nueve de Julio, which mixes with the smells of flowers and baskets of lemons, onions and fresh herbs sold by the

women who sit on the pavement. In summer they sweeten the air with
parsley and lemons, but can you smell the odours of their sex? Perhaps they
do not have underwear while they sit there with lemons and children, and
give you change while wrapping parsley. Look at their long, lustrous black
plaits and their delicate indigenous faces. Hear the song of their voices
calling the passers-by to buy their merchandise. They have singing voices
with polite accents: *'Ay señora me compra unos limoncitos, que están bién
lindos pué . . .'* ('Madam, please buy from me some nice lemons, they are so
good . . .'). See if they have their babies wrapped in cloth, hanging at their
backs, as is traditionally done, or if the children sleep in a fruit box,
protected with blankets and knitted shawls. Then, go to one of the many
coffee shops of the city, where people from my country traditionally discuss
politics, philosophy and religion. The places where they feel free to say *'curas
de mierda'* (priests are shit) and *'este es un gobierno de ladrones'* (the
government is full of thieves). These are two of the most popular expressions
of my people, almost proverbial. Go to these places where Argentinians
exercise public catharsis and vernacular confessions amongst friends and
strangers. The coffee shops of Buenos Aires, where revolutions have been
planned, liberation theologians discussed Christology and Borges wrote his
poems. Go and sit at one of the old marble tables and ask for a *cortado,* the
traditional dark coffee with milk served in small white cups, and think.
Think about what you thought. Impressions in foreign lands are so deceptive. Those lemon vendors can tell you a few things about postmodernism,
for instance. Perhaps they have not heard of Liberation Theology but they
know about the end of the Grand Meta-narrative, and not from reading
Lyotard. You have just seen the lemon vendors in the streets of Constitucion
or San Telmo. You have seen the witnesses, moreover, the subjects of one
of the most important postmodern phenomena of fragmentation and
dissolution which happened 500 years ago in Latin America. These women
may still speak their indigenous language apart from Castilian Spanish and
may also still respect the faces of *La Pachamama* (the Goddess Earth of the
Incas) in their lives, but their epistemological and theological universe
collapsed centuries ago. It lost its public credibility with the *Conquista* of
Latin America, with Christianity and European rule. Other discourses of the
sacred had come to sustain other laws and justice, and forms of love in their
countries. On the small cards they keep in their pockets, or beside the baskets
of fruits and vegetables, there is no place for The Mother of Cosmic Time of
the Incas (although *La Pachamama* never had a physical representation; she
is the earth). The daughters of the Inca Empire lost their narratives. They
now worship the medieval dressed figurine of the Virgin Mary with its
oversize crown and God-prince in its arms. Few of them may be able to
decode the intricacy of the Virgin Mary's ancient European dress and
mantle. Besides, the Virgin Mary is a fashion figurine, a dress and a cloak,
decorated with a face and two hands (the hands are useful to sustain a rose,
or some beads or a child). The Virgin Mary is overdressed, and contrary to

the lemon vendors the smell of her sex (even if statues were alive) would be difficult to perceive. Probably these women and children sitting in the streets with their merchandise do not remember that they are miraculous survivors of one of the greatest destructions of the Grand Narratives the world has ever seen. It can be dated, marked in history. It happened around the year 1492, with the invasion of the continent today we call *América* (even the name of the continent perished in the destruction) and it signified the concrete, material breakdown of everything their world knew at that time. The outcome of the destruction of the Grand Meta-narratives of Latin American high civilisations can be seen in the everyday lives of women such as the lemon vendors and the women theologians in the streets of Buenos Aires. The everyday lives of people always provide us with a starting point for a process of doing a contextual theology without exclusions, in this case without the exclusion of sexuality struggling in the midst of misery.

The continuation of Liberation Theology

A living metaphor for God, sexuality and the struggle in the streets of Buenos Aires comes from the images of lemons vendors. A materialist-based theology finds in them a starting point from which ideology, theology and sexuality can be rewritten from the margins of society, the church and systematic theologies. Our point of departure is the understanding that every theology implies a conscious or unconscious sexual and political praxis, based on reflections and actions developed from certain accepted codific-ations. These are theo/social codifications which configure epistemologies, visions of life and the mystical projections which relate human experience to the sacred. As an Argentinian liberation theologian myself, who received her theological education during the difficult times of the churches' struggle against the dictatorships of the 1970s, I am aware that in theology it is not stability but a sense of discontinuity which is most valuable. The continuousness of the hermeneutical circle of suspicion and the permanent questioning of the explanatory narratives of reality implies, precisely, a process of theological discontinuity. As part of this process, the location of areas of exclusion in theology is one of crucial importance; for instance, poverty and sensuality as a whole (and not as separate units) has been marginalised in theology. A theology from the poor needs also to be a sexual theology, a theology of economics and desires that have been excluded from our way of 'doing theology' as a second act. I am referring here to the exclusionary process of the theology which used to be called *la caminata*, or 'the walking' process of reflecting and acting–reflecting–acting on historical experiences from the marginalised people of God (Althaus-Reid 1993: 31–41). What has been excluded from Liberation Theology has been the result of a selective process of contexts of poverty and experiences of marginalisation in the continent. For instance, Liberation Theology is a rural theology and the context provided by peasant communities has been privileged sometimes at the expense of the life of the urban poor. The urban poor women of any important Latin American city such as Buenos Aires, Santiago or Sao Paulo live in circumstances which are very different from their sisters in *el Norte Argentino* or the mountains of Perú. For a start, urban poor women do not have the homogenous cultural or religious background, or even the extended family-based circle which provides peasant women with some commonalities in their struggle. The lemon vendors from Buenos Aires may have been peasant women before emigrating to the big city looking for economic survival for themselves and their families but they have then been conformed to a life which resembles more the life of guerrilla women than that of women of the countryside. The life experiences of poor urban women have the toughness of the struggle for survival in the dangerous and chaotic conditions of big cities. Not only does their economic struggle test them every day but there is a mixture of poverty and sexuality which makes of these women sometimes *unusual* poor women, and *unusual* Christian believers too. This unusualness is the condition of their indecency, that is, of the subversion of sexual and gender codes in their lives as a result of their struggle for life and dignity. I know, because once I was one of them, a poor woman on the streets of Buenos Aires and I am indecent enough to be able to reflect with theological honesty on issues of women, economic struggle, images of God and the flow of sexual desires.

My purpose in this book is not to demolish Liberation Theology *a la Europea* (in a European academic fashion), but to explore the contextual hermeneutical circle of suspicion in depth by questioning the traditional liberationist context of doing theology. In this way the project of Indecent Theology represents both a continuation of Liberation Theology and a disruption of it. I have taken Liberation Theology as my basic theological reference because this is my theological stand, in which I have been professionally educated and from which base I worked in deprived communities both in Latin America and in Britain. I still emphatically affirm the validity of Liberation Theologies as crucial in processes of social trans-formation and superior to idealistic North Atlantic theologies. However, Liberation Theology needs to be understood as a continuing process of re-contextualisation, a permanent exercise of serious doubting in theology. By 'serious doubting' I do not mean adding new contextual perspectives, such as the ones provided by the living metaphors of God and sexuality in the images of lemon vendors, to an established theological discourse. That would be good but insufficient and would allow colonial theology to con-tinue with the traditional androcentric methodology which tends to absorb and adapt the most radical elements which can arise from the margins. Serious doubting as a theological method re-contextualises Liberation Theology by questioning those very hermeneutical principles which led liberationists to be indifferent to the reality of lemon vendors in the first place. Amongst liberationists, the fact that there is no such a thing as a neutral theology is well understood; neither can involuntary omissions in issue-based hermeneutical circles be justified as mere distractions. More than ten years ago, I was involved in a church project trying to identify a relevant orthopraxis for a parish belonging to a militant Protestant church of Buenos Aires. After two years of popular bible readings and much discussion, and before reaching a conclusive decision on our praxis, we suddenly noticed that our church was full of beggars. The subjects of our praxis were already there, ignoring our meetings and discussions; it only required from us the gift to look around us. That parish was located in the midst of the city, and the area was frequented by beggars looking for food and occasional shelter during the day. When I asked why it took us so long to discover that our praxis should be one which prioritised beggars as theological partners for the ongoing orthopraxis of our church, I received a simple yet truthful answer. The city was full of beggars but we had never seen them, because one does not see what one does not want to see. Women beggars in particular are extremely deprived people who hide themselves in big cities like Buenos Aires because they are scared of the police, of men in general or just ashamed of their poverty and destitution. However, we became used to walking in the city without wanting to see them, because we were un-prepared for the challenges they brought to us. In a similar way, a materialist theology such as Liberation Theology has been walking in the streets without noticing the life of the rebellious poor urban women who do not use underwear, and the richness of the metaphors of God, based on the interface between their sexuality and poverty. This challenges us not only to ask different questions but also to undertake a different way of doing con-textual theology. This is a concrete materialist theology which understands that the dislocation of sexual constructions goes hand in hand with strategies for the dislocation of hegemonic political and economic agendas.

Feminist Liberation Theology: the *Caminata* continues

Feminist Liberation Theology, growing from a strong commitment to the life of poor women, has made a very important contribution towards androcentric dislocations in theology worldwide. However, as liberation theologians we are not immune to idealism and romantic visions of femininity in accordance with much contested, yet still normative theological views of gender and sexuality. *Machismo* in Latin America creates a strong base of assumptions and understandings in different aspects of reality by the pervasiveness of its sexual beliefs reinforced by the genderised linguistic universes of the Spanish and Portuguese languages. On many occasions, Feminist Liberation Theologies have taken for granted the male/female sexual identity and gender constructions in theology, striving not for sexual disruption and difference in order to produce an epistemological paradigm shift, but for complementarity. Gender identities have not been seen for what they are, the performative acts of the representation of sexuality (Butler 1990: 5). Sexuality is an unnatural conceptualisation of identities in struggle.

The gap between Liberation Theology and a Postcolonial Theology is one of identity and consciousness. The gap between a Feminist Liberation Theology and an Indecent Theology is one of sexual honesty. The consequences of an analysis of sexual constructions carry important implications in any contextual theology. Basically they destabilise the sexual foundations of economic and political theories, and unveil the sexual ideology of systematic (even liberationist) theology. Theology is then seen in its true nature as being a sexual project from its epistemological foundation based on a sexed understanding of dualistic relationships and its legitimatory role. Can Liberation and Feminist Liberation Theology liberate while still complying with these sexually hegemonic epistemologies?

Indecent Theology is a book on Sexual Political Theology intended as a critical continuation of Feminist Liberation Theology using a multi-disciplinary approach and drawing on Sexual Theory (Butler; Sedgwick; Garber), Postcolonial criticism (Fanon, Cabral, Said), Queer studies and theologies (Stuart; Goss; Weeks; Daly), Marxist studies (Laclau and Mouffe; Dussel), Continental Philosophy (Derrida; Deleuze and Guattari; Baudrillard) and Systematic Theology. This text is divided into five chapters, in which the process of de-hegemonisation of theology as a sexual normative ideology is contested as a methodology, while expanding the reflection on women and poverty.

Chapter 1, 'Indecent proposals for women who would like to do theology without using underwear' is an introductory chapter. It provides the methodological foundation for the rest of the book, arising from the question posited to us by the lemon vendors from Buenos Aires. Considering these women as the real subjects and living metaphors of theology, the chapter evolves exposing the economic mechanisms of production in Liberation Theology, and showing how poor women and sexual dissidents are located in the process of organisation of systematic theologies. This chapter uses postcolonial criticism in relation to Liberation Theology and Sexual Theory, including Feminist Anthropology in relation to Mariology. It engages with modernity and postmodernity from a Latin American perspective as necessary to consider the cycles of construction and deconstruction of religious Grand Narratives in the continent since the *Conquista*. The chapter as a whole is an introduction to a critical review of Liberation and Feminist Liberation Theology, and to a methodological (indecent) proposal.

Chapter 2, 'The indecent Virgin', offers the method of *indecenting* as an alternative for reflection on the Virgin Mary, as Mariology constitutes a key element around which Christianity and political hegemonies have been closely allied in Latin America. It asks questions pertaining to the figure of the theological woman writer. What is feminist theological *Ecriture*? What sort of ontological and economic investments are theologians contributing to when they create Mariologies? This chapter takes the sexual metaphors of Christianity to the border limits of the relation between metaphor and history in the Latin American context. If it is true that theology has always kept an ambiguous position between metaphorical and historical truths, Christianity in Latin America has blurred their frontiers according to convenience. In the life of the poor, and amongst poor women, there is no such sharp distinction between the metaphors of the incarnation and its factual veracity. Therefore it would be inappropriate for a materialist-based theology to discuss Mariology or Christology without accepting this starting point of blurred metaphorical truths. From there the chapter engages with indecent forms of popular Mariology from the cultural grounds of the poor urban dwellers of Buenos Aires. These are examples of the sexual deconstructions produced by the urban rebellious poor.

Chapter 3, 'Talking obscenities to theology' further develops the methodology presented in the *indecenting* of the Virgin Mary into a per/version, that is, deliberately taking what is considered as the wrong way in the *Metà-ódos* or methodological road. Per/verting deconstructs traditional elements of Liberation Theology such as solidarity, and finds in it the trace of homosolidarity (Sedgwick 1990) while using Sartre's concepts of viscosity and obscenity to reflect what is behind the theological concepts of purity and transcendence (Sartre 1956: 604). This is then applied to a Christological understanding as coming from sexual marginal epistemologies, such as the Bi/Christ (Bisexual Christ) model, and reflects on the relationship between lust and resurrection.

Chapter 4, 'The theology of sexual stories' develops the full hermeneutical circle of an Indecent Theology, based on the sociology of sexual stories, and the role they fulfil in communities especially amongst the poor. This chapter engages theologically with what Rubin calls stories from the bottom of the sexual pyramid (fetishism; 'leather' practices) apart from the stories from the top of the pyramid (*out-of-the-closet-heterosexual* stories[1]) (Rubin 1984: 279). These are sexual stories which come from magazines and newspapers engaged in dialogue with theology and with the symbolism of images and adverts in 'leather' magazines following Barthes' analysis of the *punctum*. The Latin American sexual stories help us to discern the rebelliousness manifested by the poor in their popular carnivals, discussing sexual excesses and nationalistic quests in the struggle for liberation from political, sexual and Christian oppression.

Chapter 5, 'Grondes medidas económicas: big economic measures: conceptualising global erection processes' considers globalisation from a sexual, Indecent Theological perspective. What are the relationships between a theology of sexual stories using a per/version methodology and the economic assumptions and facts of the life of poor people? How does the external debt as contracted in Argentina during the 1970s relate to the case study of the 'shrinking penis' in Ghana in 1997? Hegemonic sexuality and witchcraft mentality can no longer be considered irrelevant but on the contrary are constitutive of current economic thinking and economic relations amongst people in poor countries. Which political postcolonialist analysis can be drawn from there and how does it relate to a theology from the margins? What does the Drag Queen dressed as the Virgin Mary during a carnival procession have to say about developmental paradigms? To reflect on questions like these we explore elements from sexual theory and post-Marxist theory related to identity and representation which are used to do a sexual re-reading of Marxist theology in Latin America (Dussel). Indecent Theology is the opposite to a sexual canonical theology, concerned with the regulation of amatory practices justified as normative by economic infra-structural models where anything outside hegemonic patriarchal hetero-sexuality is devalued and spiritually alienated.

Sexuality is a complex issue and so is theology. The continuous exchange and dialogue that sexual theories, the sociology of sexual stories, new political thought and postmodernism provide us with, together with the hermeneutical circle of suspicion, are crucial elements necessary for any theological reflection which wants to disentangle liberation from colonial-ism, and gender quality theories from other quests (or the quest of the *Other*) of plurality and difference in sexual identities. Of course, in the end it is our historical experience as theologians, forged in the struggle with political, sexual and theological hegemonies, which determines the terms of this ongoing dialogue. In this case, the multidisciplinary dialogue of this book engages deeply with my own life as nurtured in the struggle against dictatorial regimes in my country, and the intellectual and Christian challenges that they provided me with as a Latin American woman brought up in the poverty of Buenos Aires.

1 Indecent proposals for women who would like to do theology without using underwear

The collapse of the Grand Narratives of Latin America: theology and sexual mutilations

The Grand Narratives, or the authoritative discourses which sustain everyday life, which Gramsci spoke of when writing about the common sense or common order of things which are ideologically constructed yet have assumed a natural and almost biological presence in our life (Gramsci 1971: 33), collapsed in Latin America over the course of a few years. Cultural, religious, socio-political discourses, economy and science, and philosophical cosmovisions which defined identity, meaning and patterns of social organisation and sexual constructions were obliterated from the earth. Even language was erased. 'Tongues' were lost; mother tongues were buried while human tongues were cut from mouths. Women's tongues were silenced for centuries. What survived entered into a covenant of silence, and since then it has never fully spoken again. Following Jacques Lacan, we may say that it was a silence of the magnitude of planets, silenced as if by a set of Newtonian laws, replaced by unified field theory and leaving behind anything outside the new cosmovision. 'We will never know what can happen to a reality till the moment that this reality has been definitively reduced by inscribing it in a language' (Lacan, in Miller 1990: 357–60). Unified field theories resolve perplexity, avoid relationalism and install laws assigned to points of space or space-time as particulars. Precisely, the resolution of perplexity (plurality) in Latin America was done in material ways. 'From some people the buttocks were cut, to others the thighs, or the arms . . . cutting hands, noses, tongues and other pieces from the body, eaten alive by animals and (cutting) women's breasts' (Todorov 1987: 151). These mutilation rituals, paraphrasing Lacan, could be compared to the cutting off of the breasts of truth, the reductionism into a new bodily order, that is, humanity reduced to one formula, one law of union and compulsion. This required a massive mutilation. The need for Grand Narratives always takes with it some cuttings and mutilations in itself. Latin American theology comes from that, a mutilation of symbolic knowledge such as theology, politics, economics, science and sexuality. It was the time of enforced martial law on perplexity, but not an end of authoritative discourse followed by deconstruction. A deconstructive path would have submitted responses 'to endless interrogations . . . overthrowing power, to preserve the opening' as Jabès says (Harvey 1986: 94). We have nothing to fear in deconstruction if this process carries with itself a problematisation of reality which opens to new questionings and visions. Instead of that, what happened after the *Conquista* was an authoritarian process, and the imposition of the Great European Metanarratives on people's lives. That was more a process of asset-stripping than deconstruction. The Latin American Grand Narratives became redundant, empty (in Spanish the name given to asset-stripping is *vaciamiento*, emptying) perhaps due to the fact that every Grand Narrative carries in itself an objectification of a *Lebenswelt* or 'World of Life'. Let us consider this point in detail. The production of Grand Narratives is in itself a way of commodifying life. These are no innocent paper moons. These are concrete intentional discourses growing from relations of production and capital appropriation. The end of the Grand Narratives of the Original Nations was an undressing process, and the native's new nakedness was then available to be re-dressed with a different (European) Grand Narrative, yet one which fulfilled the same objective as the first. Therefore, I am not claiming that the Grand Narratives of the Original Nations were better or worse than the European. No, I am only saying that the natural processes of deconstruction never happened and people were brutalised into Christian Grand Narratives and economic discourses by criminal forces. Narratives of people's exploitation and women's submission in Latin America did not change, at least not substantially. Only the masters who gave names to the planets, still following Lacan, and determined their reduced vocabulary, changed. A more brutal regime and a genocide without magnitude happened in the continent, but as a woman I cannot say that the situation of women after the *Conquista* was substantially different from before. However, as I will argue later, deconstruction is unavoidable even if forcefully obstructed. Deconstruction can be traced in Latin America in multiple forms of political, cultural and religious mistrust throughout centuries. The sexual mutilation still needs to be theologically addressed.

Lemon vendors who do not use underwear are indecent. The Argentinian theologian without underwear writes Indecent Theology. They both challenge in different ways the creation of a factual sexual order of things, one that became entangled in an alliance of patriarchy between Europeans and natives. Heterosexual Christian imaginary came to Latin America to reproduce expressive models of sex/gender by normalisation and control (Butler 1990: 24). These things are the bases of structural organisation in my country, the primal forms of normalisation and frontier patrolling systems as we know them historically. Indeed, the fact that we have been able to trace different political and cultural systems throughout human history but never a historical experience of non-heterosexual normalisation is significant, even if we take into account cultures where heterosexuality was constructed in different ways to the contemporary form with which we are familiar. Some understanding of heterosexuality is always in the origin of patriarchy. It is an understanding based on hierarchy and submission by processes of affirmation by subtraction: I am what I am not (a woman and not a man; a bisexual and not a 'woman'); and what gets subtracted is also annulled: I am what I am not, a 'woman', therefore I am not. Heterosexuality is not a neutral science and the inner logic of the system works with its own artificially created 'either/or' concepts. It unifies the ambivalence of life into one official version. Per/versions (the different versions of a road) are silenced.

When Cortes met Moctezuma in 1519, the Grand Narratives behind these two men were based on two cosmovisions which set them apart except for one thing which they held in common: the patriarchal excess of their narratives of authority. From a materialist analysis, we can think about Grand Narratives as the surplus of praxis of patriarchal power, the matrix of which is constituted by heterosexual thought. Heterosexual power therefore continues, and provides the flow between Grand Narratives linked by occasional asset-stripping processes as we have already considered. For instance, the colonisers stripped Africa of its culture, religious and economic systems but kept patriarchal power intact, if not reinforced, by Christianity. Ricoeur, in his analysis of living metaphors, has considered how symbolic constructions develop a quasi-biological life. They are born, they develop and flourish, they form alliances with other symbolic systems, and finally die and/or transmute (Ricoeur 1967: 17ff.). Grand Narratives also seem to follow similar processes, except that the primal binary construction of sexual systems remains alive (although not uncontested) and is reproduced into epistemologies and structures of political and social organisation. It is especially reproduced in our understanding of authority.

Authority defines authority, begets authority and resurrects authority. Authority is always positioned authority, Darwinian (surviving by force and confrontation) and self-perpetuating. We might be referring here to Western theological authority or USA capitalism. The authority of, for instance, the Grand Narratives of Christianity in Latin America is composed of these plus the following elements:

1 A modern conception of (Western) linear time.
2 A core knowledge base provided by the construction of the Western subject as constitutive of the real. Against that real, we position our invented lives.

The trajectory of Grand Narratives seems to follow a Western linearity and modern conception of progress, because progression also implies the notion of a point of departure, a constitutive moment, and therefore a regression, even if it is a regression to the not known or acknowledged, already there although occult. This occultist call is no doubt meaningful. Paraphrasing Chairman Mao saying that 'good ideas do not fall from heaven' (Lin Piao 1967: 206), we may say also that neither do Grand Narratives fall from heaven, but obey corporal needs of what Foucault called the disciplining and ordering of rationality, institutions and sexuality (Foucault 1980: 196–7), and we may add – of capital. We believe in them because they make us; we know we perish with them, too. However, the regressions of authority do not need to obey linear movements but can be digressions: for instance, sexual digression. If we do not have a point in our Latin American history to say that the sexual organisation of the continent was not heterosexual, we do have digressions, discordances and incongruences at any time. If North Atlantic visions of poor Latin America have been seen through heterosexual eyes, it is because the socially disadvantaged in the continent present different parameters of sexual transgression than in Europe or in the United States (Foster 1997: 7). The homosexuality amongst the Caribs and the sexual freedom of women in some indigenous communities may be erased from the theological history of our ancestors, but is strangely present in the sexual protest of the 1990s in Latin America, when people tired of militarism and repression have decided to come out as free people (Foster 1997: 13). Let us reflect, for instance, on the Maya conception of time, taking the Mayan subject as that which gives us this sense of preservation of the opening in understanding processes, which is so needed if one wants to avoid the ruling of progressive (linear) philosophical discourses (Derrida 1972: 211).

Maya theology is born of numbers and repetitions. The politico-religious Grand Narrative of the Mayas was built from the obsessive behaviour of controlling numbers, dates, astronomical calculus and construction. Each stone of a monument is part of a liturgical memory of numbers, which are important recorded human gestures in themselves. Their god was not the name of in/difference, but the numerical difference which approximated them to God. León-Portilla explains the cyclic but non-repetitive conception of time. 'The *sol* (sun) never rests. The appearance shows us that the *sol* is devoured in the *chi-kin* (the evening; literally, the sun in the mouth) but it penetrates the inner world (*mundo interior*), goes traverses and triumphantly, is born again' (León-Portilla 1986: 34). Every *sol* comes with its Grand Narrative of origins and ordering but it is expected to die a death by penetration (their time pre-fixed, divined in the sacred texts) and resurrected by penetration too. Like the biblical genealogies of male descendants, one penetration giving birth to someone else till God enters into the genealogy by penetrating a woman's womb. That is Jesus, part of a linear and progressive conception; yet resurrection adds circularity to penetration. Jesus' death is an example of tolerance, of the enduring of human life. However, the *sol's* death carries in itself the idea of some form of tolerance too. In other words, former identities were allowed to remain in the new *sol*, as a token of co-operation from the new discourse in power. The Aztecs are exemplary of that. They had confederate narratives, at least during the fifteenth century and the time of the *Conquista*. These reflected their tributary system organised around thirty-eight tributary provinces depending on Mexico-Tenochtitlan as a centre (Pérez Herrero 1992: 43). The Triple Alliance of the Aztecs did not kill but incorporated regional identities and their regional discourses of identity. That was not what the Narratives of the Spaniards were about in their construction of authority: they brought Christianity without resurrection, without the tolerance of life. Theirs was a linear, terminal conception of Christian narratives. While the Aztec Confederation expected that at least some of their philosophical and scientific paradigms would be able to rotate as peripheral moons of the Spaniards' Christianity, the Spaniards only wanted to kill them.

How did this religious philosophy of identity affect their sexual discourse? We know that women in the Aztec Empire were of low value and ill-treated. Were the alloying identity myths suspended in relation to women? Did women have a national and religious identity or a reflective one, that is, one that reflected their gender roles and positions? We will never know for sure, because much was destroyed and little was preserved in terms of books or accounts of the times before the *Conquista*. However, since we know that one of the factors in the fall of the Grand Narratives of the Original Nations was a different conception of time and the understanding of cycles of discourses of power, one wonders how they worked sexually. In short, what was the difference? There is a second factor to consider, and it comes from the fact that the Aztecs had a military narrative, which was the same as the Spaniards. The people were indoctrinated to obey and accept subjugation. It was part of the order of worship. Therefore, the fall of the Aztec Empire was a gravitational one; vertical military structures, tied to each other, collapsed without knowing how to find the space of the horizontal decisions and challenges. The military culture, patriarchy at its peak, erased the cyclical conceptions and understandings of God, also based on different compulsions on the side of Christians and Aztec: one group obsessed by numbers and metaphors of cyclical penetration; the other by a linear penetration pattern interrupted by Christ's resurrection. In the end, the Aztec Confederacy's Grand Narrative fell, perhaps because Grand Narratives have a set time for their own self-destruction. That 'progressive erosion' which Derrida identified in metaphors such as value of usury and usage (Derrida 1989: 39) is present also in Meta-narratives. The usury (*usure*) is that surplus of value which is transmitted in Aztec discursive confederations, which comes from the corporeality (*Leiblichkeit*) of the oppressed which through their oppression has given value to the Meta-narratives which objectivised them in the first place (Dussel 1988: 63). The usury, interest, continues and makes alliances and arrangements with new authoritative orderings. The story of colonial settlements and imperial control is a story of one basic alliance: the patriarchal one. Disparaged forms of patriarchal cultures find enough elements in common for mutual agreement. Languages and religious systems are banished and societal orders and political configurations are demonised by new central powers, but women's oppression continues to give focus, a sense of solidarity and reciprocity between conquerors and conquered. There is a sense of tradition and ontological continuation. Without this, and the unquestionable Western subject, Grand Narratives would be effectively deconstructed, called to subpoena. These two elements are the main surpluses of the preservation of the order of life as we know it.

However, the end of the Original Nations' Grand Narratives implied also a patriarchal crisis of gigantic proportions: husbands were required to give their wives to any Spaniard who wished to have sex, fathers to witness their daughters being taken as concubines or slaves without their agreement. Grandmothers became concubines and children sex slaves outside the control of the male eldership of society. On reading these stories, and the voices of protests from writers such as Todorov or Dussel on the *Conquista*, one gets the impression that it is authority which is questioned more than rape. When husbands came back from working in the mines, they needed to witness how their wives were forced to have sex with their bosses (Todorov 1987: 150). Guaman Poma de Ayala gives graphic accounts of Spanish men sexually abusing indigenous women while they slept (Pease 1980) which work at the level of denouncing male trespasses into other men's properties. The issue here is one of possession, of men taking the property of other men, but not a discourse about the abuse of women. The fact is that the sexual Grand Narratives of Central America and the Inca Empire worked in a frame of property, similar to the Scriptural Commandment of men's sexual rights over women. In the *Conquista*, women's sufferings are a matter of economy.

The destruction of the Grand Narratives of the Americas did not come as the result of a hermeneutics of suspicion, or the realisation of the trace in the text, that element which is a movement leading us towards what the text tries to occult, hide and negate. No, economic exploitation was the deconstructivist clause, the doubting interrogation of naturalised, assumed authoritative narratives. In that, women's oppression was to continue as part of an economic exchange. The pursuit of gold destroyed the idea of unity, the systematic thought of civilisations such as the Aztecs or the Inca Empire and introduced the plurality of European exploitation instead. As in a good deconstructivist process, it overthrew the power of an ancient monolithic discourse (built on the suppression of other discourses, those from internal processes of colonisation such as annexed cultures under the Aztec empire) and affirmed the 'coming of the Other' (Caputo 1997a: 53). However, the Other came with its own law, its own closure of interrogations, while pursuing at the same time that passion for the impossible which lies at the base of the project of supplanting one civilisation with another. To take Tenochtitlan with 400 men and some tired horses could be a metaphor for the experience of surpassing limits of the unrepresentable and unpresentable (Caputo 1997a: 33). That is to say the Original Nations' civilisations proved to be beyond the comprehension of the symbolic of colonial Europeans.

Reading deconstruction from the end of the Grand Narratives in Latin America is an interesting exercise on a marginal positioning of ourselves as indecent theologians in the context of Christian theology. For instance, the taking of Tenochtitlan by a few soldiers and horses is such a disproportion. So is the imposition of Christianity on the religiously well-educated people of vast Latin American empires. A disproportion in terms of the non-relation, of the disconnectedness between world-views and asymmetric societies. But how did the guerrilla readings of the rebellious Latin Americans understand this through the dizziness of dislocation and repositioning of their order of things? How did the lemon vendors' fore-mothers see the end of their accepted Grand Narratives? Perhaps through patriarchal patterns, the only thing they had in common with the Europeans, which provided the only sense of continuation. Without an understanding of submission there is no submission; without sexual constructs there are no *Others*. The fact that, historically, indigenous women survived through relationships with men (forced or voluntary), and men by their offerings of women to the Europeans (forced or voluntary), represents a common ritual in their efforts to reconcile and pacify. The exchange of women, together with gold, both to be 'eaten', absorbed, bodily incorporated, is the early symptom we have of the *Conquista*. There is no sense of disproportion there, although perhaps, in a general sense, of assimilation.

A simple assimilation retains by definition some of the substance of what has been embodied. If the death of the Latin American Grand Narratives had followed an epistemology of military structure, as Todorov and Dussel amongst others claim, nothing could have been assimilated and retained. A policy of '*Tierra Arrasada*' (erased land) is the territory of the napalm bomb: neither people, nor animals nor plants survive; nothing will ever fructify in those fields. The incorporation of the Latin American *forma mentis* into the Spanish one implied a minimum dialogic process at a certain point, a symbolic co-operation. Incorporation transforms what it is eaten, but keeps it. The incorporation we are talking refers to a process of nourishment. The nourishment of the European Other did not happen by capital exploitation only, but by sexual agreements. As we shall see later, the worship of the Virgin of Guadalupe is a sexual religious agreement which re-symbolises the perdurability of the patriarchal system from one Grand Narrative to the other. In fact, women provide the continuation, the element of certainty and a certain memory, the memory of their subjugation. Thus women's oppression gave a sense of normality to changing times, glossed and mythologised as in the case of the Virgin of Guadalupe.

From a surface analysis, one may think that the discourse of the sacred may have been a secondary discourse. The main one was economic. It may not have been the case of one god displacing others. It may have been instead the case of one economic system displacing a god. However, economic systems are religious systems which displace and represent sets of social relationships. Christianity, in alliance with an economic system based on exploitation, managed to create the illusion of new identities based on new relationships, but they were not substantially different because even if religiously the Aztecs' beliefs may have been more challenging of sexual patterns of oppression (which are at the roots of any economic structure), society was organised at the margins of religious symbolism. In Mexico, the priests of the goddess Cihuacoatl ('The One of the Skirt made of Serpents') were religious transvestites who dressed as the goddess. Men and women alike taking priestly roles were called the Cihuacoatls. In the Cihuacoatl worship there was a transgendered expression of the sacred matched by the sexual ambivalence of their god. Perhaps this expressed that Aztec characteristic of cyclic time and identity by annexation, or supplementary processes. However, women counted for little in their society, and were overdetermined by roles and expectations of obedience. Transgenderism did not, apparently, became a transgressive force in economic social relations. Do religious Grand Narratives displace sexual discourses according to the criteria of capital and production? Is that process the one which confers propriety, decorum, decency to our theological discourses or, at least, informs them, for instance, by removing theological transgenderism from the field of production and relationships? Or, in the case of Christianity, which is unambiguously and biologically based on a male god, there is a community of god-men too. God the Father and God the Son (not to enter into the differences in the Hebrew Scriptures' conceptions of the male-god) may show coherence but also the inclusiveness of different ways of being 'men' and different 'men' are difficult to categorise sexually. Yet, in society, it tends to support only one ideal heterosexual type of man. Theology is suggestive; the Aztec and the Christian are suggestive theological systems, but such persuasion of religious imagination is a threat to society's organisation. Therefore, transgressive elements such as Aztec transgenderism or some richness to be found in the plurality of the divine in Christianity remain opaque and disconnected. The problem is that it is easier to live without God than without the heterosexual concept of man. They need to be undressed simultaneously. The subversiveness of a religious system lies in its sexual subversions, in that disorderly core of abnormal sexual narratives where virgins give birth and male trinities may signify the incoherence of one male definition only, in the tension between patriarchal identity and difference. This undressing is the starting point for gross indecency in theology. The lemon vendors I mentioned earlier continue an indigenous tradition of not using underwear, defying the male gaze, controlling gazes, and the decency of those gazes. This constitutes in itself the base for a paradigm in our present discussion. They challenge a systematic sexuality. Systematic Theology belongs to the order of Western Grand Narratives, and although built in a make-believe dualistic opposition of mind and body, the curious thing is that Christian dogmatics is built upon bodily struggles. In dogmatics, bodies touch others, are slippery or loving or aggressive. For instance, Christianity is related to bodily functions (artificial insemination and the birth of Jesus–God, issues of control of sexuality, torture, hunger, death, and the return of the killed body in resurrection). It is also about bodily relations such as the dogma of the Trinity which is a reflection of the social understanding of what we can call 'a medieval family' pattern of hierarchical obsessions and Darwinian tensions, intrinsically male. Other elaborated dogmas such as the life of the body after death, whether the body remains in the queue of purgatory or is cremated in hell, function with the same precision of the regulation of bodies by concepts of sin which never escape the boundaries of perceived embodied needs. A body-paradigm, is therefore pertinent in theological analysis, and does not need to come from the European Other, but from the lemon vendors, who embrace in their lives the economic and sexual connotations of the survivors of the destruction of the Grand Narratives of Latin America. The paradigm is an indecent paradigm, because it undresses and uncovers sexuality and economy at the same time. Not only do we need an Indecent Theology which can reach the core of theological constructions, insofar as they are rooted in sexual constructions, for the sake of understanding our sexuality, we also need it because theological truths are currencies dispensed and acquired in theological economic markets. In Latin America, the exchange of work for the reward of the afterlife, salvation for bread and subservience for divine grace started when the Grand Narratives of the Original Nations dis-integrated. And it is a sexual exchange: not only salvation as a symbolic exchange commodity for bread, but for a type of heterosexual mode of living and producing which is expected too. David Harvey has spoken of what he sees as a re-emergence of ethical and political concerns, a 'profound shift in the structure of feeling' (Harvey 1989: 9). In Indecent Theology, we may add, there is a shift in the structure of sexual feelings which disrobes the underwear of heterosexual theology. A kind of coming-out process in which we are no longer (hetero)sexually neutral theologians. In the past thirty years, a theological movement in Latin America has questioned the ideological neutrality of theology and produced a movement of integral liberation from Latin Americans and for Latin Americans. Many forms of Indecent Theology in Europe and in the USA (Queer Theologies) have used them as their starting point for reflection (Goss 1993, Stuart 1997). Although there are many significative elements in Liberation Theology, in the second part of this chapter we shall unravel aspects of theological indifference, that is, the theological elements in liberationist thought which never undress themselves or challenge the orders of decency in Latin America.

On Liberation Theology: a history of usury

As soon as the new Grand Narratives started to work and even considering their patriarchal alliance, they established themselves without resistance. Even if the nurturer Narrative of the Original Nations was militarily oppressive and politically argued, the crisis of meaning produced by the *Conquista* was intense enough to create a distance, a critical margin with the new order. However, that resistance element is also part of the construction of discourses of authority. Every discourse of religious and political authority hides under its skirts suppressed knowledge in exile, which is marginal and indirect speech. This is knowledge which people dictate through religious and political counter symbols and mythological contradictions of the official versions.[1] Indecent Theology is therefore made of these contradictions and contradictums, and a transgression which is a regression, a going backwards to some struggle or primary resistance to the discourses of religious power, not to a beginning of sexual resistance fixed in time, but to the several openings which were suppressed or calmed down in the process of the hegemonisation of meaning. These openings are in the past, but also in the present and in the future; they work as disseminated resistances which cannot be located in any utopia of the future (teleology) or ideology of the past. This takes us to our present point of Liberation Theology as decent theology, which is concerned with authorship and the authorisation/disauthorisation of the Grand(iose) religio-political discourses of authority in Latin America. These discourses have been written in the legal structures, disseminated through popular proverbs and art, embodied in architectural designs and political functions, and have designed spirituality as well in the liturgical gestures of political symbolism.[2] Basically, they are written in political events such as the dismantling of traditional beliefs after the *Conquista*, the tax systems, the control of land and property, the legitimisation of slave work and usury. These are not only political but sexual theological discourses. Christianity in Latin America imposed a sexual economic order of usury, of usage of people in relationships. In colonial marriage, women were given according to interest rates of work, basically reproductive work, but also according to the needs of peasant or urban populations. Non-heterosexual marriages were not approved because there was no usage, no usurious interest evident in them; for instance, they did not produce children. Sexuality was defined in terms of usury, given for an interest, usually high and with no end; divorces were not allowed. The rates of interest invested in marriage were prefixed, unchangeable, monotonous. What difference can we make between this usury of love and sexuality, of bodies institutionalised and the usury methods of the Jesuits? For instance, between the seventeenth and second part of the eighteenth century the Jesuits in Latin America owned more than 400 valuable haciendas in Mexico, Peru, Ecuador, Bolivia, Colombia and Chile (López-Cano 1995). In Ecuador alone, 10 per cent of the best agricultural lands belonged to that religious order. Apart from that, they had control of a vast workforce of slaves in Brazil and Peru. Whenever indigenous people during colonial times appealed against the Jesuits' abuses, they lost. The Jesuits were highly influential in the *Consejo de Indias* (Council of the Indies). They practised usury; they lent money to their allies in power at high interest and the high interest of work was paid to them by their workers. At the same time, sexuality and marriage in Latin America exemplified the concept of the *mala vida* (bad living). *La mala vida* was a concept which signified the abuse of women at the hands of husbands, fathers and brothers in a household. It meant sexual and economic abuse (Lavrin 1992: 21). *La mala vida* was more than a sexual metaphor of women's exploitation in marriage and family life: it was a metaphor for workers' exploitation, for slave work, economic usury but also usury in Christian theology which exploited people under threats of religious damnation. Bartolomé de las Casas, in his defence of the Original Nations, mentions the analogy of Latin America as a woman who, instead of having a good husband, has one who gives her a *mala vida* (Las Casas 1953: 69) Therefore, in the *Conquista* of Latin America there was a Sexual Theology which followed patterns of sexual legal arrangements such as marriage in the following points:

1   Deprivation of economic support and basic infrastructure of the home (the site of the female); international policies of exportation of raw products thus neglecting infrastructures in the countries.
2   Legal physical punishment as the duty of a male to teach a female. The native as a minor.
3   Regulation of sexual practices inside and outside marriage. Regulation of sexuality in Latin America under Christianity, even for non-Christian people.

How theological work is alienated from the workers

Behind any discourse of liberation in Latin America which breaks with patterns of authority at social, religious and political levels there is a hidden worker who produced that discourse in anonymity. Discourses of liberation have a value which comes not from their textual force, but from the realm of human activity, that is, from the rebellious people. Such rebellious activity is what interpellates the reader in her struggle against oppression, and gets objectified in the text of the discourse of liberation. What we are identifying here is the role of the *Lebendige Arbeit* (Life-Work) as conceptually developed by Marx in his *Grundrisse* (McLellan 1979: 109). Before a discourse of liberation such as, for instance, Liberation Theology became valuable in a theological market, there was a first face-to-face dynamic relation, a production of a claim for liberation or denunciation of the Meta-narratives of Christianity in Latin America which came from the 'naked, poor bodies' of the oppressed (Dussel 1988: 64). In the same way, an Indecent Theology should also come from sexual transgression or 'Coming Out' stories: the experience of finding one's own sexual identity in community, of a refusal to accept *la mala vida*, for instance. Theology of Liberation likes to locate itself at the point of the fall of the Grand Narratives of Latin America in the sense that it wants to locate its theological subject in the concrete work of the people who made the centuries-old counter-discourses in Latin America from their suffering bodies. The point is that Liberation Theology is not a self-contained entity or peculiar category of analysis related to God and a particular theological subject such as the poor, independent of the structures of a theology which is always and foremost, a Sexual Theology. Based on sexual categories and heterosexual binary systems, obsessed with sexual behaviour and orders, every theological discourse is implicitly a sexual discourse, a decent one, an accepted one. It would be naive to consider that Liberation Theology has been indecent, that is, that it broke with the sexual imaginary of Western theology by using class analysis. Liberationists were somehow Hegelians, and right-wing Hegelians at that, seeing in the institution and structures of heterosexual, *Machista* Latin American society the movement of a *Machista* God, a god of the poor, but a *Machista* one. Liberation Theology suffers from what in Argentina people call a chronic 'pancake' syndrome. This means that like a pancake in mid-air, it changes its original position according to its context or interests. Liberation Theology has been turning from Materialist approaches to Idealism in mid-air, like a pancake, before landing again in the frying pan. In a sense it would be right to say that Liberation Theology belongs to an idealist theological market, because laws and offers and demand in this theology have been thought around certain faith presuppositions (which are unchalleangeable as a given). I have called this property of idealist theology an ex-centricity, that is, to have a centre core of theological issues nurtured by humanity's historical perspective but reflected upon by closed, established theological truths working as faith-given. This means that idealist theology is neither dialogic or democratic. It takes a set of unchallengable theological truths, which are the referents for any theology including theologies of liberation, for instance the virginal conception by Mary or the theocratic filiation of Jesus. These are referents in the background of any theological praxis and popular theology has always had difficulty in doing a theology in dialogue with a community of faith without perturbing those ex-centric theological referents. Our point here is that the commonality of all ex-centricity in theology is sexuality. The virginal coitus, the filiation of Jesus and the sexual pattern of relationships of the Holy Family are crucial. However, we are establishing a sexual story and history as foundational for Christianity and theology, and a sexuality informed by what Daphne Hampson called faulty biological understandings (Hampson 1990: 17) and sacralisations of sexual orders of masters and subordinates. Although our understanding of biology has evolved and, moreover, our understanding of sexuality has became independent of medical spheres of definitions, theology is still desperately clinging to what gives it an ultimate sense of coherence and tradition: not God, but a theory of sexuality. To challenge God is not as indecent as to challenge the sexuality of theology. Sexual idealism pervades theology, including Theology of Liberation.

The liberationist hermeneutical circle has proved to be politically materialist and sexually idealist and is therefore a basic decent discourse (contained;

limited). It is in the insertion of Liberation Theology in the Western theological market where the overdressing of the theological motives and methods usually begins. The (hetero)sexual Latin American assumptions get affirmed and the potential challenge to the system that Liberation Theology represents loses efficacy. Why? Because sexual suspicion has not been introduced to the economic and political realms of life in Latin America. Theology of Liberation is also a (hetero)sexual idealist theology, based in the systematic traditions of the West.

The market of Systematic Theology: lemons, *señora,* and some hermeneutical circles, *me compra pué* . . .

Theology is basically an incoherent art. If we were going to use a metaphor inspired by the New Testament, we would say that theology is the art of going to bed with God while avoiding full sex. After all, this is the first thing that Christian faith tells us: that the beginning of the historical relation between God incarnated and humanity is to be found in the metaphor of going to bed with God for the first (unique) time, and without a condom. Such was Mary's experience. If the first Eve had a fetishist penchant for a serpent, the second went for unprotected sex with a God-Cloud. Sexual metaphors which determine the beginnings of religious symbolic constructions are like that, chaotic, unpredictable and immoral. That is why we like them; something in them reminds us of real-life patterns and the chaotic order of sexuality. However, if we are going to suppose that God is procreated by humanity going to bed with God (as in the narratives of Mary in the New Testament), the metaphor may prove ample enough to accommodate other forms of sexual activities too. Different positions and sexual subjects may be hidden in this story. As the Hebrew Scriptures start with a myth of God and humanity based on the sexual legitimacy of societal order, in the story of Adam and Eve, the New Testament starts with a quasi-woman (Mary, a de-biologised being) and her sexual intercourse with a God, or to be more precise, with an idealist sacred Meta-narrative. Jesus Christ is conceived then as the unique production of a meta-narrative and a quasi-being, which although it sounds fantastic is the origin of the in-credible in Christianity. Beyond that, the entire sacred text is concerned with sexual control and the effort to make of the in-credible a real, material substance. This has been done, at tremendous cost, but let us not get to this point yet. There is a thread of sexual obsession alongside the sacralised discourses on power, commandments and ethical definitions which have permeated our so-called Christian Latin American societies. Such discourses on power have been systematised, classified and organised in Systematic Theology. They are Western based in the sense that their subject, the idealised Western, white, elite man, the source of philosophical–theological reflections, can be found in the main representatives of the constructions of hegemonic discourse of political and economical power in our world. The point is that the political and economic constructions of this world are based on sexual experience, or the interpretation of sexual experience. Theology is from that perspective a sexual act participating in the ideological construction of God from the idealist discourse of what it is supposed to be going to bed with God, and the regulations and control discourses based on some heterosexual falsifications or alienations of what is due to reality, and to the people who live under the threats of the naturalisation of sexuality or decency codes in theology.

Decent theologies struggle for coherence, the coherence that sexual systems also struggle for. Yet, we may ask what is wrong with being incoherent theologically? Liberation Theology, as a discourse from the 1970s in Latin America, understood (even if only partially) the economic esoterism of the Christian dogmatic and imperial traditions of systematic theologians. Imperialisms are, by definition, criminal activities of expansion, possession and control; theology's permanent search for coherence is only an expression of its hegemonising objectives, a taxonomy. As in Latin America the narratives of political power are imperial and Christian (not Aztec, Mayan or Inca), the liberationist discourses started from a critique of economic (Western) Christian Grand Narratives. In the oral traditions of the early years of Liberation Theology (which received other names, such as 'Pertinent Theology', for instance, which a woman theologian, Beatriz Melano Couch, started to develop based on a Ricoeurian framework), people spoke about the possibility of theological dissemination. At that time, in Argentina, theologians of liberation such as Revd Alberto Blatesky, José Miguez Bonino, Beatriz Melano Couch, Mario Yutzis and J. Severino Croatto did not agree with the idea of Basic Ecclessial Communities as a return to the primitive (Apostolic) Church. To sustain that idea may have resulted in a regulated polysemy or a coming back in the ecclesiological discourse in search of some original meaning to be re-enacted. On the contrary, Liberation Theology was promissory, and spoke in terms of dissemination and the possibility of the unknown breaking into the old narrative of being the church in Christian Latin American. That dissemination is crucial for processes of liberation. At a pastoral level of work, it is easy to see how the subordinate discourse of Latin Americans needed to find ways of surviving by invoking an older authority such as the Apostolic Church, some ex-centric authority. At the level of theological discourse, this was not the case. The discourse was less constrained than the practice of Christianity. More congregations were killed than theological corpuses. Books survived better. Therefore, some traces of indecency were present in the genesis of Liberation Theology. Women and (closetted) sexual transgressors welcomed it.

Marxism disclosed and made public the fact that politics is not only what parliamentarians and political parties do, but is the superficial expression of deep socio-economic realities. Liberationists declared that theology was not what the theologians did. Instead of that, theology was the realm of the expression of deep ideological realities which reflect people's sense of sacralised oppression. However, it was obscure. It lacked representation because it lacked transparency in the positioning of the Latin American subject of theology. Were the poor the *colonised subject*? Moreover, were the poor the Christian colonised subject that Christianity felt it was possible to help? This did not take into account the fact that the Christian Meta-narratives in Latin America have the historical responsibility for the construction of the subject called by liberationists 'the poor'. Why is it then, that the Latin American subject as early defined by Gustavo Gutierrez amongst others, is seen as Christian and poor, as a homologated category? The Latin American Christian discourse of liberation was following previous paths of a *Criollo* route, a road of nativisation. It needed to assume that nothing had been outside Christianity, no Mayans in Guatemala nor Candomblé worshippers in Brazil, for instance. It needed to start with totality even if against totality. It needed to declare the poor asexual, and not challenge women's subordination or the sexual insubordination of the *fabelas* or shanty towns. Anybody who has been in Latin America during the yearly carnival celebrations knows that carnivals are the festivity of the poor and sexual indecency: 'the revolt of the Queers' (Lancaster 1997: 19–20). Political and sexual transgressions are the agenda of carnivals, yet the subject of carnivals, the poor, have been obliterated in Liberation Theology. What happens then is that if the shanty townspeople go in procession carrying a statue of the Virgin Mary and demanding jobs, they seem to become God's option for the poor. However, when the same shanty townspeople mount a carnival centred on a transvestite Christ accompanied by a Drag Queen Mary Magdalene kissing his wounds, singing songs of political criticism, they are not anymore God's option for the poor. Carnivals in Latin America are the Christmas of the indecent, and yet they are invisible in theological discourse.

When one rereads a text such as Gutierrez's *A Theology of Liberation* nowadays, it is striking how traditional and conventional his theological discourse appears. With the exception of the attempt to dislocate the theological subject with the 'cut of class' (to paraphrase Althusser[3]) Christianity as a totality was left wanting. More a dislocating theology it carried within it the element that with the passing of the years would produce the crisis of Liberation Theology: a re-location, that is, an incorporation of the poor Christian. It is a movement from the margins into the central discourse of theology. It is surprising that this work could have produced such havoc in theological circles at that time, but we must understand that the then prevalent Systematic Theology was extremely self-identified, undifferentiated, a kind of cultural mirror act which considered any discourse from the south, barbaric. But 500 years of the construction of the Christian Other and the permanent war on the Latin American subject by colonial definitions of reality and theological meaning could not go like that. However, Liberation Theology was meant to become a recognised theology with a clear denunciation of ideological and theological historical links which perpetuated poverty in Latin America, and it was a commercial enterprise too. Perhaps the latter factor was the more decisive one in the history of the dialectics between Western and Liberation Theology at that time. In a few years, people in Europe who had never read Barth or Schleiermacher in their lives were reading Gutierrez, Bonino or Segundo. The incorporation of the margins into a central discourse was not yet a point of discussion, as has happened today with the advent of postcolonial theologies. People who supported the liberation of Mandela in South Africa or the end of the Cuban boycott were people who usually contributed money to charities and agencies related to the Third World. These people and agencies were suddenly reading texts and sub-texts from Liberation Theology. Booklets, journals with articles and chapters in edited books popularised obscure theological terms such as the hermeneutical circle, Freirean conscientisation processes and the reading of the prophets in the Hebrew Scriptures. It meant that, suddenly, theology was fashionable. And what is fashionable, sells. Suddenly, the market was inundated by theological books, Latin American crosses, articles in journals and indigenous music: it was a receptive market. Meanwhile, European theologians, professional and amateur, booked trips to Brazil, Argentina, Chile and Central America. They came and asked us where were the communities of the poor? The demand was so high that at times we needed to produce Christian communities on demand for the foreigners. I even found myself in the situation of being called on to be part of a popular Bible study group for the benefit of a bishop from abroad visiting Buenos Aires. It was like one of Gary Larsson's cartoons, the one where the squirrels are preparing to beg for food from a man in the park: 'Now, try to look cute, and you Carl, stop smoking.' I remember the absurdity of that bishop addressing me with the evident satisfaction of a man talking with a native woman whom he presumed was illiterate, simple and poor but with a strong faith. In fact, I was a university student and if I was very poor, it was not through the lack of a job (I had two at that time) but hyperinflation. Moreover, I was an indecent woman. The sort that at that time, when the military regime was promoting family values, had decided not to marry, but to live on her own and to love a gay man. However, even the authentic illiterate and poor in the group were carefully responding and covering other people's faux pas in order to give a good impression, that is, the colonial image of Liberation Theology. It was the beginning of church tourism and theological voyeurism, and a theological performative role was developing, dangerously repeating the colonial understandings of Christianity and the natives. No doubt it did more for them than for some of us. They came with notebooks and cameras to take photos, and returned to their countries of origin suntanned, with some traditional shirt from Latin America and notes for a future book to be published on Liberation Theology. Meanwhile, the liberationists were losing the initial indecency of their project of theological dissemination. Too much clapping and admiration was as bad as the criticisms.

Indecency and liberation

It is within the logic of the centre that a discourse about the poor can result in a profitable enterprise. When I watch the news on TV concerning Third World disasters, sometimes it becomes evident how even our dead keep alive the economic markets of the West. Disasters and massacres such as Rwanda become books which sell, theological books included. Issues of sexual indecency have historically produced tons of books on homosexuality and Christianity. Over the dead bodies, the bodies of people who suffered and felt their life to be sometimes intolerable, theology was written. The market fixes the price and the value of merchandise, but it also determines what is merchandise. An item of merchandise is 'objectified work'; 'used *Lebendige Arbeit* (Life-Work)' (Dussel 1988: 30). The decency of the system lies in a network of authorisation and censoring; naming a merchandise as such fixes the decency of a society – for instance, the value of a person as merchandise, as the value of women in the economic markets of marriage. The Latin American system of decency which rules and regulates how women should dress, how they should speak, the sexual activities they should perform, is based on this. Systematic theological production has traditionally made reflection on human suffering its object of exchange. In Eurocentric theology, the material suffering of the people was expropriated from the oppressed classes and became the intellectual property of the owner of the intellectual system of production, the theologian. The real suffering of the oppressed, as presented in the *Lebendige Arbeit* of the exploited, becomes an item of merchandise which, following Marx's analysis, becomes an abstraction separated from the system which nurtures and locates it. Moreover, theological discourse became one of the only presentable aspects of what is now hidden and forgotten: the complex pattern of the human praxis of suffering. Following Marx, we can locate theology precisely at this moment, as a category under which the wealth of the bourgeoisie is represented (Dussel 1988: 26). The wealth of the theological Western bourgeoisie is then represented in the Systematic Theology which has forgotten in its abstractness the living suffering and praxis of the oppressed which precedes it, that is, the real 'theologians' who are the people who reflect and act from their sufferings under theo/ideological structures of oppression. Therefore the laws of market production apply to theological production. For instance:

1 *The law of reversal*: The more the worker produces, the less the worker consumes, means in this context that theology is a surplus value of human suffering. It alienates by taking possession, extorting from others what belongs to them, dismantling any relation that the workers may have with the sacred. The process gives value to human suffering as merchandise, objectified as an abstract commodity and sold for a price: the continuation of oppressive political systems in alliance with ecclesiastical ones. Meanwhile, suffering becomes ontologically and

theologically devalued. The richer the theologian grows as a person by the world's recognition of her ability, the poorer become those whose experience of suffering is the subject of reflection. Theological reflection which has not disengaged itself from hegemonic Christianity or the construction of sexual order and law (decency) which repositions people into subaltern political positions, impoverishes people's suffering which cannot find an authentic expression in theological sexual categories.

2 *The law of ownership*: The suffering poor provide, in this process we are describing, creativity and questioning of theological relevance, but they do not own the means to produce their discourse, neither the end product which is a fetish (in Marx's terminology) of their labour power. Theological reflection, even in Liberation Theology, becomes a commodity. The doctrine of salvation as if it was a pound of sugar reproduces endlessly the misery of the poor in abstract discourses based on real material suffering. The poor person as a theological author in her own right (the right of her experience of sacralised forms of oppression such as sexism, racism and classism) is thingified (reified) in the process, by the intellectual producers who get their profit in terms of power.

This system of theological production has been, like many other markets, controlled by the North Atlantic production line of theology. The elaboration and choosing of theological themes and methodologies belonged, according to the fashions in authority discourses, to Germans, USA or British theologians. When I started to study theology in the 1970s in Buenos Aires, I was still told that I needed to learn German and English in order to be able to read classic works from systematic theologians in their original languages. Latin America then imported the theological goods in the two senses of the word: as theological products and as theological merchandise in exchange for the Other. Our poverty and physical hunger was exchanged for theological concepts such as 'the bread of life', which objectively did not have much use, and was the equivalent of giving a cookbook with colour illustrations to starving people. Concrete suffering was the currency we exchanged for systematic promises or descriptions of the bread which satisfies more than real bread, but alas, how ridiculous that was when hunger cramps took over the body. This is what Juan Luis Segundo was referring to when in the 1940s he sought to find a theological reflection 'which would not leave us on our own at the time of having a meal' (Segundo 1948: 8). We could further extend this now: a theological reflection that does not separate prayer times from meal times cannot separate prayer times from those of intimacy; from times of going to bed with someone. That is the point for a theology without underwear, made by people whose sexual misfortunes, personal or political, need to be reflected upon as part of our theological praxis.

All theological markets fluctuate, and decline is usually perceived in two senses. First, theological discourse starts to lose value, including the invested authority which covers with excess traditionally ideological discourses of political and moral inventions in society, such as the justification of monarchies and the hierarchical apparatuses from the wide field of Gramsci's commonsense constructions. In a secular Europe, Liberation Theology has lost novelty as it stands against several attractive theological positions, such as Gospel and Culture, or Ecotheology. Second, church and academic discourses no longer collaborate with and reinforce each other, as they have done traditionally. Previously students attending certain Bible Colleges, Seminaries or Faculties were linked to the production of specialised workers such as ministers of religion. They were appointed workers not only for the spiritual development of the churches but also for the financial aspects of the institution. The minister's work has always been closely attached to the upkeep of church properties, their repair and maintenance, to the economic contributions expected from members during their lifetimes and to donations of capital and property through legacies after their death. Many stories of successful ministers are strangely attached to the building of a new church, the reconstruction of an old one, or to some economic development of one kind or another. Theology is an actuarial science. Liberation Theology perhaps does not sell so well nowadays and, moreover, it has produced a de-centering of the church/academic discourse in the sense that it was meant to be critical and not supportive of the church. Theology has received value and meaning in terms of how many people/dollars have been attracted into the church through it. But Liberation Theology in Latin America was bad for business, because the middle class abandoned their congregations while the increase in areas such as the Basic Ecclesial Communities movement was among the poor who contributed almost nothing to the church in economic terms. The BECs were not accountable in economic terms. The point is that although in the beginning the North Atlantic discourse contested and rebuked Latin American theology as Marxist, atheist or simply illogical and incompetent, very soon it became absorbed in its market. It was the beginning of their prosperity and our ruin. We had not understood yet the laws of theological markets. We knew enough Marx, but we did not apply his thought to our own system of theological production, still dictated by the West. The point is that liberationists forgot that for Marx ideology was more a style of living and thinking than a product: a Marxism without a teleology. Paraphrasing Althusser in his presentation of aleatory Marxism, we could speak of an aleatory theology, which works from contingency and encounters, instead of a teleological theology which implies idealism (Navarro 1988: 33).

There are two elements to consider here: one, the apologetic production and second the assimilation process of Liberation Theology. The apologetic (Latin American) production was a counter-discourse which confronted the critiques produced in North Atlantic academia at that time. It made Latin Americans elaborate on the issue of the theological subject of Liberation Theology, finding in it the category of 'the poor' as distinct from the North

Atlantic subject. It made the North Atlantic theological discourse come clean with what was behind their elusive 'men' subjects and the cultural, racial and economical assumptions (not to say sexual) behind 'mankind'. Although a category may be seen only as a component and a conceptual moment in the dynamic tension of the construction of a theology, the poor was a hasty concept. It referred mostly to the male-perceived peasant world of the poor, not to the urban poor, and to the Roman Catholic poor. It reflected the homogenous tendencies inherited from the Western framework of thinking theology. There was little discrimination amongst the impoverished masses or understanding of mechanisms of oppression in their own community. Basic Ecclesial Communities also suffered from that domestic violence which sends Latin American women and children to early graves. Leonardo Boff's *Ecclesiogenesis* was a welcome book, but already perceived as idealistic by many Latin American activists at the time of its publication in the 1970s. When translated it must have been a delight to Europeans but many people in Latin America were aware of the romanticism infiltrating our supposedly materialistic theological reflections. Sex was out of the question, but a sexual shadow covers many triumphant writings with doubts and ambivalence. Not only did 'the poor' subsume women, it also subsumed lesbian, gay, transgendered and bisexual people. The reality of the old traditions of Latin American poverty such as incest and abuse of girls in their communities was ignored. Abortions in the back street (or at home with a knitting needle), a common cause of death amongst poor women, was not on the agenda of the theologians although it was part of the life of the communities. The poor, as in any old-fashioned moralising Victorian tale, were portrayed as the deserving and asexual poor. Very few studies were done on the life of the marginalised at that time, in spite of the well-known discourse which started with the claim that Liberation Theology used mediation sciences such as sociology, anthropology, psychology and economics in order to understand reality. Conceding that some economic analysis was produced, there are no theological works which reflect psychoanalytic studies such as those developed by Lacan, Pichon Riviere and Alfredo Moffatt in the Argentinian school of the Psychotherapy of the Oppressed. We have not seen any ethnographic methodology pursued with rigour, and the sociological analyses were only pertinent to fragments of the population. On the economic side, Marxist analysis lacked nuance and agency. There was poverty and brutal dictatorial regimes at that time, and liberationists were in the vanguard of resistance. Of that there is no doubt. Paulo Freire, although not a theologian but a philosopher of education, was detained, tortured and managed to leave his country to go into a long exile. The priests of the 'Third World Priest Movement' were persecuted and killed, and we cannot now recall more than a couple of names of what was at that time a considerable movement. This was our reality at that time, but the problem was trying to equate our theological discourse to a given theological structure inherited from Europe, with a centuries old sexual logic. The apologetic years of trying to present Liberation Theology as a 'proper theology' damaged the creative movement of what started as a break with the Grand Narrative. This apologetics is responsible for the parallel categories system which uses old concepts in new frames, thus rendering the challenges minimal. Therefore we had the Christ of the poor, the Virgin Mary of the poor and the Church of the poor, as if just by adding the formula 'of the poor' was enough to produce any substantial structural or epistemological challenge. Far from that, it reinforced Western theological features which should have been departed from, except that it was prevented by this adaptation syndrome of Theology of Liberation. Apologetics still exists in Liberation Theology, and in recent years it has seen a surprising revival in the writings of influential Roman Catholic theologians from the UCA (Catholic University of Central America) in El Salvador. Their main intention for several years has been to demonstrate in a quasi-scientific (Stalinist) way how 'proper' (dogmatic) Liberation Theology really is. Their recently published works have been collected into a volume entitled *Mysterium Liberationis* (Sobrino and Ellacuria 1993). As Latin is not spoken in Latin America except amongst certain Roman Catholic priests, we wonder what readership they had in mind for this publication. The book is organised thematically, dealing with classical topics such as 'The Trinity', 'God the Father', 'The Virgin Mary'. Liberation Theology, far from liberating itself from systematic Western patterns, has become domesticated, a decent basic construction without the transgressive elements one might have expected.

The Western theological market took that very important first attempt of a Liberation Theology in search of its subject and methodology and forced it to become marketable and decent. That was the Liberation Theology of which my lecturers at ISEDET used to say to the students: 'Remember there is more value in a piece of paper or a letter written by a priest in the name of a poor community demanding clean water from the government, than volumes that may be written on Liberation Theology. We are not going to write a new version of Barth's *Dogmatics*!' To become marketable in Europe, Liberation Theology needed to go native. There was my previous example of the European bishop visiting Buenos Aires, and myself, a university student, who needed to play the game of belonging to the poor community together with a heterogeneous small group from the church. We did not lie to the bishop: we allowed him to misrepresent us. It was a piece of theological science fiction. The community of the poor that he wanted to visit only existed in his imagination, composed in his colonial ancestral memory of stereotypes of such degrees that he could not have recognised a community of the poor if he had spent a month amongst them. Recently, in an interview, Gustavo Gutierrez recognised the mythical forms into which Liberation Theology was cast by the makers of what we may call Theological Hollywood, or Disney-Churches (Gibbs 1996: 369). The effect of this theological myth-making was very interesting, producing almost an opposite cross effect in the market, creating different reactions in the theological productions of both

Latin America and Europe. In Europe, it was the return to the ecclesiology of the primitive Christian Church, as if a hidden meaning was being rediscovered, thus validating what it means to be a theologian and a Christian in this secular era. It was also the reinforcement of old cherished sexual stereotypes of Christian family values and women's roles outside feminist discourses in Europe. The feminist consciousness of Europe and the USA was sometimes contrasted with that of the down-to-earth, poor Christian Latin American woman. The former was characterised by idle talk of human rights coming from individualistic privileged positions: the latter was grounded in reality. Yet, the male establishment of Liberation Theology was supposed to be grounded in reality and simultaneously in a search for a higher consciousness. However, the poor down-to-earth mother suited romantic ideas of Europeans in search of the utopian *Shangri-La* of theology. These European academics made haste to publish sometimes against, or sometimes in favour of Liberation Theology. It is interesting to note now that few if any have continued with that line of theological reflection. Their books on Liberation Theology were products of the law of the theological markets of that time. Their books on Liberation Theology were reviewed and sold, and after that, they moved to new theological fashions, Ecotheology, Pentecostalism or New Age movements, if not back to an unrevised Barth's *Dogmatics,* written before feminist and postcolonial consciousness. It is understandable why Liberation Theology does not sell books in the European market anymore. The criteria are those of merchandise. But during the 1970s and 1980s, Western theologians found an original script in the Latin American discourse both in terms of taking the discussion into popular realms, and outside the spectre of feminism, for instance. When some of them tried to use the liberation methodology in Europe though, they found it difficult. Their conclusion was that Latin Americans were different: which was not in any case an original conclusion. The Pope had reached the same conclusion in 1492 when he decided that Latin Americans were not human beings. This time the academic conclusion was that Christians in Latin America were far more Christian, far more poor, far more humble and far more grateful to the church's envoys than people in Europe. The description of the natives holding to a childlike, innocent faith in the midst of their suffering, produced tender smiles in the romantic European Christians. Women knew their role in society; sexuality outside heterosexual systems did not exist amongst poor Christian communities, and men were real, caring gentlemen. If they beat their wives it was because the structures of sin had deprived them of jobs. The descriptions of the Latin American poor produced at that time echoed the descriptions in the *Sunday Strand* of London, at the beginning of this century. It was a moral construction of the poor as native. They never thought about the poor as, for instance, a sweet transvestite who needs to prostitute himself in a nightclub to survive in a life of extreme marginality and oppression. The poor native Christian was conceived according to a restricted heterosexual model. We have already considered that there is more to heterosexuality than the caricature persistently sold as heterosexuality. Heterosexual people in Latin America also live in asphyxiating closets.

Is Liberation Theology a theology of dialectics (reconciliatory stances) or revolutionary changes? The answer is historical. In Latin America, the main concern is still to show how Liberation Theology has come of age and can be considered the equal of western theology. That is where the *Mysterium Liberationis* ends, in an anything but mysterious, predictable way, absorbed by the Western theological ethos. In the past few years Liberation Theology has lost markets in Europe. A minority remains, repeating historical Liberation Theology (discourses and anecdotes from the 1960s and early 1970s) without producing anything substantially new in what was a promissory movement. Whatever happened then to Liberation Theology and its position in the capitalistic theological market? A cultural shift took place. In recent years, in order to produce some difference in its analysis, especially since postcolonialism was underlying the liberationists' contradictions on issues of identity and agency, liberationists discovered the native people from the Original Nations who sometimes were not Christians. Once again the adaptation method was used. Instead of Christ and the poor, the new discourse was on Christ and the Mayan. Christianity suddenly became more plural. It was Christianity and *Mestizaje*; Christianity and *Santería* worship, or *Umbanda*; Christianity and Andean theology. The market was receptive to Christianity and Culture, which was more acceptable than class analysis, especially since Savage Capitalism had ruled out political alternatives, leaving only Cuba as a socialist state. European theology took up the theme of 'the future of Liberation Theology after socialism' without realising that Latin America still has, and very proudly, Cuba. Cultural Liberation Theology was relaunched, leaving the political and economical analysis aside. It was a return to idealism in the guise of the new marketable fashion product of Gospel and Culture, which tends to ignore the fact that culture is an economic and sexual variable too.

On *Teología Feminista Latina*: the poverty of sexuality

It is important to notice that in these complex relations between Liberation Theology and its western masters, it is the work done by women which has been producing the diaspora of orthodoxy, that is, the constant movement and migration of patriarchal Western assumptions in Liberation Theology, for instance, by the mere fact of challenging the gendered subject of Liberation Theology. Marx distinguished two types of work: one is social work, and the other is community work (Dussel 1988: 30). Liberation Theology mistook one for the other. What the liberationists saw as distinctive community work was social work, that is, the result of production (religious, theological and ecclesiastical, such as in the case of the Basic Ecclesial Communities) done by individuals inside a system of theological production, but not of a community. It was women who rediscovered the latter, through the fact that they were excluded from centres of study (even Liberation Theology centres) and from places of responsibility and decision-making in the church (except in the traditional roles of wives or lovers of important men) and concentrated their efforts in community work. There is an extensive bibliography written on the work done by poor women in *comedores populares* (soup kitchens) and social work in the voluntary sector of society. In a way, Liberation Theology exploited their work. These poor anonymous women organised BECs, but the analysis of BECs subsumed their work; their work in theology was invisible even if highly productive. It was productive because 'the poor woman' became part of the fashionable spectrum of Liberation Theology. 'The poor' and 'the poor woman' were in fact fetishisations, reified phenomena extrapolated from the reality of people's lives, concepts which lost any relation to the context which produced them. Therefore, liberationists produced a discourse of the native woman, succesfully sold as 'the poor mother', 'the poor but strong Christian woman' fitting the patriarchal romantic idea of womanhood in Latin America. It was never the poor woman who was fighting to be ordained as a minister in her church, nor the poor mother trying to get an abortion or struggling, not against capitalism, but against abusive Christian men in her family. If the poor were an asexualised construction in theology, and in Liberation Theology, women fitted the bill for the Mary-machine model. As a result of this process, liberationists wrote and reflected on this ideal woman, the only model they respected. It was not the so-called white middle-class woman (although middle class and white is relative in Latin America where class and race are not always clear-cut), but the poor, ignorant but faithful Christian mother as the model they praised. However, ignorant and poor women (as I have myself been) also have aspirations. I wanted to study in a university and be a trained theologian as my leaders were. Unfortunately this was a transgression of my boundaries and I did not get sympathy or support for that. Their model of poor women excluded our rebellions, our vocations and struggle to be whatever we wanted – poor but intellectual women, active in theological praxis, informed by serious study and reflection. The model of womanhood constructed by the liberationists was as deceptive in their benignity as the Jesuitical reduction models of Paraguay and the north of Argentina. They were fine models as long as the natives regressed psychologically from their maturity as people to some sort of childhood (a European childhood, to be more precise), with patterns of obedience, good behaviour and rewards. Yet, we know that many *Chamames* (Guaraní spiritual and political leaders) called their people to burn the missions and reclaim their right to be the Guaraní nation, with their own beliefs and systems. 'Stand up as mature, adult people for your nation and your beliefs' was the call of the *Chamames* (Liboreiro 1992: 49) Such was, in a way, the call that came for poor women such as myself who refused to play the part of the poor, but happy in her place, Christian woman of the militant church. In reality, we poor Christian women were supporting that theological enterprise that was Liberation Theology, but we were not supported by it in equal terms. When someone recently called my attention to the fact that BECs, are disappearing in Latin America, I said that I was glad. BECs although very valuable at a certain time, are artificial structures. You cannot keep people in artificial structures for ever. You cannot expect people to live in restriction for the rest of their lives. Moreover, that would defeat the purpose of the very structure which is supposed to be a creative device to bring about something else that needs to happen in society. Instead, what we see is the failure of economic plans, which produce more hungry and dependent people every month. The continuation of the BECs could be measured in the same way. The fact that the BEC people organise themselves into popular (interfaith/secular) movements shows the maturity of people in setting aside reductionist projects that, if perpetuated, are of benefit to some theological market but not to the life of real people.

The construction of knowledge, and theological knowledge in our present world, is technologically mediated. A truly liberationist, materialistic based movement ought to know that. Where are the popular publishing houses to give voice to the voiceless? Why did liberationists need to print their book in the USA? Why did they not change the production of theology in order to produce a Chiapas' style of 'Intergalactic Flowers', that is, really a communitarian work of expression and reflection? Where were the new institutions to train poor women and give them theological degrees? Evidently, the organisational standpoint of capitalism has not been challenged. Women started to articulate, to give voice to these concerns in the domestic fields of theology in Latin America, in their BECs, in their churches, or in my own case in the midst of my struggle to study divinity against a church which threatened to expel me from my seminary unless I agreed to study just a few subjects, not for a qualification, but to help me to be a better Sunday School teacher. However, the difficulties that Feminist Theology in Latin America was going to encounter were not only the patriarchal construction of Liberation Theology and Christianity itself, but a methodologically inherited trap. That trap comes from the underdevelopment of gender materialist analysis during the last twenty years in the continent. Feminist Theology in Latin America started from the concrete experience of women, but never reached the peaks of social and political gender analysis that male liberationists had in their time. Dussel read Marx and theology, but the feminists in Latin America did not. Comblin produced a detailed analysis of the church and the national security doctrine, but feminist theologians never engendered that. The analysis of 'women's experience' remained at an undifferentiated level, which happens when experience does not consider the difference between religious and political meaning and its actual signification. Both are different things. Reification occurs in part where that distinction is not made. Thus, Latin American women struggle between what can be considered factual realities of exploitation and discrimination in the religious and political discourse of the continent and the subjective religious experience or meaningful discourse of liberation. The problem is that in the discourse of liberation, women are already disembodied in the category of the poor woman, which is a romantic conceptualisation, a universal which fits the invention of women and the invention of the poor at the same time. In a theological materialist feminist analysis, women need to be studied in certain contexts, and not from a mere struggle of ideas about womanhood constructed in opposition to hegemonic definitions, say by reading life in opposition to the Bible, but by a process of de-abstractionism or materialist reversal. What is the material basis of the construction of women in Latin America? It is judicial, enshrining women's behaviour in law, in customs and in traditions, and can be classified in an index and viewed historically. They need a historical materialist analysis, but Feminist Theology in Latin America did not engage with the sociological and cultural studies made by Latin American women in our century. Instead of that, it started with ideas, and superstructures not to de-authorise them, but to reverse their power in this case, in favour of women. Take for instance that piece of cultural materialism that pretends to be the discourse on Mariology in Latin America. In this case the discourse on the Virgin Mary constructed Latin American reality. As a result of that, the Mariology of the Latin American women befits the Gospel and Culture theological fashion which seems to think that cultural realms are outside sexual economic ones. The dialectical praxis between economy and genderised culture in Latin America is not explained, and no strategies for change are elaborated. The only trans-gressive act produced in these years of Feminist Theology in the continent has been feminist exegeses on the Bible, which are for the most part limited exercises of symbolic value and Mariology, with its doubtful results. Mariology of liberation, by the way, is not only the realm of women theologians; male theologians pioneered the field and authenticated it for women theologians to follow. Men have been writing and exaggerating on the premises that the worship of Mary is a feminist thing for years. Mariology is a decent field of work for women, approved by male theo-logians. This is precisely the point. Feminist Theology follows liberationist decency based on tight sexual constructions. It makes little difference if they are Western or native constructions because both are patriarchal, deter-mining constructions for women. One can say that sometimes women enjoy more freedom under the prevalent Western construction, which, based on liberal systems, allows them to study. Some indigenous groups will not allow their women to study. In other cases women may enjoy more sexual freedom in some indigenous groups than in the Western world, but we are talking of concession systems which always present a decent construct of womanhood. We are in the realm of the ex-centricity of women's decency as a presup-position of the hermeneutical circle. Theology is a sexual act, a sexual doing, based on the construction of God and divine systems which are male and worked in opposition (and sexual opposition) to women. It was women who historically stabilised the discourse of theology, dissolving gender tensions into afterlife equality systems. Specifically, the sexual regulation of women's life has been the element which gave coherence to theology, considering how pervasive and sustained has been that reflection through the centuries. Therefore, Latin American women have been going to bed with God the Father and the Son or with Mary at the same time, without questioning that sexual act of theology which is simultaneously economical. It regulates numbers, fixes positions and pre-empties intimacy and meaning. To undo that will require something more than cultural materialism; something that will require us to take our pants off at the moment of doing theology.

Theology 'with women's eyes'

'. . . *Tus ojos para mi, son el reflejo fiel, de un mundo de ilusión . . .*'
Your eyes are for me the faithful reflection of an illusory world . . .
(Tango: *Yo no sé que me han hecho tus ojos*)

'*Ojos negros, traicioneros . . .*'
Black eyes, you betrayers . . .
(Cueca: *Yo vendo unos ojos
negros*)

Why does the Feminist Theology of Liberation select the female gaze as a privileged place of discourse? Why not a theology with women's hands, legs, breasts or head? Why not a theology 'with women's sex?' Moreover, why a theology from a fragmented female body, in this case, a cornea, a woman's retina? 'Theology with women's eyes' is not only a Latin American trademark of feminist hermeneutics. In the Third World Feminist Theology movement, the image of eyes has been used extensively in the titles of books, edited works and articles. It is a popular if tired metaphor used in Latin America which has not been renewed or recreated after those first years of theology as a polite gazing from women's eyes into the male philosophical wonderland of Liberation Theology. Feminist Theology was born from the realisation of unequal power relations in the theological fraternities of the liberationist 1970s and early 1980s. It was not initially, at least, a simple cry of protest at the exclusion of women in theological education or the limitations to priesthood or ordained ministries of the Church. It was the realisation that the few women, counted on the fingers of one hand, who had high theological education during the 1970s were enjoying the privilege of being the token presence amongst the all-male delegates at international conferences, without helping the rest to do the same. The early account of the birth of Feminist Theology by Virginia Fabella (Fabella 1992) is interesting in the way that the key motives for uneasiness are presented, as related to a power struggle, and a right to be there, while feminist consciousness seems to come later. No wonder theology done by women was a gaze, a penetration by what we can call the female phallus into the sexualisation of the theological enterprise which confronted it. In this Feminist Theology, eyes and erotic desires projected themselves in a voyeuristic methodology of looking at, as the divine impregnation of the Virgin Mary happened in old iconography, a gaze (light) passing through a window and directed to her womb (Graziano 1997: 159). From all the senses and imaginary of a fragmented woman's body the eyes have been perceived as the most innocuous because they are the religious authorised spare parts of a woman in any patriarchal society. Women's eyes represent the lightness of what is supposed to be women's knowledge, circumscribed around issues of seduction and subjection. Latin American women's eyes are always lowered in confrontation with men, and never keep their gaze into men's eyes unless a woman is an easy, indecent woman (sexual deviant). That is precisely the point of the metaphor with women's eyes in Latin America: it marks the boundaries and regulates female sexual transgressions. Theology with women's eyes is another form of the female boudoir's little arts, a boudoir theology. It is just an authorised point of view, a perception from a different angle or in a different light but of the same issues. The issues of theology, even if they are of women's concern, are those belonging to a patriarchal structured social reality, including the reading of the Scriptures and legislative texts of church practice. In the end, they are organisational standpoints which are never challenged in the theology with women's eyes: the definition of womanhood is a conceptual heterosexual given, as is the idea of the family and the material base that masculinity confers on the sacred. It seems that the issue is reduced to looking at conflicts differently, but not challenging who decides what are conflicts in the life of women or not, and how they decide. Finally, it carries the idealistic illusion that by just looking things can be changed.

Theology with women's eyes carried out exegesis, re-readings of the Bible, but never developed a serious feminist theological materialist analysis or hermeneutical circle, except for some flirting with a general description of women's conditions under different oppressions (better and more effectively developed by Latin American women sociologists than by theologians). The pattern of the exegesis has generally been a curious one. Exegesis tends to start with some description of women's condition of labour, or a recounting of a story from the memory of the Original Nations or the history of liberation in Latin America. The theologian usually starts as a cultural raconteur, who continues with a biblical account of the issue related to the story. For instance, if the story is about poverty, the theologian will proceed generally with an account of the meaning of poverty in the Hebrew Scriptures and New Testament. Finally, the study tends to end with a paragraph in which the name Jesus, the words Kingdom of God and/or justice or hope will be mentioned as in a spellbinding exercise. A statement of hope, but of ex-centric, miraculous hope and not of concrete challenge tends to be the result of feminist reflections, unless we are able to come out with realism in theology and accept the lack of answers which have overwhelmed us.

What is evident in this common pattern is that the gaze method is a yo-yo, jumping from materialist promises to historical criticism and back to idealism. The women's gazing into male theology ends in idealism, because there has not been a sustained effort to develop a truly materialist approach which would redefine women's issues in Latin America, starting from a sexual enquiry into patterns of doing sexual theologies and confronting the abstraction process of women's life into patriarchal categories. Women have become things in life and the divine pantheon alike, and male ideas (including Christian gods) have become people. This is particularly true in Latin American Mariology.

In bed with the Madonna

To choose Mary as a departing feminist theological criticism is another example of idealist methods in a theology which is supposedly Marxist influenced. If it is true that the first inscriptions (of hunger, pain and sexual desire) are always written in the body, one wonders how a women's theology can start with Mary, the icon of a no-body. To start with Mary is to start with an idea, a gas-like substance, a myth of a woman without a vagina which discloses in a hilarious way the fact that half of humanity has been constructed around ideas of ghostly simulacras. As a woman theologian myself, I need to struggle against the idea of using 'she' for the Virgin Mary. The Virgin Mary is not a woman but a simulacra in which the process of making ideologies and what Marx calls 'mystical connections' is exemplified (Marx 1976: 43). It is not only that our idea of a woman who does not reflect the human experience of womanhood in the least has been made a narrative of authority, but this 'thing' called the Virgin Mary has interfered with other political and social conceptualisations. It has become natural for Christian women in Latin America to identify Mary as a goddess because goddesses and gods are not expected to be human or to have human characteristics. For me, if the Virgin Mary had paws instead of hands and her vagina was in her ear, thus making it easier for the Word of God, the Logos, to 'say its Word' and penetrate her, it would not make any theological difference. Mary is in the realm of the fantastic and phantasmagorical. Used to rape and incest in their poor overcrowded conditions of living, Latin American women are not necessarily the ones to question why a young woman needs to fulfil a vocation of accommodating God's desire when God pleases. Many women and poor women in my continent are forced to marry very young and become pregnant with their first child when they are barely past childhood themselves. The Virgin Mary is a theologically casuistic case presented in feminicide. A life that cannot have any choice because it is a woman's life, and no other reason, is a life which suffers many forms of assassinations. After the sacralisation of the Virgin Mary legend and its incorporation into a universalising discourse, it is there that we find the first *'cuerpo del delito'*, that is, the body of crime where sexual behaviour and punishments can be ascribed. Why did God need a woman to procreate? And for the defenders of non-anthropological deistic conceptualisations, of a God who is supposed to be neither female nor male, what if God approached Joseph and asked him to help in the divine intercourse? The legend of Mary does not stand up to any serious disquisition, but could do with some bold denunciation exercises, such as those advocated by liberation theologians when they fulfil the prophetic task of unmasking structures of oppression. But feminist theologians from Latin America have not done this. To be specific, the subject could benefit from a sound materialistic analysis, an ontological materialism and a materialist dialectics. We need to discern the construction of sexuality and gender roles in Latin America as political subordinates which have been naturalised by colonisation processes using the sexual order of God the Virgin in the continent. It is not what dogma says which affects people, but the raw relationship to the Virgin Mary's theo-ideology which has shaped our common sense and limited our hermeneutical circles. However, the most daring thing liberationists have courageously said is that Mary was poor, as if adding a socio-economic perspective to the woman who is not a woman was enough. For sure this requires more nuance in its analysis. It is interesting that in every recently edited collection of essays on Liberation Theology, published by someone of the first-generation liberationists or some of the self-appointed male inheritors (so called 'second-generation liberationists'), most of the articles written by women are on Mariology.[4] Audre Lorde has said that 'the masters tools would never dismantle the masters house' (Lorde 1994: 54) and we may add to this that one must beware when the masters feel so pleased with Mariological studies.

Mary Mother of God, *Mummy* of the Poor?

The passion for idealism and the constant use of ideology as a method has never been so blatant as in the case of Latin American Mariological Theology. Articles and chapters in books repeat almost the same thing, the theme of 'Mary and the poor' without any serious materialist attempt to analyse Marian false consciousness in Latin America. The most consistent example of this has been the text produced in Ivonne Gebara and Maria Clara Bingemer *Mary, Mother of God, Mother of the Poor* (Gebara and Bingemer 1989). The reader can be easily misguided into believing that theologians (and women theologians) in Latin America write together, in some sort of 'community style'. That has never been the case. Moreover, in many countries of the continent the liberationists have not even produced disciples or encouraged younger minds to follow their path. In fact, *Mary, Mother of God, Mother of the Poor* is probably the only work written in this way, and the authors have not written another book together again. It is true that some authors such as Pablo Richard and the late Guillermo Cook tend to sign their chapters and articles adding at the end of their names the words 'and friends'. Sometimes these names are disclosed, sometimes not, but the task of the liberation theologian, female or male, does not follow guidelines very different from the pattern imposed in North Atlantic theology. The ways of producing theology have not been challenged in their mechanisms of production: the communities of the poor are sometimes the resource (hidden work) but not yet the visible authors of any text. The sad thing is that the limits of materialist methods in Latin America are not imposed by lack of creativity, but of coherence. We tend to feel happier creating legends such as 'the theologians work in community' for the benefit of Western consumerism, than for the sake of doing things in a different way. We have the vision of doing theology in community, of writing as a 'we' and not an 'I'. We announce it but we seldom do it.

The main thesis of Gebara and Bingemer, two Roman Catholic lecturers from Brazil, has been to uncover the anthropological conceptions of traditional Mariology and thus rediscover a Mary who would stop being the opium of women (in the narcotic sense out of boredom, as well as of oppression). In order to do this they want to produce a realist anthropology, as opposed to the idealist one which the authors think has pervaded Virginal studies till now (Gebara and Bingemer 1989: 7). Anthropology, that science which had its origin in the colonisation of Africa, and the scientific ordering done under the colonial gaze, becomes a concern for their analysis. Obviously, the authors are not referring to the taxonomic catalogues of the end of the nineteenth century, when British theoreticians were trying hard to divide barbarous from civilised, explaining their different racial character istics and moral qualities alike. But, equally, one would think that liber ationists would be as suspicious as Althusser of using a philosophical anthropology which can elaborate upon the nature of humanity, based on some sort of model of general human features or characteristics. However, the authors do not quote a single anthropologist or philosopher in their entire book. There is not a single endnote to guide us into what is this anthropological enterprise that they are analysing. In the final bibliography only the mention of Husserl's *Ideas* might gave us some clue concerning the intention to integrate phenomenology with the methods of comparative biology and social enquiry which started in 1920 but which were later superseded by biological–cultural understandings – as seen for example in Scheler *Man's Place in Nature* (Audi 1995: 580–1). Gebara and Bingemer do not refer to anything specifically recognisable as coming from an anthro pological field of studies, cultural or philosophical. However, they do engage in a light discourse against idealism, dualistic world-views and apolitical conceptions of humanity in the framework of a mild feminist critique. Basically, the following summarises their main contentions (Gebara and Bingemer 1989: xi).

1   Latin American Women have an important alliance with Mary at this moment in time, because they are 'stirring up to win their rights . . . .'.
2   Their proposal is for a new anthropological foundation in Mariology, which must be 'unifying, realist and pluri-dimensional'.
3   In order to do this, they want to begin with a reflection on the idea of the Kingdom of God as relevant for women in Latin America and Mariology.

The alliance that real women in Latin American can or may have with a highly complex religious symbol developed for centuries through the oppression of women (and particularly, colonised women) does not look like a promising starting point for realism. Women's rights are not necessarily homologisable with the ideal discourse of the patriarchal state of rights, because the construction of sexual and gender roles limits so-called rights and shapes needs and duties. The fiercest arguments against the right of women to vote were fought in Argentina under the banners of the Virgin Mary. Would women still be feminine if they voted?[5] Even Evita declared of women, that after all 'we are neither in the Vatican nor in the Kremlin' (Perón 1951: 284), when confronted with the fact that poor women seemed to be considered to be fit only for sacrificing themselves for others. That is precisely the theme of Mary in Latin America, the theme of human female sacrifices, because it touches the core of the colonial construction of sexuality in Latin America. Women dying of domestic and public violence; women dying of backstreet abortions; women dying of hunger due to the discrimination in education and jobs. Moreover, women sacrificing themselves on the altar of the false consciousness of the worship of a virginal mother. This construction started with the word *Indios*. The concept of the 'Indian' as a masked concept which hides the fact that there is no such thing as a continuity between the inhabitants of our continent, specifically the women of our continent, and the present situation after the genocide of America (Dupeyron 1992). Mary is a concept which comes to the continent at the same time as the concept of *Indios*. The presence of the icon and its nativisation produces a sense of continuity which is false, unmasks the oppressive role of the foreign religion of Christianity in the continent and keeps endorsing women with boundaries, aspirations and ideals which are imperialist in nature and ideological in method. According to Dupeyron, the concept of women in Latin America is similar to the concept of *Indios*. They are equivalent illusions under the heavy weight of a metaphysical and logical conquest. It is an ethical victory for the colonisers, under the banner of Mary, the icon which shows women why they are not real women. From this perspective, what might be a unifying realist perspective by which to read Mary? Certainly not one that starts with 'the idea of the Kingdom'! Has any poor or rich Latin American ever lived under a monarchy? Is it realistic to speak of Kingdoms as in middle age Spain? Were liberationists not socialists? And why unifying? The metaphor of the Kingdom is useful in denunciation of what needs to be reflected again in the

Gospel's message, but pluri-dimensions in theology are not without risks. It is similar to theologians speaking with poor communities and finding that they are re-reading the Bible against the traditions of the church (C. Boff 1987: 136). What can the theologian do? If the theologian is committed to doing theology with the people, then the theologian must recognise that sometimes people do theology without underwear.

It is a pity that Gebara and Bingemer have ignored the rich sources which come from the 1960s in Marxist anthropology and feminist materialist anthropology, which could have helped in the clarification of their so-called realistic anthropology, starting with real lives and *historias* (histories/stories) of Latin American women. Classical work from anthropologists such as Michelle Zimbalist Rosaldo and Karen Sacks are particularly relevant for a Third World materialist (or realist) Feminist Theology. Rosaldo and Sacks were amongst those pioneer women who challenged male assumptions about gender structures in society, linking elements such as patriarchal hier-archisation and the division between private and public spaces so crucial in the lives of poor Latin American women. Other anthropologists chose to re-read Marx and Engels to analyse the family structures with a hermeneutical suspicion which was lacking in a field as male dominated as theology, including the liberationist version. In this case, the work of Kate Young in *Of Marriage and the Market* would have provided material for a realist anthropology relating poor Latin American women and a sacred text which starts with the arranged marriage of a pubescent girl such as the Mary of the New Testament. In that case the claim of so many Latin American women forced into early marriages by a mixture of economic needs, patriarchal destiny and religious sanction of a woman's fate in life could have had a voice. But no, Gebara and Bingemer criticise an imaginary anthropologist or philosopher, repeating the following key postulates of Liberation Theology:

1   *That history is only one*: This is a very contested position in Feminist Theology. For instance, we can argue that Mary is not part of history since she has broken the historical nexus of women as non-menstruating, conceiving outside the realms of sexuality and procreating by unnatural[6] means.

2   *There is a unity of soul–body in humanity*: But in this, Gebara and Bingemer have missed the point that Mary, as a religious symbol, behaves in a strange way, which disembodies theology by its negation of sexuality and de-souls women who only through a bodily function such as reproduction become spiritual beings. This is a complete contra-diction which ends by negating body *and* soul alike in women.

3   *Theology is contextual*: However, Mariology cannot be easily contextual-ised. Furthermore, in Mariology it is necessary to recognise the complexity of our contexts and to avoid falling into idealist contexts which are indebted to a Christian ideology of faulty sexual under-standing in the first place.

These three interesting postulates, if taken seriously, mean that Mary is not historical but is a religious symbol in the history of women's oppression. Re-readings of the Bible, important as they may be, cannot unmask the fact that women have concrete lives ruled by Marian performances. If Mary is a symbol for the Latin American women's liberation movement, how is it that in 500 years we have seen exactly the opposite? Where does *Marianismo* come from then, if not from Mariology and popular Mariology? One wishes that everything in the symbolic field could be reduced to a case of literary criticism illiteracy, but the dynamic of symbols cannot be ignored, nor their living reality beyond the realms of good exegetical intentions. Re-reading the gospel cannot hide the fact that Mary shows the disunity of soul–body by the anomaly of her representation. Only by using a contextual theology is it possible to make the break with the citation procedure or repetition which is the only clue to Mary's religious credibility. Unfortunately, the anthropological debate with *Mary, Mother of God, Mother of the Poor* cannot be an extensive one. The anthropological Marian enterprise in that book lasts less than twenty pages of a book of nearly two hundred. Beginning from a declaration of materialist commitment, the authors take us into Platonism, to the world of biblical texts, dogmas, selected traditions of appearances of the Virgin in the continent (the traditions which fit the thesis, not the ones which are against) and five final pages on Basic Ecclesial Communities, as a way to ground the discourse. Realism, which Mariology of Liberation wanted to be grounded in, is lost.

The questions which Gebara and Bingemer ask concerning anthropology and hermeneutics are relevant indeed, because Mariology is powerful in Latin America. Moreover, in Mariology lies the possibility to deconstruct the sexual and political foundations of the continent. Mary is a machine which processes multiple Othernesses and oppressions and returns them in the image and similitude of the onlooker, and in this lies the dangerous trap of the worship of Mary. Mary interpellates men and women, especially amongst the poor, and produces the false consciousness that is Marian faith, concerned with the perpetuation of capitalist models of marriage, biological sexual definitions and universal faith constructions of women believers, submissive or courageous, but always determined by their relation to the symbolics of Mary.

Does theology need an anthropology or *Mujeriology*?

Let us consider a move from anthropology to *Mujeriology*, for the sake of a love for differences, not equalities. After all, equal discourses confront us with the fact that the centre fixes the equation for the margins. The 'Equal to Whom?' is never favourably resolved unless one accepts previous structures of power and definitions of relationship. A *Mujeriological* (Womanist) perspective is that which starts by asking who is she? Who is that Latin American woman subject of Marian discourse that liberationists present to us? To give the answer that the subject of women's theology is 'the poor' (identified as women, in this case) would be an essentialisation not only of Latin American women but specifically of poor Latin American women. There are poor women in *fabelas* and in shanty towns, and there are poor women on factory night-shifts and living as domestic workers in the most exclusive residential mansions of big cities. There are rural poor women, and urban poor women. There are poor women who define their sexuality in relation to other women as there are poor men who love other men. Poor women do not come with the sexuality of dogmas; that is the reason why dogmas exist in the first place, to re-order reality. An orthopraxical approach (the liberationist standpoint theory, as classically developed) can also commit the mistake of thinking that the real woman is equivalent to the theological presupposition of what real poor women believe for their own good. Behaving like ethnologists struggling to respect the host culture while looking at it with the eyes of the Other, theologians always keep the Latin American woman inside the margins of the decent discourse of society. Decency is the theory of the proper in Latin America, which is a theological concept inherited from the disruption of the *Conquista*. The *Conquista* is, first of all, a theological disruption and hegemonic theological statement. *Mujer Latinoamericana* is a theological concept too, and made to fit this discourse of the proper, specifically in the sexual order imposed by Roman Catholicism. This is not to say, romantically, that civilisations before the end of the Great Narratives were non-patriarchal: they were different, it is true, but the Aztecs, for instance, were known for their hatred of women while the Incas allowed women a degree of sexual freedom sadly denied when women fell under the Virginal influence and the construction of theological decency.

The contradictions are many. Unfortunately, theology has become the art of erasing them. The homogenisation of sexuality and, specifically, the sexuality of the poor, serves as a basic pattern from which behaviour, aspirations and relationship to God and to economic systems are worked out and sacralised with an aura of immutability and eternity. It is interesting to note that the economic nature of theology has been unveiled many times in history, and before Marx's critique on religion. The Hebrew Scriptures and the New Testament are critiques, although only partially, of economic structures of oppression. The so-called Fathers of the Church criticised usury and private property. So did the Reformers. Theology of Liberation only produced a more organised economic and political critique than its predecessors did, but the sexual nature of theology, closely linked to theological understanding, and the sanctioning of mechanisms of power and control in patriarchy have been missed. We have not had a sexual analysis of systematic theology, or dogmatics. The reason for this is that economic systems may change, but the sexual nature of theology is too close to the final product. It is because of the sexual nature of theological systems which always, unfailingly, start with a declaration on compulsory heterosexuality and gender roles as part of their distributive system, that a closeted heterosexuality has been developed and assumed as a natural thing. Decency is the name of the Latin American closeted heterosexuality, that is, the assumption that even heterosexuality can be moulded according to a prescriptive way – which is not true. Heterosexual women need to come out of their closet like anybody else, speaking the truth about their lives, heavily domesticated by patriarchal definitions of what it is to be a heterosexual, monogamous, faithful woman with a motherly vocation. The whole strength of women's Liberation Theology may lie just in this point, because it has the opportunity to disclose and to encourage women to come out of the closet also as heterosexuals. This cannot be done by making the Virgin Mary an un-employed woman. The symbolic action of the Virgin Mary throughout the history of Latin America is part of the problem, not the solution. Obviously, it will require from Latin American women more of a passionate, lustful love for women than commitment to a hybrid humanoid theological represent-ation such as Mary in order to leave the closet of decency and hypocrisy of Latin America. It is not an anthropology but a *Mujeriology* that we need in order to stop subordinating women's political experiences to ghostly talks of apparitions of Virgins in the Hills. How far is this apparitional theology from an orthopraxis approach! Yet, articles and books from Latin American liberationists are still dedicated to the starting point of an apparition, such as the Virgin of Guadalupe, for instance, which relates the questioning of our lives as women (and men) in Latin America to the image and likeness of the theological project of the *Conquista*. The danger lies in the fact that by adding the themes of nationalism and the struggle against imperialism in our continent to the worship of the humanoid Virgin, women's loyalties are split. We are constantly being reminded that poor women are devoted to the Virgin, but it is also true that they are equally devoted to husbands who abuse them. A simple case of false consciousness, such as the Marian devotion in Latin America, cannot be criticised easily, under accusations of not being committed to the poor, or to the cause of Latin American liberation . The truth is that closeted heterosexuality as embodied in the quasi-human imaginary of the Virgin Mary is what cannot be challenged. This is the reason why the theological indecenting of the Virgin Mary or the homoeroticisation of Jesus are more an economic threat to structures of political and economic oppression than the political, mental structures which in Latin America came as part of a theological medieval Roman Catholicism. The time has come for Latin American women theologians to remove their underwear at the moment of reflecting theologically and, as in the image of the lemon vendors in the streets of Buenos Aires, allow the smell of their sexuality to mix with their reflections on feminism, theology and economics.

2 The indecent Virgin

Sexual positions: locating the G(od) spot of virginal reflections

It was an inspiration. I suddenly realised that for the next carnival in Buenos Aires I should go out as a female impersonator of the Virgin of Guadalupe. I therefore started to look carefully at pictures to find dressing clues to help me with the dying of bed-sheets and other home-made manoeuvres to be the *Guadalupana* for one night. Pasting silver paper half moons to the skirt? Making my hair look even darker than it is? The little carnival number could then consist of me and two other friends (Mary Magdalene and the other Mary) with me, as the principal of the trinity of Marys, addressing the carnival multitudes with a mimicry of Virginal discourses starting with words such as 'My children!' The original inspiration came from a painting called the *Portrait of the Artist as the Virgin of Guadalupe* by an important Chicana artist, Yolanda López. She has painted her self-portrait as if coming from the opened cloak of the Virgin of Guadalupe, which, if looked at carefully, has the appearance of an open, gigantic red vulva. The image of the Virgin of Guadalupe has been described in terms of the dark colour of the skin of the image and the style of her clothes, but curiously, nothing has been said about this tender, swollen reddish vulva from where she emerges. López, as the Virgin of Guadalupe, emerges from this divine vulva looking like a young Latina, dressed with a modern skirt and trainers, and in a jogging attitude.[1] Looking at the portrait, one of the implicit metaphors in the image of Yolanda López as the Virgin of Guadalupe could be a point for self-identification. That is to say any woman (not only a Latina) could theoretically see herself in the picture. This would work as a sort of funfair photograph, creating the illusion of being whoever is in the picture painted on a board: you simply put your head in the hole in place of the head of the person or animal represented. In our example, it is a case of sexual positions. To put your head through the hole, to see yourself as the Virgin emerging from a divine vulva, requires a sexual option. For instance, you need to consider where God is in this, because God's position is a sexual option in itself. Sexual identities are usually found in the places we are accustomed to inhabit and in the way we position ourselves and are positioned in the narratives of the past (Stuart Hall, quoted in Weeks 1995: 97). We can consider, for instance, whether God is a female divinity represented by a vulva, but even beyond that, whether God relates to an autonomous sexuality or a reflected one (such as in the case of women's sexuality in traditional heterosexuality). Or is God a pleasurable site, a G spot somewhere hidden but built around mythical (sometimes exaggerated) proportions? In that case, we need to consider the mythical proportions of penetration in traditional theology. Traditionally, theology has seen the world as coming from God's dissemination which has been represented by the Highest Phallus *men* could conceive of: the Word of God. Systematic theological thought has been made by these forceful seminal disseminations and their discursive reproductive powers. Christian issues of humility and submission to God come from that premise; the ejaculatory movement of the Word of God requires an immobile receptacle, such as the Virgin Mary, for instance. However, there are many varieties of sexual positions which Systematic Theology has not considered yet. For instance, that sex does not need to be penetrative disseminations, as the portrait of the artist as the Virgin of Guadalupe seems to convey. The G(od) spot does not need to be located as a supplement; the G(od) spot belongs to the vulva and her pleasure; to the embrace of the lips and the hardness of the clitoris. From that undifferentiated sexual position we can then think about ourselves, as the portrait of the theologian as the Virgin of Guadalupe and her challenge to reconsider the sexual position of God in this.

In a way, to write theology is similar to the act of putting our head in the hole at the funfair photo-booth. It is an act of identification with religious symbolism. When the photograph from the funfair is revealed, we can see ourselves as if we were monkeys or pirates. Men become young women and women old men. Funfair photographs are acts of transcendental dimensions; they transgender us, and this is done at the crossroads of sexual definitions complicated by age, culture, gender, race and social classes. The point of the funfair photograph is precisely to contradict as much as possible the identity of the person portrayed. Humble people want to be portrayed in expensive clothes and men like to appear as nude women. Theologians who write on the Virgin Mary as 'Virginal liberationists' seem to be also pursuing this transcendental act of putting their heads on the Virgin's photograph. They do not seem to notice the vulva of the *Guadalupana* but would like to think that every Latin American woman (and man?) can see herself in the Virgin of Guadalupe. Obviously, many Latin American women will say 'No thanks'; in my case, I am a woman who prefers to choose sexual companions, and therefore, I cannot identify with Virginal submissions by requirement. Moreover, I am not keen on elderly divine figures looking for sex (such as God the Father) due to some bad experiences I had with men in my life, such as bishops. However, I can see why the idea of the theologian as the Virgin of Guadalupe may be appealing instead of appalling for some women. To put the head on the vulva of the Virgin, for instance, for the photograph, may be part of a short-circuited kind of goddess-empowering ritual. If the Virgin of Guadalupe is powerful, but also poor, I as a disempowered but poor woman have something in common with her (social class status). Due to my worshipful attitude towards her (or what she represents, since the Virgin does not have a life outside of our theological imagination) she may share her power with me. However, this empowering circle is a short circuit, because in worshipping Mary women need to go through a spiritual clitoridectomy, in the sense of mutilating their lust, in order to identify with the Virgin, get her approval of their behaviour and never question the social and political order built around such religious ideology. This happens because the Virgin and the vulva have become disjoined and separated, which is a tremendous contradiction since the term 'virgin/virginity' usually presents us with the mental picture of a vulva, as a specific sexual location for the purposes of identity.

The point is that the Virginal liberationist does theology without lust. Lust suffers a theological clitoridectomy and therefore no real sense of empowering can come from the worship of the Virgin. Of course, we can also consider that the divine empowering women have received from the worship of the Virgin has been the power to suffer that theological clitoridectomy performed by the church down the centuries. For instance, the power to endure the closeted heterosexuality of a society which is particularly cruel towards poor women; the empowering of imagining that our shoulders are broad enough to carry the usual oppressive load. Moreover, any form of transcendental meditation done through the Virgin is suicidal, since the first thing that needs to be denied is the material body.[2] The greatest paradox in this transcendental quest comes also from the fact that poverty and virginity do not fit together in the lives of women. Poor women are seldom virgins, because poverty in Latin America means crowded conditions of violence and promiscuity, where girls get raped before puberty or married as adolescents as part of the few available economic transactions on offer, except for several forms of prostitution and sexual bondage. Women thus get pregnant before they know what their own sexuality is, before they can discover the divinity of lust in their lives. The idea of the life of the poor but decent women is as illusory as the apparitions of Mary on Latin American hillsides, and as hypocritical as Karl Barth writing on the values of the traditional family while he obviously could not suffer the occasionally idiotic nature of married life. However, liberationists can argue against that, saying that since poor Latin American women are devotees of the Virgin, we as theologians must honour this while finding liberative elements in Marian worship. Do you remember the old premise of Liberation Theology? First comes reality; theology is only a second act. However, what has not been clearly thought out is how reality is conformed; what is excluded and what is included in that definition of reality needs a more thoughtful reflection. For instance, discourses on women and poverty say nothing related to the vulva and the G(od) spot in the lives of poor Latin American women. Not every poor woman is heterosexual, nor do heterosexual women have homogenous behaviour either. Sexuality and poverty combine themselves in different ways and reality is constituted with variations. Oppression ramifies itself and is less contained than liberationists used to think.

Let us consider further this argument which is twofold, for it comprises two key elements of the ethical standing of liberationists. First, the fact of doing theology from people's own spiritual world; second, the engaging in a theological conscientisation project to distinguish oppressive from liberative cultural elements. In these two statements we have the core of Latin American liberationists' ethical values: solidarity and a vow of never betraying the cause of liberation.[3] However, in the case of the Virgin, they are clearly not compatible. Let us consider these elements, and if it is possible to become the Virgin of Guadalupe just because poor women have such a heavy spiritual investment in her.

Worthy speculations: investing in the Virgin

Anthropologist Wendy Holloway's notion of 'investment' is a useful one to consider here. According to her, in any society (such as the Latin American) where there are several simultaneous discourses on femininity and masculinity competing for hegemony, a woman can get some reward for her support of a certain discourse on women which promises to be beneficial to her (Holloway 1984: 238). For instance, to be a Marian worshipper may give some reward to poor women in Latin America who invest in the Virgin's worship in order to get some emotional satisfaction, and some material rewards too. These usually come from theological investments in the Latin American decency system: the idea of the good daughter, good mother and wife have been constructed around virginal/whore dichotomies according to the hegemonic production of the moral system of the country. That decency system relies on regulation and order to facilitate penetrative discourse regulating the insertion of women in society. Outside these, there is prostitution, that is, a public stand of women outside their domestic realms of life.

By investing in the Virgin, a poor woman avoids being classified as a prostitute, meaning by this a woman who takes a public stand of deviant or subversive power. And this is done in a continent where sexual subversiveness is usually associated with political terrorism. The price to be paid is high. Even in Basic Ecclesial Communities women need to avoid the social ostracism and disapproval which is non-beneficial to the art of surviving poverty. They risk losing their contact point in the homo-solidarity of the system. Going back to Holloway's concept of *cathexis* as investment in a particularly defined positioning of the female subject in society, may help us to understand the positioning of poor women in Latin America in *Machista* theo/social structures, but also women's rebellions. What happens is that the promises women obtain from the worship of the Virgin and their insertion in the *Machista* church are seldom fulfilled. In any case, much sexual dissatisfaction comes from adherence to idealist systems supported by Virginal worship, such as marriage, no sex without a reproductive goal and life in a sacramental community such as the BECs. What happens is that the return for a woman's investment in decency is so poor that in the end it allows her to keep a rebellious spirit in spite of her sexual/gender investment. For instance, in *Machista* theory, motherhood is a great investment in Latin American society by a process of Marian *cathexis*. Motherhood supposedly gives a Latin American the highest investment rate in terms of status in church and society. However, the bank of historical reality has never paid any interest on these promises of respect and status made in romantic Christian literature. On the contrary, motherhood is the most devalued position for women in Latin America in real value terms, except for the status symbol of aristocratic women who like to boast of having large families while supported by wealthy husbands (or by a considerable fortune from their own family) and who enjoy the home care provided by ill-paid poor women who need to neglect their own children in order to look after those of the rich. In that case, wealth and not motherhood gives women a societal and church based position of respect. The lack of critical insight into the devalued position of motherhood in Latin America has created several analytical mistakes and misjudgements, amongst them the understanding that the Mothers of *Plaza de Mayo* were able to produce a unique movement for the defence of human rights during the dictatorial regime of the 1970s in Argentina, due to the respect that a Marian society pays to mothers. Nothing could be further from truth. The Mothers of *Plaza de Mayo* have been tortured and killed. It is due to their courage and intelligence as women, not as mothers, that they have been able to organise themselves and present a challenge to the government on issues of state terrorism. They stood publicly. They were called *locas* (madwomen, prostitutes). Some of the Mothers remember with irony that they were usually sent to 'go and pray to the Virgin Mary' by priests, bishops and men of power, perhaps with the hope that the Marian worship would domesticate them, make them decent mothers who would educate daughters into decency and not political subversion. Testimonies from tortured victims of the *Junta* describe how, in the concentration camps, they were forced to pray 'Hail Marys' before bedtime (CONADEP 1994: 348). The virginal worship appears here with another face, that of affective theo/political investment. It is not a novelty though. This kind of religious investment in the Virgin of Decency may date from the *Conquista*, and presents a simple case of the reproduction of false consciousness.

Vanilla Mariology

If it is true that Latin American women since the *Conquista* in the fifteenth century have been drawn to worship the Virgin of the Conquistadors as part of a false consciousness process whose goal is economic oppression, and that this cannot be challenged due to the spiritual investment of affection from today's women, then we cannot talk of domestic violence anymore. If theology condones sexual violence on the basis of the accepted and cherished, what then can we say of women who refuse to abandon the partner who beats them because he is their partner, the father of their children, and they love him? The problem increases when women theologians in Latin America do not realise that their Marian Theologies are also part of making an investment in the Virgin. This kind of women's theology calls for an identificatory act with the Virgins (in the plural, for there are thousands of images with different characteristics and personalities) in Latin America, and this is the crux of the problem because the promises of such an investment are not fulfilled except by bringing resignation and false consciousness into our lives under the guise of liberation. The point is that to write about the Virgin will always be 'the portrait of the theologian as the Virgin of Guadalupe' because it cannot avoid showing considerable degrees of (dis)investment in that gigantic vulva, that history of beginnings which surrounds the picture of the Virgin of Guadalupe. To put our heads, as women theologians, in that vulva is, in itself, a statement of sexual identifications, which are closely linked to the production of ideological discourses in the continent and the challenges presented in them by conscientisation processes. Those challenges are based on the fact that gender and sexual discourses are, cross-culturally speaking, variable and unstable (Moore 1994: 58), and theology tends to stabilise them in alliance with ideological stances. Have Gebara and Bingemer not seen this point (which comes from feminist anthropology), in their claimed anthropological study of the Virgin Mary? If they had done so, the issue of conscientisation may have been taken more seriously in their work. Conscientisation depends on questioning and problematisation of 'given' realities. The problem is that the theologian as the Virgin of Guadalupe is always such a hybrid product, a kind of émigré from lands of patriarchy who still retains the full cultural values of sexual oppression. It is a case of Vanilla Theology which cannot question more than the approved script on women and Christianity in the continent, and which does not risk anything, because it does not come from women who love women enough. In leather, S/M and fetish erotic styles, 'vanilla sex' has been defined as the area of unadventurous lovers, without clear initiatives into different ways of expressing themselves sexually (Baldwin 1993: 59). The feminist theologians of Latin America are mostly of the unadventurous, vanilla kind; they do not want disapproval from their churches or institutions; they are orthodox heterosexual women (or pretend to be) with a minimalist insight into sexual difference and little hunger for more pleasurable theo-logical options. For instance, the pleasure of freeing ourselves from the decent constraints of restricted political life. Curiously, some Latin American men have been far more adventurously advanced and critical of sexual issues in Christianity than women,[4] but, of course, men can afford to be indecent. Their 'feminist' theology has also been taken more seriously than women's theology.

The problem presented to the conscientisation processes in relation to the worship of the Virgin are obvious. The theologian as the Virgin of Guadalupe sooner or later needs to identify herself with a fabulous virginity, and a biographically located inscription of sex/gender in that of God in history. Gender is usually considered in linearity and punctuality. It has never occurred to theologians that gender, for instance, can be thought of as processual instead of punctual, but the processual is the location of conscientisation with which Virginal liberationists seem to feel ill at ease. The fabulous virginity comes from the Christian narrative itself. According to the Russian Formalists, that group who wanted to dissociate 'art from mystery' (Eagleton 1992: 3), the fabulous can be defined as that basic story material which has been arranged at some point into a mythical biographical structure. It is important though to remember that fables are biographical in the sense that they follow patterns of chronology in a biological sense: beginnings and ends of recommended behaviour or the life adventures of moral patterns and the dangers which await them in life. The difficulty with sex/gender as biographically constructed in this way is its almost exclusive dependence on citational techniques, which act as replications of models of sexual constructs (Butler 1990: 31). For instance, the femininity of the Virgin Mary is consolidated every day by a theological citational process which gives human coherence to Mary, a humanoid symbol. In fact, Mariology creates a history of gender from an artefact: a supposed woman who does not have a recognisable sexual performance is made into a sexual code. This is a case of gender without sexuality, and the core of the repetitive citation on virginity, for there is no other so-called biography, as in the case of Jesus, supporting the Christian myth. Liberationists are in fact supporting the uniformity of this hegemonic practice of 'quoting' the Virgin Mary and increasing it by trying to add new elements of constructed coherence for women to continue to identify with that ghostly idea which is the Virgin. Take for instance, the theological writings produced about the Virgin of Guadalupe, from Dussel (a Marxist theologian) to Leonardo Boff and Gebara/Bingemer.[5] What they tend to have in common is the repetition of the performances of the Virgin as compiled in her fabulous biography, plus nationalist identification points which can be much discussed from a postcolonial analysis. Also, none of them has ever considered a de-coding of the Virgin in Latin America. The fact that materialist theologians can be so naive when reflecting on the invasion of America as to rescue the gods of the invaders as the true gods is another case of sad ex-centricity in theology. A conscientisation attempt needs to consider more seriously the theological construction of the Virgin's biography. For instance, how it is that the Virgin in Latin America is not a case of speech acts but of visions. The Virgin presents us with the case of a visual biography.

I have said elsewhere that the Virgin Mary in Latin America is a rich, white, woman who does not walk (Althaus-Reid 1994: 55–72) and whose authoritative discourses are visual more than scriptural. The vulva of the

Virgin of Guadalupe is for showing off, not for written reflections. Sacred Christian writing has been a production area privatised by men, from which women and even the Virgin have been excluded. Male theology is the area of the W/word of God or the 'Spermatic Word' (*Logos Spermatikos*). Christine Battersby has produced an interesting work on this point in her book *Gender and Genius: Towards a Feminist Aesthetics* (Battersby 1989). According to Battersby, the New Testament Logos or Word of God (who is described in John 1:1 'In the beginning was the Word') has been associated with the capacity to produce rational (male) discourses. Logos is then a concept which took substantial meaning from ancient Greek thought and Roman Stoicism in the concept of the Spermatic Word (Battersby 1989: 8, 49). That Spermatic Word is the word of origins, the word and embodiment of God the Father who produces praxis (actions and thoughts) by a process we may call 'Spermatogenesis'. This Spermatogenesis is the creation of discourses of rationality in the testes (testicles; the place of the divine testimony) of God. From God's testicles, as his divine witnesses, we find a process of auto-dissemination of the Word from which women in Christianity have been excluded. Therefore, God the Father is the scribe of his lonely creational pleasures, for His is the pen/is (Battersby 1989: 50), the power and the glory. However, the Virgin Mary has no sharing in her symbolic construction of God's speech acts. She is no word; she is only appearance. Her biography is not that fabulous writing as in the case of the Hebrew Scriptures and the New Testament. The Virgin Mary's biography is made basically of a sexual story written by automatic Spermatogenesis, a fable where non-human characters (the angel; God; a woman who is not a woman) interrelate and copulate. It may be a short and spectacular copulation, but it is not much of a piece of writing, rather a visual showpiece of pregnancy. There is a phenomenology of the look and it is the looking in Mary's biography that has influenced the credibility of her appearances and not the word of Mary through the history of Mariology before, during and after Theology of Liberation. In this sense, we can say that Mary's life is a Christian symbol which involves an intentional act of looking at images and apparitions: of the Virgin, of the conceived child and of supernatural annunciations, although, curiously, not of expectations of sex with God. This is an interesting point, since we all know how the biblical characters are cited through the lives of Christian people. For instance, young boys in the church may be expected to grow faithful as Abraham or repentant as King David. They could be stubborn fiery characters like Peter, but as 'Peters' they will be understood and corrected in their congregations. Yet, no young woman is supposed to get pregnant by God or at least to have that historical possibility as a second coming of God in history. No young girl thinks 'perhaps if I am humble enough God will have sex with me'. The second coming has been spiritualised and dematerialised, but there is no reason to do so since we have grown into that understanding of God in history. It may seem ridiculous to speculate in these terms, yet it is legitimate to extend theological enquiries into the incarnational area of reflection since in this way we are able to perceive how Mariology cannot stand the test of time. We do not believe in virginal incarnations anymore and although we may keep some vague expectations of bodily resurrection, virginal conceptions are not part of our horizons.

It is interesting how an eternal God only had one registered case of procreative sex in history. We may assume that the rest of his lonely pleasurable activities were of a non-procreative nature. Where do the churches then get the idea of sex being divinely approved of only if done for the purpose of procreation? It is not so in the scriptural account of God's sexual activities where masturbation seems to belong more to a divine order than sex with someone else. Moreover, if God could be conceptualised beyond anthropomorphism as neither male nor female, we may then ask ourselves who is who in this story of sexual encounter with Mary? That does not need to be so clear either. On the contrary, a non-anthropomorphic theistic reading should not have any objection to the further development of the birth narrative as non-heterosexually constructed. For instance, it may be read as an encounter between two women. We have said that Mariology is visual, made of paintings, icons and medals which are more public than writings. God's sexual act with Mary carries in itself an intentional act of looking: a gaze on her womb is directed outwardly, and it is an act which, through the history of Mariology, has been opened to the conscious perception or absorption of what we have been looking at (Spiegelberg 1989: 109). That looking at the Virgin is not a neutral act but is already committed, and it requires a sort of intertextuality of interpretation coming from other visual discourses transmitted through theology. However, the fact that the discourses on the Virgin refer frequently to the gaze on the womb and not the vulva is significative in itself. The image of the *Guadalupana* does not come from a symbolic womb; it comes from a vulva. In the scriptures God is sometimes referred to as compassionate by using a Hebrew word which means 'compassion from the womb' (Tribble 1978: 45). The womb (*rahamin*) as a site for reproduction can be appropriated easily by the male. In fact, during the times of the Hebrew Scriptures the understanding of conception was basically a male perspective. It was thought that only the man had the forces of life to reproduce humankind; women were no more than receptacles or laboratories to give a place to that life to develop. The idea of a sterile man was nonsensical. If men carried with them the possibility of life, no one could have thought that for instance, by sin, a patriarch was not able to conceive. Yet, women are depicted in the scriptures as the ones who for some religious reason (God not listening to their wishes, for instance) could not have children. The men were entitled then to divorce them. However, the vulva cannot be so easily appropriated by male religious discourse, although someone can argue that clitoridectomy is precisely that, the ultimate appropriation of the non-reproductive sexuality of a woman, done for religious reasons. The point is that a Mariology which may concentrate its attention on the divine gaze on the vulva will have far more possibilities than the discourse of the womb, which was co-opted centuries ago.

Unfortunately, the Virgin seldom shows her vulva in her numerous apparitions, although sometimes she shows her womb (represented by a baby Jesus), but the womb is the area of words, of seminal speeches while the vulva is that shocking pink swollenness which speaks by its mere presence. Perhaps the time has come to make the Virgin indecent in this respect. A modern example of this point is to be found in the recent apparitions of the Virgin of San Nicolás in Argentina which have been reported as happening between the years 1983 and 1990. Señora Quiroga de Motta (the visionary or seer as the Roman Catholic Church calls her) claims that many of her questions to the Virgin who appeared to her were visually answered, in the sense of internal visions. However, the words of the apparition were unusually abundant and recorded in two unpublished collections; they amount to 1884 messages (Laurentin 1995: vii). However, these Virginal speeches are of a citational nature. They consist in the citation of chapters and verses of the Bible, expressed in inelegant ways, as for instance, 'My daughter... read 2nd Corinthians 6:13' (Laurentin 1995: 101). (There is no specification of which version of the Bible the Virgin prefers.) This is an unusual effort to make the Virgin credible, by invoking that *Logos Spermatikos* of the Bible, in a time when Latin Americans and Argentinians amongst them have started to read the Bible and depart from authority as a divine visual investment. However, it is not only a point of authority but of sexuality which is made here.[6] Scriptural citation represents patriarchal perspectives on conflicting behavioural interests: for instance the womb versus the vulva at a time when Argentina debates the legalisation of abortion. However, to give a voice to the image of the Virgin requires other processes of authorisation. It is not only male authority which is required here, but a colonial male authority. All the Argentinian apparitions, including the one just mentioned, do not speak the current Spanish of the country but use pronouns and verbal forms from the current usage of Spanish from Spain. The result is worthy of postcolonial reflection on why the words of authority from the Virgin Mary need to refer still to the Spanish Crown instead of the Latin American cultures. Thus, for instance, some of the texts by the Virgin say:

> *Os doy las lecturas bíblicas con mis mensajes para que el mundo vea . . .*

or

> *Id y evangelizad, no os fijéis dónde. En el lugar donde esteis, evangelizad . . .*
> (Bajo García 1991: 180–1)

Instead of that, an Argentinian Virgin (or at least, in my own Argentinian neighbourhood) would probably express herself in the following way:

Che queridos, les doy las lecturas bíblicas con mis mensajes para que el mundo vea . . .

and

Vayan y evangelicen, che. No se anden fijando por donde vayan. Uds, en el lugar donde estén, evangelicen . . .

These words would make an Argentinian apparition, indeed! But the Virgin always speaks like a Spanish lady relating to the colony and, moreover, she uses sexist language, referring to brothers, men and mankind, instead of using words such as sisters or humanity. One wonders what sort of education Virgins are receiving nowadays in Heaven? The point is that the citation of the Virgin at this time and age is basically effective only as a visual exercise, which in Latin America is abundant. In Argentina even in the subways one finds statues of the Virgin. But the 'voice' betrays the Virgin, who then appears as the toy sitting in the lap of that great ventriloquist God the Father: and there is an end to any female identification with the Virginal image. Moreover, the voice sometimes takes sinister turns, as if it is difficult to keep to the subtle ways of theology when it is a case of Mariology. This may be seen for instance when the Virgin of San Nicolás tells the seer during a mass, 'Today, with the Father's blessing, you will be fed with my son' (Laurentin 1995: 91). The Virginal voice gives reality to the cannibalistic elements of eucharistics, elegantly suppressed and represented in theology.

Making theological violence sexy

Paraphrasing Marx, we can say that the Virgin Mary came to Latin America the first time as a tragedy, and the second time, during the current discourse of Liberation Theology, as a farce. One of the main elements of the farce is the making of violence sexy. As a tragedy, the stories of apparitions of the Virgin and Christian apostles such as St James, which are censored from Liberationist Theology, speak for themselves in terms of the killing Madonna. That violence as exercised in the Virginal legends, was a vital element in the understanding of hierarchical relations such as those of men and women in Latin American *machista* systems. As an example of early Virginal violence, the following is a text written by Inca Garcilaso de la Vega in his story of the Conquest of Perú.

> For there were a thousand Indians [sic] for every Spaniard, and they were determined not to give up the struggle until they had slain them all. But the Spaniards attacked the Indians with the same courage and ferocity, calling aloud on the name of the Virgin and on their defender, the apostle St James . . . Prince Manco Inca watched the battle from a hill and encouraged the Indians by calling on the various tribes and provinces . . . In this hour of need our Lord was pleased to favour His faithful with the presence of the blessed apostle St James, the patron of

Spain, who appeared to the Spaniards . . . on a splendid white horse,
bearing a shield showing the arms of his military order and carrying in
his right hand a sword . . . Whenever the Saint attacked the Indians fled
. . . Thus the Spaniards took heart and fought on, *killing innumerable
Indians who could not defend themselves . . .*

(Garcilaso de la Vega 1996: 801–2; italics mine)

Explaining the mythological origin of the name given to a hill, Santo Cerro
(Holy Hill), we find the following explanation:

After the battle, the Spaniards prowled through the Vega, plundering the
natives, and shortly came to the hill known as Santo Cerro . . . [In that
place] Columbus erected a cross... It seems that after the Spaniards had
departed, the Indians espied the cross, and approached to revile it. As
they did so, they saw a woman descend from the clouds and alight upon
the cross. It was the Holy Virgin, but the savages did not know her . . .
[Nothing the Indians did] seemed to affect her determination to remain
and protect the cross. Seeing this the Indians recognised her saintliness
and fell down... Since then the hill has been a sacred spot . . .

(Ober 1883: 314–15)

The text of Guaman Poma de Ayala in his *Nueva Corónica y Buén Gobierno*
(Pease 1980), where he recounts the Conquista del Perú, has drawings
showing St James on his horse standing upon a dead native man. There are
many other texts, such as the following:

Saint Mary of the Peña from France is a beautiful lady, all dressed in
white clothes, which are whiter than snow and she has a face which
shines more than the sun. The indigenous people were terrorised to see
her, and it is said that she [the Virgin] threw earth into the eyes of the
unfaithful indigenous people [to blind them].

(Pease 1980: 295)

In other texts he is even more explicit about the killing role of the Virgin
Mary, till the point is reached of making violence a sexy issue. Mary was the
beautiful killer woman of the Americas. The following is an example from
the many texts which exist associating the dominatrix virginal beauty with
criminality.

Enciso speaks a lot about the devotion the *Indios* felt for the Virgin
Mary, whom they venerate especially under the guise of the "Auxiliary
of the Christian Chief", that is "as a very beautiful woman who came to
help [the Spaniards] with a stick, that is, she killed [the Indians] with a
stick (*Que los mataba a todos a palos*)," but that they finally recognised
her as the *Vera Dea* (True Goddess). And since they saw that happening

they said that the Holy Mary was a good Chief . . . (*e como vieron aquello dijeron que Sancta Maria era un buén Cacique . . .*)

(Pease 1980: LVI-LVII)

These texts are just examples from many written during and shortly after the time of the *Conquista* about the apparitions of the Virgin and her collaboration in the genocide of America. That is the tragedy, that the Virginal presence killed with a stick children, women and men, who had become through her symbolic presence in the continent poor children, poor women and poor men. Because these testimonies are plentiful they stand as witnesses making us wonder which are the selective criteria by which the apparitions of the Virgin in Marian Theology in Latin America are presented as liberative. In our more recent Latin American history, the association of the Virgin Mary's apparitions with support of military dictatorships has continued. Augusto Pinochet, the Chilean dictator, after having suffered an armed attack while driving his car, from which he escaped unharmed, expressed in this way another apparition of the Virgin:

> After the attack, people started to talk about a miracle that had occurred... After the gunfire, and when I arrived at my place of rest, I looked at the car and I saw that in the window there was the appearance of the figure of the Virgin... Later on, other people made the same comment to me, that they felt the same [that there was the image of the Virgin in the car]. Now then, the image of the Virgin that I saw, is the same image of the Virgin that I have always with me [a medal] hanging from my neck.
>
> (Oyarzún 1992)

Or again: 'I am a believer, and if God allowed me to continue living [after the attack] and He showed me the face of the Virgin, this has a profound meaning for me . . .' (Correa and Subercaseaux 1996: 215).

Pinochet, in his own words, has always been a devotee of the Virgin Mary, and he attributes a miraculous healing in his childhood to the *Virgen del Perpetuo Socorro* (Correa and Subercaseaux: 36: 201). In Argentina, during the 1970s, the dictatorial regime was a Marian one. Emilio Mignone condensed the absurdity of the role of the Virgin Mary in the construction of fascist regimes in the following anecdote about a religious procession in Luján (the Virgin of Luján has similar status in Argentina to the Virgin of Guadalupe in Mexico): 'A foreign priest said the following through a megaphone: "The Argentinian person who does not venerate the Virgin is a traitor to the Fatherland [*Patria*] and deserves to be shot in the back"' (Mignone 1986: 170).

Personally, I heard a priest during another demonstration who was even more graphic than the aforementioned. He shouted to passers-by like myself who were not following the procession that 'Argentines who do not show respect for the Virgin are Communist sons of bitches [*comunistas hijos de puta*].' As we were suffering a high degree of State terrorism at that time, associated with a Communist witch-hunt, we were all ready to bow our heads, while at the same time praying for better times in the future. At this point, we need to consider if the Virgin Mary can be saved, not for the liberation of women but at least for the liberation of nations, as liberationists affirm. Let us then consider the biography of the Virgin of Guadalupe, *la Guadalupana*, whose prominence as the paramount source of liberation in Latin America, has been taken to absurd limits, even to the extent of her being called 'a feminist champion' of the continent.[7]

What does the *Guadalupana* have under her skirts?

I need to concede that the Argentinian Virgins, in common with some of their holographic counterparts in the rest of the continent, seem to have a formidable architectonic vocation. They tend to come barefoot from the Heavens but always require the construction of temples. One wonders how the Virgin Mary has not become the patroness of architects, engineers and masons in the continent since she has supported their industry so much. Yet, she never demands houses for the poor to be built, and has never said 'My children, I want a free school (or a hospital) to be built on this site'; but temples for her statues and medals to be coined are obsessively demanded from the poor, who make collections and donate what they can for such purposes. All Virginal biographies are built around three aspects, present in more or less a similar fashion:

1   There is a statue and/or an apparition which appears/moves in a mysterious way.
2   The image expresses with words or other images that she wants a chapel or sanctuary to be built in a certain specific location, and sometimes she wants a medal with her image to be made and sold.
3   Once the chapel has been built, the original biography gets embroidered with people's stories of miracles, usually the petitions of the poor, healing from illnesses and toothaches, jobs or extra cash, and help with legal procedures. Thus, some Virgins get bridal dresses as presents because they seem to be effective in helping women get married; others get small metal legs because their speciality is to heal leg pains. Their speeches (or 'messages' as they are called) seem closely linked to moral discourses from children's books of the last century, concerned with young people swearing or drinking (Laurentin 1995: 93) Apart from that, the end of the Cold War has made references to the demonic Communist system as the enemy of God irrelevant. There has not been a single apparition of the Virgin in Latin America condemning abuses of human rights or exploitation. The Virginal word is always a devalued,

small word. It is about good manners and obedience to ecclesial hierarchies and gestures of courteous submission, because Mariology belongs to the discourse of motherhood, in which mothers 'do not write, they are written' (Suleiman 1985: 356).

The Virgin of Guadalupe has a more refined biography than other Virgins. Hers is related to the wars of independence (although not the independence of the Original Nations) between the Creole elite (*Criollos*) and the Spanish elite. Yes, she also has an architectonic vocation which requires a temple, and since Virgins are only presences and not authoritative words, issues of buying land to erect buildings and financial speculation, as well as the colouring and sizes of statues, are deeply important. Once the statue of the Virgin is in its place, nobody can see what is hidden under the skirt. Alas, the Virgin is just her skirts, and skirts made from a mixture – as in the case of the *Guadalupana* – of patriotism, cultural links and the devotion of the poor. Women theologians have been too fast to see in her what every woman wants in her life as an individual and as part of a community. However, nobody has taken the trouble to lift up her skirt to see what is under it. This is not a biological point. In discussions with colleagues, the point has been made to me that it would be too reductive to keep continuing to discuss Jesus or Mary in a biological context. Although one can see the point of producing a counter-argument as far as our feminist interests are concerned, by stressing that Jesus had a penis (allegedly), we must recognise that we are in the presence of a sexual religious imaginary. This has come to us from narratives of divine copulation and patterns of sexuality in Christianity which are deeply indebted to how our gods are or have been sexually involved in history.

The *Guadalupana* story is too well known to be repeated here, and this is not the kind of biography to which we want to refer. Liberationists present this story with Virginal candour, repeating a legend written in a book from the sixteenth century called *Nican Mopohua*. The story is about an indigenous man who saw the apparition of the Virgin of Guadalupe. She told him to ask the bishop for a temple to be built in that place where she appeared. As the indigenous man was distrusted, the Virgin sent a miraculous image of herself in a painting. The bishop believed in the apparition, and the temple was built. This is the whole biography. Guadalupe is the name of a place and a Virgin venerated in Spain. The image of this Virgin of Guadalupe from Mexico is more autochthonous than others: it is a painting of a Virgin as a sort of young Maya woman (although this may be an exaggeration), dressed in attire which resembles the traditional Mayan costume. Obviously the story of the myth is more complex than that, and has political overtones – which the Marxist analysis of liberationists has missed – concerning some disputes of authority between friars and priests, and which of the two should have a more relevant place amongst believers. Apparently, the legend of Guadalupe helped one of these groups to establish itself. However, the liberationists usually concentrate their Mariology on the following three aspects:

1   The supposed identification of the Virgin with the natives' oppression.
2   The relation between two religious female symbols: the Virgin and the goddess Tonatzin.
3   The role of the worship of the Virgin of Guadalupe during the Independence Wars, in terms of religious support and courage.

The issues of the Virgin and native people's identification is, apart from being a case of false consciousness, a point of fashion and of 'paintability'. The pigment used to colour the skin in a painted image and a dress design, together with the words attributed to that ghostly image, which, refreshingly, were not in the official Spanish of Spain but in that of the indigenous people, have formed the basis for a theological identification between Gospel and Culture. We wish it were that easy. In reality, this argument is part of an old idea that, metaphorically speaking, God could walk amongst Aymaras in Perú, looking like an Aymara, speaking Aymara, but quoting Vatican doctrines and texts of the Scripture in Hebrew. I would call it a case of 'paintability' or decorative abilities which abound in Christian theology especially around issues of gender. What the Virgin has under her skirts, no matter her decorative dress design and mantle (the swollen vulva), seems to be a hegemonic phallus which in this particular case may conceptually correspond to a male penis. However, it is not the phallus under the skirt which concerns us but what she does with it which is the motive for reflection. Her hegemonic phallus is theologically relevant for the sake of the coming out of the closet of female human sexuality. If there is a hermeneutical circle in Mariology one hopes it is the hermeneutics of coming out, because until now theology has got away with murder by naturalisation. By naturalising a closeted heterosexuality and not allowing the sexual imagination of religious symbols to identify with sexual reality, theology has missed the point of religious imagination. God, Jesus, the Prophets, Mary and the Apostles they all live in our religious imagination and their biographies can be changed, opened or closed down for ever following a material criterion or Orthopraxis which starts at the point of reality first, and theology only as a second act. However, Black Theology, Liberation Theology and much of the Gospel and Culture movement starts from the criterion of Sexual Orthodoxy, that is by sexual/political dogmas first, and reality only as rearranged to fit this model. Reality is here the second act; therefore, for methodological purposes it is important to open the divine biographies and undress the performances which are in function for our consumption. Feminist theologians who do not disrupt, contribute to the regularity of the permanent referral to the past as conscious experiential levels, for instance, or as ill-repeated semi-historical local mythologies. This procedure marginalises to the realm of curiosities that which is outside the regular constructed areas of intellectual knowledge, approved described ranges of experience and even feelings, which are structured according to degrees of affinity with hegemonic systems or rebelliousness (Williams 1977: 35). Feelings, like material practices, are the main area of patriarchal manipulation related to divines biographies. Therefore the uncovering of Mary's phallus, apart from a patriarchal critique, can also contribute to discoveries of sexual novelty in a closed symbol which has exhausted itself. The hermeneutical key is related to that double dialectic of the vulva and the womb. The womb has been appropriated by male theology but not the vulva. Therefore, following the visual imaginary of the *Guadalupana*, one may say that there is no deep discourse in Mariology which can be of interest to us. The discourses under the skirt are not authentic ones. However, it is at the surface or superficial level where theology has more possibilities of creative analysis. The vulva of the *Guadalupana* is not hidden, and does not say anything. It is simply there, making connections for every woman who knows her body and can recognise a drawing of her sexuality beyond the original intention of the author. The relation between Tonatzin and Mary is highly artificial. One is an agrarian goddess of the Aztecs and the other the virginal mother of a Lord and Saviour, both of them working religious symbols of different if not opposite systems. The legend speculates with a kind of religious symbiosis or ambivalence. Guadalupe appears upon the ruins of Tonatzin's temple. From a perspective of liberation this has a negative value. In the same way, to say that the banner of the *Guadalupana* was used during the independence war can be done only if we remember that such independence was not a native one. Moreover, indigenous people who fought during that war did it with the belief that they were going to become a nation again. Nothing could be further from the truth and from the intention of the independence war, which was fought amongst elite men: Creoles versus Spaniards. How liberationists can make a feature of liberation and Mariology from these elements is difficult to know. There is nothing authentically indigenous in this discourse of the Virgin of Guadalupe and the people of Latin America.

Mary, *Queer* of Heaven and Mother of Faggots . . .

> [We] certainly believe that your God and this Great Lady [the Virgin Mary] are very good. But remember that you have only just come to our land. In the course of time, we shall do what is right.
>
> (Bernal Diaz 1963: 176)

> Christianity is an ancient form of sex education.
> (Bright 1997: 29)

Historically, the Virgin makes violence sexy but not pleasurable. Mariology lacks the refined etiquette of sadomasochism, and does not even acknowledge consensual theological acts. Violence is the path of the religious coloniser and generally comes with sexual impositions on people's identity. However, as the Latin American ancestors said, 'in the course of time, we will do what is right', and in this case, what is indecently right. Following one of Adrienne Rich's famous arguments, I would like to claim that the compulsive, closeted heterosexuality (Rich 1980: 631–60) which makes 'systems' out of theological reflection, works by pathological devices which enforce (by use of force and threats, including an imaginary of violence and false consciousness) the privilege of the legislative camp of that *ménage à trois* of ideology, theology and sexuality. We may gain little by turning back to primal definitions of 'women', for instance, as Gebara pretends to do in her co-authored book on *Mary, Mother of God, Mother of the Poor*. That is to say that Mary was (is?) a poor peasant woman, with courage and inspiration and a list of relevant virtues for the modern, peasant woman full of courage. Really? But suppose I am not a woman from the countryside: not a *campesina* (a peasant). But what if I am what I was during childhood, adolescence and early youth – a poor urban Latin American, brought up in the streets of run-down neighbourhoods of a big city, and a woman with gender troubles and contradictory representations. Should I not use, then, a style of analysis from my own area of possibilities which are not included in the central hegemonic repertoire of peasant feeling, experiences and epistemological validations on truth and methods used till now in Liberation Theology? If we move from centre (essentialist) definitions of identity and womanhood in Latin America, not only thematically, but methodologically, by the delegitimisation of central methods, then we go indecent because we introduce risk to higher theological forms of stability and security such as Mariologies. Here we are using 'Queer' as the category of indecency: 'a zone of possibilities, always inflected by a sense of potentiality that it cannot yet articulate' (Jagose 1996: 3). An Indecent Theology will always come from the margins of imprecision and mismatches. This is what is flagrant in liberationist-cum-feminist theologies: the centre-based theological definitions which we already have regulate and fix the so-called marginality of the margins. However, Indecent Theology is a process founded on opposite grounds; the idea is one of a concurrence or 'coalition of culturally marginal self-identifications' (Jagose 1996: 1), and not of the firm, set identifications which prolifically sprouted up during the centuries in our religious *imaginaire*, such as the Virginal one. What it is important to remember here is that Indecent Theology is also a contextual art. In the Latin American reality, indecenting the virgin may be more important than in other continents due to the heavy *machista* investment in her worship, and the pervasiveness of its influence in politics, from Cortés to Pinochet. A Queering of Mary in Latin America, becomes then an indecency (Indecent Act). It is this indecency as a theological category which allows us to put Queer theory and analysis in context. An Indecent Theology is not necessarily one which is obsessed by definitions and places for reordering realities, but one which acknowledges the diversity of sexual and theological behaviours existent in Latin America which can be compared and articulated neither 'diachronically nor synchronically' (Halperin *et al*. 1990: 46). This means that at the same time, at the end of the 1990s in Latin America, the poor, for instance, do not have any uniform sexual behaviour, neither can it be compared historically to the sexual referential cosmovisions before or after the *Conquista*, or before and after the Virgin of Guadalupe going native, or before and after Liberation Theology. Nor can their sexual behaviour be compared with North Atlantic experiences. For instance, according to Foucauldian chronologies, 'homosexuality' was ordered as a category in Karl Westphal's article on 'contrary sexual sensations' in 1870 (Van der Meer 1996: 138). In the Caribbean, by contrast, homosexuality was constituted during the *Aperramientos* in the fifteenth century (the ritual killing of what Spaniards identified as contrary sexual sensation practices amongst the native population, which consisted in setting dogs to eat men alive).[8] In the same sense, the concept of woman can be dated to the Virgin Mary. Consider, for instance, the following text from Bernal Diaz, a witness of the *Conquista* of America. In it we have the narrative of how Cortés was offered some women (daughters of chiefs) for himself and for his soldiers' pleasure. Cortes accepted, but only after a theological discourse, reported as follows:

> Cortés showed them an image of Our Lady with her precious child in her arms, and explained to them that this image was a likeness of the Blessed Mary, who dwells in the high heavens and is the mother of Our Lord . . . whom she holds in her arms and whom she conceived by the grace of the Holy Spirit , being a virgin *before, during and after* His birth . . .
>
> (Bernal Diaz 1963: 177; italics mine)

The identification of 'woman' and everlasting virginity, is the foundation of the theological and political enterprise of Europe in the Americas. Although the definition of virginity used by Cortés in his inaugural theological lecture amongst the natives, seems to be related mainly to that patriarchal myth of the hymen (which not every woman has and which is not the physical closed door of the vagina as popular imagination thinks), there is more to this membranous theology than one may suppose. For instance, Susie 'Sexpert' Bright, in her book *The Sexual State of the Union*, asks herself if 'losing love and compassion is in fact the price of suppressing lust's natural, original feeling' (Bright 1997: 76). The texts of the *Conquista*, including the testimony of Bernal Diaz, seem to confirm her words. Bright, who is making a point about what she calls 'lust suppressors' considers how lust and love are impelled to never integrate in our societies (Bright 1997: 74). The Virgin imaginary in Latin America is the permanent dichotomy of lust and love: this is why poor people are presented in the Theology of Liberation as decent, that is, asexual or monogamous heterosexual spouses united in the holy sacrament of marriage, people of faith and struggle who do not masturbate, have lustful thoughts at prayer times, cross-dress, or enjoy leather practices. However, if we keep falsifying human relationships in the name not only of God (a habit to which we have grown accustomed) we must remember that we do it also in our love for justice. Gillian Rose thought that erotic passion and faith passion were twins (Rose 1997: 64), and if one flees, so does the other. At this point, someone may ask if this is relevant to the Gospel of Justice, or the plight of the poor. Of course it is. Who do we think the poor are? Virgin Marys coming from heaven with a rosary in their hands? I remember when, in my early youth, I lived in a very poor neighbourhood of Buenos Aires, which was so deprived that it did not even have public transport to reach it. I used to come from work every day in the evening, and leave my bus quite far from my house, covering the remaining distance by walking through the streets which were muddy during winter and oppressively dusty in summer. Leaving the bus, I needed to cross a major highway (*La Panamericana*), and I always remember the sight of prostitutes, women and transvestites who were there stopping cars and looking for clients. Nearer my home was the noise of a factory, working away, night and day. Groups of women used to wait at its doors during the night hoping to get a casual job, perhaps replacing someone who was sick, and doing an hour or so of paid work. They were there, waiting for the supervisor to come out and choose one of them at random while they shouted their names ('Me, please, because I have a sick child' used to be a plea). In my mind, there was no difference between the transvestites and these women. I knew both groups from the neighbourhood. Some of the women waiting at the door of the factory would occasionally exchange sex for money. Those were hard times of poverty and political dictatorship. Exchanging money for sex was not that unusual; many women just married in order to eat regularly. In my experience, there was very little concern for sexual moral judgement but plenty of political criticism of the government and politicians, including the church politicians. It may have been that we were lucky enough not to have a church in the neighbourhood so that people were not brainwashed into Virginal discourses and sexual categories. For us, discourses of liberation came from the factory's activists from the Socialist Party, and not from priests. It is not true that the poor trust more in priests than in socialists. In Argentina, one of the most common sayings has always been '*curas de mierda*' (priests are shit). The poor have a considerable capacity to accept reality in all its complexity.[9]

Does this personal recollection of life in a very poor neighbourhood of the suburban area of Buenos Aires fail to reach the peaks of the narratives concerning the life of the poor made by the declarations of Basic Ecclesial Communities? If so, it is only because BECs are constructed figments of the romantic theological imagination of many Europeans and some Latin Americans. Lust and love, and lust and justice do come together. No hymen separates them. Love for justice and Christianity, on the contrary, do not historically come together. This is because Christian theology is based on unjust and stable sexual configurations, and because there is a premise in Liberation Theologies which considers that justice requires that everybody behave in the same way. On the contrary, justice can take on board plurality and contingency in life. If it is going to be real justice then these should come first (Weeks 1995: 64). Political injustices (ideological alliances) are simply a consequence of these dichotomised hierarchies' visions of hetero-sexual patriarchy.

These categories adjudicate sexuality to our gods, and not vice versa. Our gods are Queer, because they are what we want them to be. There are no final definitions or models, just rubber-like, flexible identities ready to perform a divine act according to patterns of power. Even the rape of the Virgin, that illuminating theological reflection from Mary Daly (Daly 1987: 85), can be seen from a Queer perspective as not a definite sexual revelatory act coming from God the Father, or to put it in other words, it does not locate the G(od) spot so easily. The problem is that sexual identities and preferences do not necessarily go hand in hand. Having sex with a woman cannot be taken as a proof of God the Father's heterosexuality, nor should Mary's pregnancy be related to a heterosexual conception of womanhood. As sexual identities emerge amongst relations of subordination and political domination (Weeks 1995: 96), this point is a crucial test of our religious imagination. Suppose for instance, that God was a faggot. Why not? His phallic desire could have been somewhere else. This is so at least of God the Father of Jesus, for there are many different conceptions of God in the Scriptures that require from us theological options, with different characteristics, as liberationists rightly pointed out years ago (Croatto 1983). God the Father's identity is sub-ordinated to genealogies (the God of Abraham; or the God of our fathers, for instance), to class struggles and racial and sexual tensions in the Scriptures. The fact that we know about the gender roles of God (the aggressive God of Israel, or the tender God of the New Testament) does not entitle us to homologise such gender performance with his sexuality. In Christianity, this has been done by following the assumed pattern that truth is equal to social truth, to life, and sexuality is associated with sin and death (Weeks 1995: 47, 168). That is, truth is equated to a particular form of sexual action. Therefore, God as a sexual divinity must have sex without sex and fix a pattern of life and truth for people; an aesthetic pattern of sex such as the granny's nightgown which used to cover her whole body with the exception of a hole in the area corresponding to her genitals. (I recall a granny who told me that her husband never saw her body and yet she had several children by him.) Let us suppose, continuing our argument, that God is outside traditions; that God transgresses sexual traditions and, on the contrary, God imagines new traditions all the time. Why not God the faggot? Why not Mary the Queer of Heaven? The fact that nothing is known of Mary or God's sexual identity liberates them; nothing is fixed, except for gender roles, and these are already well contested inside and outside Christianity.

If we were to follow that dictum from the Reformation, that we know nothing about God except for what we know of Jesus, then we need to confront a Jesus/God whose theological identity has become a unique mess of being the One who fucked Mary and is yet her son at the same time (interesting if not very edifying material). That Jesus who had a preference for men disciples, beloved disciples and a Lazarus who was so close to him that the Gospel presents Jesus in his infantile denial of his death. So Jesus may be a faggot, or a transvestite, so little we know of him except what other people saw in him; sexual appearances are so deceiving. Or Jesus as a man who desired both men and women and met those men and women's desires whoever they were. Systematic Theology is full of assumptions. Why do we assume what we assume? Mariology assumes a certain relation between Jesus and a family group integrated around certain sexual identities, but it does not need to be so, especially if we are talking about a group of people (Jesus, Mary, God's presence) who show the location of divine and human interrelations. That location cannot be construed so conventionally and in such a provincial pattern, for sure. In Systematic Theology, Jesus' divinity was all in his genes, but in Indecent Theology we consider that it was formed around relationships with people and cultural, religious and sexual belongings. We shall work deeply on Jesus' identity crisis in the next chapter, but there is no reason to assume that the Virgin Mary and Jesus could not also be the same person as my neighbour the cross-dresser who was an Umbanda worshipper who used to cover himself with the cloak of his statue of Mary. Indecent readings may find the need to leave the biographical style of reading and construct, for instance, a Mariology in a style remarking the imprecision of borders when illuminated by theological imagination. Theological imagination means a creativity which allows reality to speak out, while Systematic Theology's pretence of factuality (virginal births are not facts) denies historical experience. Mary does not exist beyond our religious imagination, but that existence is significative, especially in Latin America, and moreover, it is an existence. A more honest position in our adjudication of gender roles and sexual definitions to Mary and God is not only necessary but enlightening for theological assumptions which have suppressed chaos in normal existence. Sexual chaos and the chaos of death are the two suppressed forces of Christianity although paradoxically they constitute the Christian paradigm. Sexual stories of God in relation to humanity are foundational in the Hebrew Scriptures and in the New Testament; they are part of the *Credo*: 'I believe in God the Father almighty, Creator . . . who was conceived by the Holy Ghost; born . . .' Second, the theological elaboration of a God who is born in order to die in a crucifixion has put not only sexuality in the realm of the public, but also death. Why should it horrify people to talk about God the Faggot, since (a) sexuality belongs to the order of the public domain in Christian theology and (b) God is as unstable a category as sex itself (and cannot be fixed with certitude for ever)? If God or Jesus Christ cannot be called faggots it is simply because we cannot see the divine outside the reductive structures of a Systematic Sexual Theology which knows little about love outside decent regulatory systems of controllable sexual categories. The point is that what cannot be made indecent in theology is not worth being called theology because it will mean that 'God', 'Jesus' and 'Mary' only may have meaning in a determined heterosexual economic system. The Virgin Mary story and the tales from women of my country buying alum sticks to create the mythical hymen before a wedding, work in the same close, fixed, obsessive circuit of property–people categories. God the faggot challenges, for instance, the contingency of love; its transient nature and the different laws of fidelity which are present in queer love relationships. Gay and lesbian relationships are characterised by fugacity and transience (Weeks 1995: 68); heterosexuality out of the closet (not as ideology) has no historical experience of fidelity but of adultery. Weeks argues that there is value in transient relationships and the love which can be found in the contingent, casual encounter, since as human beings, contingency and fugacity are our nature (Weeks 1995: 48). Also, as sexuality is always located (Weeks 1995: 86), one can also reflect on what is the heterosexual transgression of God. For instance, as homosexuality or bisexuality or lesbianism cannot be identified with universals but only with the specifics of a contextual situation, God's sexual identity as, say, a faggot, needs to be located too. In that we shall not be looking for a God coming down to earth in search of his boy or girl, but our search will be for styles of relationships and understandings. We may consider how our quest for eternity in Christianity has led us to stray from the category of the present moment, which is more related to the implication of the story of sex and the death of Jesus/God than theology would like to accept. From the sexual experience of Queer people who experience love and intimacy in the casual and in friendship relationships, we may learn that God is a God of moments and that moments can be different but the momentary is also divine.

It is evident that indecenting the Virgin may be the counterpart of the membranous theology to which we are accustomed and which consists in constructing women and other lesser heterosexually thought beings with shut lips (not only their mouths), and closed sexualities – at least in the sense of forbidding the erotic use of the non-reproductive body. That has direct theistic implications. To indecent the Virgin means to indecent God and Jesus, as their identity is relational. Indecent Theology works here as a coming-out process which consists of simply doubting traditions of sexual presuppositions, a process that being public can have transformative political implications.

Hermeneutically speaking, a per/version of something is a way, a path chosen or a turn taken in the journal of everyday life. Indecenting Mary is therefore the act of per/verting a religious symbol, choosing another path of allowing fixed identities to be, as life is, more imprecise and mutable. Robert Goss, in his study on Queer Christology, does that by considering 'how natural it is for Queer Christians to reclaim Jesus as Gay/Lesbian-*sensitive* and construct a Queer Christ' (Goss 1993: 82). This means that Jesus can be a figure with whom gays, lesbians, transvestites, bisexuals, heterosexuals and transgendered can identify, without making of Jesus a transvestite or lesbian each time. Goss's main Queer theological points on Christology, which we can consider as related points for the indecenting process of the Virgin, are as follows:

1   The historicity of the religious symbol needs to be considered. In this case, the fact that Jesus is a historical man is relevant.
2   There is the androgynous look of the symbolic construction. Jesus has an androgynous appearance.
3   Are there any suspicious relationships, or skeletons hidden in Jesus' wardrobe? The old hermeneutical speculations and rumours, hard to die and very credible, about the true nature of the relationship between Jesus and Lazarus are there. Robert Williams (quoted by Goss 1993: 81) has made a clear statement about the loving relationship between Jesus and Lazarus as evidence of Jesus' homosexuality.
4   Beyond uncontrollable lust? Elaborating upon Rosemary Radford Ruether's view of Jesus not controlled by sexuality but by friendship, Goss considers that Jesus gives us glimpses of non-heterosexist and non-homophobic sexual social patterns.
5   Jesus died because of his high degree of solidarity with the marginalised and the cross 'symbolises the terror of internalised homophobia that has led to the closeted invisibility of gays and lesbians' (Goss 1993: 81–5).

Goss is a theologian who works on Queer Theology with a strong passion which comes from his commitment to justice and compassion in our society. As Susie Bright has said, love and lust, two dynamic terms whose relationship is essential in Queer studies, come together (Br'ght 1997: 76). While basically agreeing with what Goss presents to us as the basic elements for Queering a religious symbol such as Jesus, I would like to engage his points further, addressing them here to the Virgin Mary and constituting the basis for the next chapter, finding the traces of obscenity in Jesus. Goss's points are important because although presenting a very radical option, they also leave us with that space which is a yearning, an incompleteness, which is Indecent Theology: a process that is never finished. The last theological word cannot be produced except at the risk of continuing to build that membranous theology, that systematic dogmatic hymen made of stone which has contributed to the formation of sound doctrines in the past. Contrary to what Christian theology has taught us, it has not been the perennial which has embodied salvation, but the transient, contingent relationship of God with humanity, through processes of mobility and change. The saving forces of humanity lie around breaking those hymen-like conceptions which constitute the real base of sin. Sin is that lack of erring in life, that obstinacy in traditions, and that passion for the acceptable, unmoving, solidified ideologies and stagnant theologies.

There are several conceptual difficulties in building a Queer Mariology which makes the enterprise much more complex than constructing a Christology. Although Mary and Jesus' biographies are by historical stand-ards very weird ones, Mary has more non-human characteristics than Jesus. For centuries, the Vatican has been building layer upon layer of what we could call proto-alien characteristics in Mary: first, the stone-walled hymen virgin conceiving by copulating with a kind of divine cloud and giving birth in some unimaginable way. Then, it was added to her biography that her mother was also odd in that same way, and Mary was also conceived from a cloud. No wonder Jesus is presented in the Gospels as sexually apathetic at times! One can easily argue that the Virgin Mary is the strangest thing in Christianity and scarcely needs anybody to Queer her, but Queer is not oddity. Queer is precisely the opposite: it is the very essence of a denied reality that we are talking about here when we speak of 'Queering' or Indecenting as a process of coming back to the authentic, everyday life experiences described as odd by the ideology – and mythology – makers alike. Indecenting brings back the sense of reality, and not the commonsense reality politics denounced by Gramsci which constructs not only objectivity but subjectivity too (Gramsci 1971: 333).

Mary as a historic figure? Now, that is Queer

Goss's Queering of Christ is an interesting project because it is based on Liberation Theology . This means that, first of all, he needs to consider Jesus as a historical man. That is the stumbling block of Mariologies of liberation, especially of the kind which pretend to do some anthropological analysis in their theological reflection. Curiously, they always start by reclaiming or reconstructing Mary as a human being, the peasant Mary of the Americas, for instance. Whereas in Jesus there are some elements of solidarity in his biography, we cannot find them in Mary. First of all, we would need to define what was women's solidarity with women in New Testament times, or the current politics of gyn/affection, that 'passion that a woman feels for woman' (Raymond 1991: 7). Moreover, that gyn/affection would need to take into account what was women's solidarity in a country under Roman colonial occupation, and which kinds of new conflicts and dis-affection amongst women were created by that geopolitical situation. We are aware that under colonial patterns of domination, issues of nationalism divide women's struggle by forcing women to choose between 'tradition' (including the oppressive elements of it) and political independence on one side, or 'cultural innovations' (a different, perhaps even better social position for women) and political dependency. This false binarism is usually imposed as part of the same commitment: your country and its oppressive traditions (which usually get romanticised during conflicts) or the enemy country and their traditions. Which was, then, the right action and affection to stand by as a Jewish woman in a country under foreign occupation? Mary was not Judith, the liberator of her nation. The biblical Judith was a mature, experienced, well-educated and politically conscientised woman. She was almost a female proto-Messianic figure, who unfortunately was only developed in time around her struggle for independence but not as a religious symbol. However, Mary is the opposite of Judith. Mary is the colonial spirit of servitude to patriarchalism incarnated to such an extreme that she could not be represented as a common human being. She is a patriarchal gender performance going solo. However, the narrative says that she knew a poem. Does an old poem of liberation supposedly remembered by a woman, make of that woman a liberator? Such is the argument of the story of Mary and the Magnificat. Yet, according to liberationist criteria, it is only action for liberation, and not poems, which count. Even Pinochet declared his love for God (Correa and Subercaseaux 1996: 200) in the midst of one of the bloodiest *coup d'etat*s of Latin American history. The indecenting of the Virgin Mary needs to accept the fact that Mary is not a historical figure, which does not mean that some Mary mother of Jesus did not exist historically. She may have, but that person is not relevant for us theologically. The Mary of Christianity is something else; her real existence is the religious alien Virgin symbol. This is what needs to be made indecent, not the illusory virgin, whom of course, if she existed just as Jesus' mother, had nothing to do with the symbolic of the Virgin Mary. The point is that the religious alien Virgin exists as a powerful discourse of distorted humanity, and from that perspective, we are not denying the existence of Mary, but on the contrary, establishing the real existence of Mary in our political and religious imaginary. But it needs to become what Ricoeur called an *Imaginaire* of Rupture, and not of continuation. *Imaginaires* of rupture are the disruptive discourses of utopia which remain critical of symbols which have become fixed and fetishised in the community (Kearney 1984: 29). The cultural formation of a nation or group depends on the retelling of stories which, by their own power of affirmation, can become stagnant. A religious myth can become a mystification supporting an elite in power and hegemonic control instead of bringing symbolic elements of liberation to the community. Mariology is sexually stagnant. Only a rupture at the level of theological imagination can liberate her and the communities who worship her.

Is Mary an androgynous person? Androgyny or hermaphroditism are terms which come from sexual dimorphism. This happens because heterosexuality has difficulties in understanding sexuality outside the biological discourse, that is, outside the epistemological boundaries of reproductive organs. Therefore, it is easy to understand why hermaphroditism as a concept used to be a sort of liberation in the field of symbolic production associated with the notions of 'third sexes' sanctioned by nature (Herdt 1996: 19). For instance, Miss Poppy Dixon, in her website of 'Female Characteristics in Christ and Christianity', develops a simple line of argument in this matter. If, according to Paul, in Christ there is no male or female, therefore, Miss Dixon says, the gender of Christ can be found as being dual or 'intersexual' (Dixon 1998). In her own words, Jesus 'represent(s) the range, from female to male, of the sexuality of God' as it comes from Genesis and the creation of humankind in the image of God. In a way, we all carry phalluses and clitorises at the same time, and we all use them in different combinations and proportions with much creativity and originality or according to time-honoured scripts. What may worry us theologically is not necessarily what real phalluses may do, but the symbolic ones. What alarms us is not what role real clitorises fulfil, but the imaginary clitoris's function in the dialectics of membranous theologies (hymens) and life. To say that God has a range of sexualities does not tell us anything about those located sexualities. It may well be that God has a female sexuality without a clitoris, but with a hymen and a vagina for penetrative reproductive purposes, and this can then make the femininity of God irrelevant for women. Indecenting the Virgin can make femininity relevant but it will require us to recall the clitoris; that is, recall the pleasure principle back to the discussion, but not necessarily by the norms of closeted heterosexuality (in fact heterosexuals should not get pleasure in the straight ways prescribed in Vatican documents. Ideal heterosexuality rules out pleasure even amongst heterosexuals). Therefore, let us consider that Mary is not the woman who conceived by inhaling the smell of Fatherly semen. Let us think that she is the woman who has had 'seven times seven' clitoral sexual pleasure. Let us say that she may have conceived by pleasure in her clitoris; by self-given pleasure, perhaps. In this way, lust and love may then be re-linked together in the same way that love and solidarity for justice, in Patriarchal Liberation Theology, has been reconnected effectively. However, solidarity for justice has never been developed in relation to love–lust. When some years ago, the Metropolitan Community Church in Argentina sent a letter to a selected group amongst the main liberation theologians in Argentina, Perú and other countries of the Southern Cone, asking them to sign an open letter repudiating the killings of homosexuals in Argentina by a right-wing group, none of them agreed to do so. They were not being asked to sign a letter declaring their support for lesbigay issues, but one declaring that the Bible did not support the killing of homosexuals. However, the theologians of solidarity did not want to show solidarity with victims of sexual persecution, some of them saying that homosexuality was not their issue. The lesbigay Christian community, which was at the time working on the lines of liberation theology, manifested textually that those famous Liberation Theologians had stopped walking in the path (of liberation) years ago. I was impressed by the young man who told me that the liberationists did not walk with the people anymore. And why? Simply because they exercise solidarity on their own lusty grounds only, as their heterosexual drive for power leads them. Solidarity as the expression of a relationship with someone else also reflects a way to relate sexually, in hegemonic dominions, or in a welcoming community of free people and beyond sexual acts. It refers to the understanding of hierarchies and binarism in economics and in theology too. An indecent hermeneutics of suspicion, well applied, will Queer the Virgin in what counts as having sex beyond hermaphroditic patterns of sexual organs, reproductive sexuality and expectations related to biology, but also in patterns of thought and relationships with people and institutions.

Are there any skeletons hidden in the Virginal cupboard?

The process of becoming human is related to that permanent need to claim our identity in community. Concretely, this also means the need to say, paraphrasing Ortega y Gasset's 'I am myself and my circumstances', that 'I am myself and my skeletons hidden in the cupboard'. This essential ontology of the corpses from the past makes our identity as much as our complex relationships in our community, in a combination of race, class, gender and sexual cultures. As a Latin American theologian in Diaspora, I have learned that those hidden peccadilloes are part of cultural universes too. Differences between some European patriarchies such as the United Kingdom and the *machista* Argentina produce substantial changes in perception and sharing of peccadilloes. Sexual stories which would be celebrated and illuminated meaningfully amongst women from my culture could produce social ostracism in Britain, or vice-versa. However, the important point is to recognise their formative importance in our lives, because they ground us theologically in dialogue with ourselves and God, and with the current ideologies which are persistently trying to suppress and distort our identities with a politics of denial. Peccadilloes are an important part of a theology of storytelling, or sexual storytelling where real experiences and fantasies get mixed. Heterosexuality is basically founded on a denial of reality, and works by creating a Christian culture of secrecy. One meaning of virginity in Mary is the denial of a past of sexual experiences. Indecenting Mary needs therefore to reclaim the divine peccadilloes of the Virgin. The repetitive narrative of virginity has erased that, in favour of notions of patriarchal motherhood exalted to the point of having become the sustainers of women as unspoiled private property, located in economic units such as the family. The apparitions of Mary always quote her saying 'my children'. Someone has decided that she is our mother and the mother (and casual partner of a one-night stand) of divinities. Yet, real mothers have peccadilloes and skeletons in their cupboards too. I suspect one of the reasons why the Virgin Mary cannot be dressed as a common woman in the Liberation Theology style of contextualising icons is related to the fact that such a representation would confront us with the sexual story of the Virgin, and her companions. In Liberation Theology, the image of a peasant Mary is still one of a clean-faced smiling child–mother simply dressed, and perhaps with a scarf on her head. The young poor women from the *villas miserias* (slums) go around with dirty faces, short, ill-fitting dresses and vulnerable little plastic sandals, while their whole pubescent bodies start to tell stories of sexual abuse and harassment. Their bodies can tell stories of what happened to them as children, in their one-roomed, tin-covered huts or under the bridges of the city, stories of having been sexually molested by fathers and brothers or occasional visitors, episodes which happened in the same room where the statue of the Virgin Mary stood, beside the TV and some plastic flowers. In Argentina, my generation reached puberty by having become experts in avoiding men who would masturbate and ejaculate over young women on public transport, or touch them in the streets while making comments about their breasts or legs. Indecenting Mary: her virginity is the first thing that must go because poor women are seldom virgins. Theological virginity must go because it encourages hegemonic memories, false memories to be shared in the false environment of heterosexuality, while the real skeletons in the cupboard are excluded from our sharing and learning as mature people in community. Theology requires pleasure which comes from the provoking side of sharing our ideas, in the recognition of the other and also in the points of identification from our sexual storytelling. This is important in order for us to come out as human beings from the closets of false consciousness, and unless Mary can stand with her fantasies in front of us, then she excludes the historicity of our sexuality. As Susie Bright says, 'Without fantasy, your cock or your clit may as well be as erotic as your elbow' (Bright 1998: 139). By that she means the formative side of sexual fantasies in our erotic identities. That sharing of erotic fantasies locates our peccadilloes of lust in history and through an interrelation with other's stories gives us a sense of humanity and continuation, and not a sense of sexuality as disruptive of history as Christianity tends to present.

Have we, theologically speaking, been moving beyond lust? Rosemary Radford Ruether's article 'The Sexuality of Jesus: What the Synoptics have to say' considers how Jesus' notion of friendship was developed with men and women alike. So she favours the notion of a Jesus 'controlled not by sexuality, but by friendship' (Ruether, quoted in Goss 1993: 82). The difficulty we may have with this statement is that it seems to be so obviously connected with the heterosexual model of friendship, as a de-sexualised relationship, and also with the phrase 'controlled not by sexuality', which, following the same pattern of thought, puts sexual relations in the sphere of the 'uncontrollable' of our lives, or the animal side that needs to be disciplined in order to find favour with God. There is no sexual novelty in this argument. It is the same one that Systematic Theology has used for centuries, under the guise of a friendship-without-sex model. As Goss comments, there is nothing we can say about Jesus' historical sexual practices because they are not recorded. However, this whole concept of divinities beyond lust is problematic from an indecent perspective. Mary's sexuality can be considered using the same paradigm. First of all, friendship is always a sexed/sexual encounter between sexual people. The problem is how do we label what is sex and what is not sex. At the time of writing, the case which the media brought to public attention concerning President Clinton was an example of heterosexual hypocritical manipulations around the issue of sexual relationships. The patriarchal definition was linked to penetrative sex, but penetrative sex is not necessarily linked to a 'relationship'. Their combinations are multiple and reach sometimes fantastic proportions. When is it lust or when is it a relationship? Was Mary's sexual encounter with God committed love, or a one-night stand with the unknown? Did He or Mary have someone else in their lives at that time? Did she give God a blow job? Is a blow job a sexual relation or not? Can committed mutual masturbation count as love or not? Heterosexual thought divides and subdivides what is sex and lust and what is love and commitment, while in reality things do not stand easily in such categories. Greta Christina, in her essay 'Are we having sex now or what?' (Soble 1997: 3), confronts us with the issue of trying to determine what counts as sex or not. In her article, she describes how fascinated she has been since her youth in counting the number of people with whom she has had sex. At the beginning she found the experience amusing; from number one to number seven, no problem. Reaching number seventeen was equally easy to count. After that, she confesses, it became increasingly difficult. She was no longer able to discern so easily if sex was still to be counted as sex when, for instance, not penetrative, or while her and her partner were fully dressed, or in bondage games of sexual restriction (without involving genitalia), and of course, depending with whom she was having sex. A heterosexual grandmother and a gay? A lesbian and a transvestite? The combinations are multiple and complex. Therefore, we may ask ourselves how do we count who is having sex with whom in the New Testament, although probably we may reach the conclusion that counting is just part of another heterosexual strategy. Friendship in heterosexual terms has been hierarchical, unequal and built on the borders of cultural and racially acceptable definitions, but basically asexual. Moreover, heterosexual people suffer greatly from the asexuality of the constructions of friendship. Monogamous marriages become the end of friendship and nurture in community because the sexual fear which lurks between every married man and woman goes beyond asexual friendships. This is paradoxical, since heterosexual friendships are constructed as asexual, and yet, distrusted through experience as sexually engaging. Heterosexuality makes people's lives lonely and produces unnecessary suffering because in reality relations are more fluid than fixed, and we are confronted with that elasticity and sometimes uncontrollable lack of boundaries which exists between bodies and communities (Epstein and Straub quoted in Weeks 1995: 89) . If Mary's sexuality remains within the boundaries of asexual friendship and 'controllable' lust, this will be of little liberative value. It is possible, however, following the arguments of Ruether and Goss, to say that a bisexual woman or a lesbian can identify with a heterosexual Mary under such an 'embrace' of sexually detached friendship, but only to a certain point. One cannot expect our friends to have our same sexuality, to identify ourselves with them, but one must relate sexually to sexual beings or divinities, or we run the risk of making an Android Theology (God the Machine and humanity: any sex is virtually out). We do not need to speculate biblically on Mary's sexuality, but we must be ready to be that sort of reader who can understand texts sexually through our experiences: to name what is not nameable; that is, that Mary may have slept with women, with men but even more than that, that sex is a very narrow definition in heterosexuality and that it needs to be theologically revised too.

What we need to discuss now is one of the most important liberationist standpoints: solidarity with the poor. We have already seen how Liberation Theology falls short of its liberationist intent, basically due to its colonialist stand and its stereotyped heterosexual principles. However, liberationist declarations of principles have been attracting well-known Queer theologians such as Goss and Elizabeth Stuart (Stuart 1997: 81ff.). Both of them talk about Jesus' project of the Kingdom of God, or *Basileia*. *Basileia* is an interesting word in Greek. It has feminine implications to which I have not so far referred. Since my country is a republic, it is difficult enough to explain the meaning of the word 'Kingdom' without first beginning with a Greek lesson.[10] Moreover, the term *Basileia* tends to obscure precisely what we do not like in the concept – theocratic notions, hegemonic threats and values which, although good in principle, come from the same colonial–heterosexual religious matrix we are trying to Queer, make indecent and destabilise. To call Kingdom 'Kingdom' acts as a denunciation of the theocratic project of the New Testament at the same time as it highlights its commendable points; moreover, 'Kingdom of God' is a concept in conflict with itself, unstable and ambivalent, and perhaps we should not try to stabilise it. The Kingdom as a divine project for a society in which mutuality of service and equality is provided is very commendable, but the problem lies in the fact that the theological principles which sustain it are not commendable, because they are sexual principles of order naturalised and consolidated in a divine thought. One main point which liberationists accept, for instance, is that Jesus died as a consequence of his solidarity with the people. Therefore, the resurrected Christ may be Indecent, a Queer Christ, standing up for people from the borders of our descriptions of reality. Let us not argue here if more solidarity may have been shown by a Christ living amongst the lepers and dying of leprosy, than being tortured to death by an Empire which he did little to oppose. The point is that if Jesus died young and beautiful in his early thirties, and this gives meaning to the story of eternal life and resurrection, the Virgin Mary's life does not have the same meaning. No life is given up in solidarity, except with that 'little death' or sudden sexual urge of God. What solidarity with the poor (and poor women) does Mary present us with? Which challenges the sexual contracts of marriage for pubescent girls, and property laws related to their reproduction? Which challenges menstruation taboos, and strict religious codes? Indecent acts in theology demand of us creativity to see the unseen, but also courage to denounce what does not work. In this case, the indecenting of the Virgin demands from us the integrity to stop the citational process about the liberative actions of the Virgin Mary and her standing for the oppressed.

I have said elsewhere that Christ is 'Christ in Community' (Althaus-Reid 1995: 150). Christ grew up in a community, not in isolation. From that community he learnt social and religious expectations. That community taught him to be a messiah in dialogue, with the limitations of the historical consciousness of the time. Christ may still be incomplete and growing with us, in a process of refining Jesus' limited historical consciousness and sharpening his perceptions, while we continue learning in community and re-reading our faith from a perspective of liberation. I have also said that women made Jesus from their own assumed heterosexual constraints: they projected them into Jesus, and they taught him them. It is the same with the Virgin Mary: we have made of her the stone-hymened icon against which generations of young women have crashed their heads and hearts in infinite desolation and terminal sadness. We have made of her the lust-killer, the destroyer of surplus pleasures and the legal clause of women as property in family structures. No liberation discourse is going to change that, especially if it persists in repeating and thus fixing notions arising from a false sexual consciousness. As for liberationists, both in Latin American and in North Atlantic theology, I admire their candour and romanticism. Twenty-five years of Liberation Theology in Latin America has not changed an *iota* of the sexual constructions of our *machista* society. This has its own significance. The indecenting of the Virgin should then be a collective process of undressing her, and superimposing onto her the lives of women showing her liberative irrelevance, unless a new religious *imaginaire* of the Virgin can be rebuilt on the base of the old. This of course may be relevant because the Virgin Mary is a powerful sexual and gender religious identity, with much power still over the lives of people in Latin America. However, as in the case of Jesus, one could think about the limited Mary and her lack of consciousness being supplanted by ours, although there are also questions raised which are deeper than in Christology, done from a dialogic perspective. For instance, whether we think Jesus should be born or not, at least outside a loving relationship amongst equals.

Mary, the drag queen (or is it Jesus cross-dressing?)

Why is Peter Pan played by a woman? Because a woman will never grow up to be a man.

(Garber 1992: 168)

Did you ever wonder why the Virgin Mary is always young in the icons? Because, like Jesus who died young, she never grew up. Moreover, in the popular religiosity of the Latin American Christian poor, an indecent imagination about Mary, making of Jesus a young Mary, has been exercised for many years. As a point of grounding our Indecent Theology, we can consider the worship of ambiguous Christ/Marys and cross-dressed Christs in the popular Christianity of Argentina. For instance, *Santa Librada* is worshipped as the female crucified Christ of the urban poor. The Deceased Correa (*La Difunta Correa*) is a complex example of Jesus and Mary in the same person, with highly sexual overtones. In both these examples there are crossings of sexual, class and political borders. In other countries such as Brazil, there is a transvestite Christian community which has adopted the Virgin Mary as a divine Drag Queen. Such a community challenges the biography of the Virgin who now speaks sexually through her Drag Queen appearance, and has became the Virgin Mary of the transvestites. In Argentina, that role amongst the secular transvestites was taken by the image of Evita, and many transvestites claim that Evita inspired them, or that they feel a 'reincarnation' style of affinity with her. For liberationists claiming to develop a theology from the roots, it makes us wonder how selective have been the procedures of finding the people's original theological standpoints. Could this mean that the closer to the normal accepted colonial theological pattern people are, the more accepted are people's experiences in theological reflections? The point is not only that the real marginalised people have not been accepted in Liberation Theology as 'people' or as 'poor'; it goes beyond that. The problem is that in Liberation Theology we have been consistenly missing different categories of analysis already there, for instance in the worship of *Santa Librada*, the female Christ. However, these categories of cross-dressing in theology exist and they also carry with them their own theological orthopraxis, as popular theology is pragmatic and materialistic and makes deals with God for issues of survival in daily life. Curiously, as we do not seem to have presented dangerous memories of liberation in the Virgin Mary, indecent poor people just invent them.

The popular theology of transvestism

Santa Librada

The *Santerías* of Buenos Aires display statues and stamps of a young woman who looks like the Virgin Mary, yet she is crucified and her body hangs from the cross, reminding us of Jesus. She is called *Santa Librada*, and her worship is very popular amongst the poor urban people of Buenos Aires. As in the case of the Virgin Mary or Jesus, there are prayers and rituals associated with her (Christian) worship, prayer cards, candles and the customary novenas with the 'Our Father', 'Hail Mary' and 'Glorias' at the end of the prayer. *Santa Librada* means literally Saint 'Liberated' and the origin of the worship goes back to a Roman Catholic saint (*Santa Liberata*), a virgin and martyr who as such has never been popular. However, she is important according to the worship developed by people around her. From a phenomenological perspective, relating to how people perceive her is far more enlightening than finding historical explanations which the majority simply ignore. Some people would say that *Librada* is the crucified Woman Christ of the poor; others tend to see her as a crucified Virgin Mary. Who is *Librada*? She is not *Christa*, the crucified Christ woman icon of the Anglican Cathedral of New York. *Christa* is the iconic image of a female Christ without ambiguity; *Librada* is the popular ambiguous divine cross-dresser of the poor, the unstable image of a Christ dressed as a Mary. *Librada* as a cross between Christ and the Virgin Mary is a much sought after icon. The demand for her statues and printed cards is high in the *Santerías*, which are the traditional shops in Argentina selling herbs, potions and charms together with worship objects for popular religions such as Umbanda. *Librada* is represented as extremely young, white and blonde, as old-fashioned Christs used to be (and still are), with long blond hair and blue eyes. It would be difficult to find a representation of Mary as blonde, but not one of Christ. There seem to be different traditions in the representations; the Virgin Mary comes from Spain, and her images are white but with brunette hair.[11] The blond images of Jesus come mainly from Protestant traditions with different racial codes. Therefore, *Librada*'s face could well represent a feminised Christ. The issue of *Librada*'s body is ambiguous: sometimes she has a well-defined female body with full breasts and round hips (especially on prayer cards) but in statues she often looks elfin, like a Peter Pan who will never grow up, as Jesus will never be old. Her clothes are similar to the Virgin Mary's traditional attire, including sometimes a head cover. In some other representations, the only difference from the Virgin Mary's clothes is the choice of colours; for instance, *Librada* may have a red shawl and red necklace, which is a colour which never appears in Mary's statues or prayer cards. And *Librada* is hanging from a cross but smilingly, as a Virgin Mary transgressing by her presence the traditional site of Jesus, the cross. *Librada* is neither Jesus nor Mary, but a dress, a cross and superficial gender challenges which present us with a pattern of divine transvestism.

In the particular religious situation of a Roman Catholic Latin American country such as Argentina, Christ has traditionally played a very small part in the life of the people. The religious colonisation of the people was done through the worship of the Virgin Mary and not through Christ. The traditional saying of the Roman Catholic Church in Argentina, 'To Jesus through Mary' (*A Cristo por Maria*), has left Christ as an ambiguous deity, difficult to approach in his identification with God, and God is definitively inaccessible for the religious imagination of people. *Librada*'s worship fills that gap, because it is located at the intersection of Christ and Mary, with enough ambiguity for anybody to decide for herself her true identity. In practice, with *Librada* we do not know who is who and that instability is part of a transvestite epistemology, which by doubting the binary pair in religious opposition (Mary/woman and Jesus/man) succeeds in doubting the stability of the whole theological gender system. In the words of Marjorie Garber, transvestism is a critique of binarism (Garber 1992: 10) because it presents us with a third alternative, something unique which transgresses and emigrates from male/female locations. A transvestite has a clear gender location, but not a sexual one. Transvestites can be heterosexual married men, 'lesbians trapped in male bodies', or any intersection between two different things, sexual attraction and gender construction (Garber 1992: 132). *Librada's* sexuality is not an issue; her gender is.

Librada's worship has originated around legal and social transgression. An old traditional prayer asks her to deliver a person from the police because she is the protector of petty thieves and bandits, those who are understood in Argentinian society as thieves by necessity, not choice. The petty, small robbery as performed by poor people has not only been accepted amongst the poor as a fact of life, but also praised as an act of courage by a person who risks herself in order to feed her family. The traditional Argentinian worship of the *Santos Bandidos* (Bandit Saints) is an example of this. They were 'good bandits' who stole from the people who denied them jobs and had taken their lands and rights. They redistributed the wealth in their communities. The prayer to *Santa Librada* I am referring to simply says: '*Santa Librada, librame de esta disparada*' (*Santa Librada,* liberate me from this flight (from the police)). The prayer is short and rhymes well in Spanish; it is a protective formula. The life of the poor is filled with enemies. Loneliness means not only lack of love but lack of support in the community and help, therefore it is an 'enemy'. Lack of jobs, health problems are all perceived as enemies from which one needs protection and *Librada* protects those who cross legal boundaries in acting to fulfil these necessities. That is the starting point for her worship; acts of legal transgression where Christ or Mary cannot be invoked for protection. Yet the crossing of legal boundaries requires also the crossing of other, divine boundaries and new forms of legitimisation. If transvestism is a category crisis (Garber 1992: 16), it operates by making obvious (on the surface; at the level of dressing) that there is a 'conflict somewhere' on the ground of culture and religiosity which, for instance, destabilises the system. In this case, the category crisis is presented by this Christ/Mary figure, and the conflict somewhere is a faith which does not respond effectively to the economic injustices of society. The divine boundaries are then remade but at the surface level, of the dress codes of *Librada* in popular pictures and prayer cards and cheap, affordable painted statues. This is the transvestite theology of the poor. The transgressive praxis accumulates one thing after another. One thing is to bless thieves; another, to be a Mary occupying a Christ space (the cross), or a Christ in his space, dressed as an elfin woman.

The destabilisation produced by *Librada* is done at the gender level, which is the surface level of names and dresses (Hirshfeld, quoted in Garber 1992:

132). *Jesucristo liberador* (Christ the liberator) becomes *Librada* (liberated; in the passive voice; an action of liberation not announced, but already performed). At the level of dress codes, Christ is a Palestinian woman. Interestingly, *Librada* does not make of Christ a woman, neither of Mary a man. It makes of Christ a Christ dressed as Mary, and of Mary, a woman occupying the male divine space of the cross. The point of this popular transvestite theology is that it is a theology on the move, or on the run (as the people protected by *Librada* seem to be, escaping from poverty, and/or the police) from one place to another, and without settling. Perhaps this is a theological response from people to what does not fit into their lives, symbolised by what is considered indecent in Christian circles: to dress as the opposite sex (as condemned in Deuteronomy 22:5), to transgress sexual limits but also other limits as class barriers and the fixed locations of poor and rich in a Latin American country (Garber 1992: 32). The paradox is that people's theological symbolisation processes are always impersonations. Gender, as Butler has said, provides and nurtures the Grand Narrative of heterosexuality (Butler 1990: ix). The heterosexual matrix of Systematic Theology is permanently under threat of dislocations of divine gender identities, because Christian gods are also the products of sexual fears and misconstructions organised under gender characteristics. Thus, the YHWH of the Hebrew Scriptures is treated as a fetish penis or unnameable organ (its name cannot be spoken; see Butler 1990: 48), whose only visibility is the male cultural performance of the Hebrew narratives. For instance, in Hosea, the Gender-God (whose presence works by sanctioning or disauthorising narratives) 'speaks dirty'. That is, pornographic material of women as sexually abusable is presented as the heterosexual matrix of the relationship with God (Setel 1985: 87). However, that does not say much about God's sexual construction. Lesbian, bisexual or gay partners can be abusive too; gender performance and sexual desires cross and meet at different points. The same can be said with relation to Jesus and the Virgin Mary. From theological speculations, we have only received gender constructions of deities, and some, as in the case of the Virgin, totally absurd and disparate. However, their sexualities remain a mystery. This is why when theology is performed with honesty and with transgressive indecency, we are all impersonating gods. The Virgin Mary is a gender type, a dress code, and Mariology is the impersonating act of making of Mary a she/heterosexual; or a she/lesbian, or the ambiguous sexually transvestite of *Santa Librada*. What popular theology is teaching us in this case is that Mary and Jesus are subjected to the same *assujettisement* of the subjectification process as everyone else (Braidotti 1994: 61). Rosi Braidotti has considered how the subject is defined at the crossroads of multiple variables (sex, gender, race, class etc.) and by the interaction of both material and discursive practices. In theology, this interaction is an intertextuality and intersexuality. The material practices of theology are the institutions and the discursive gender/sexual symbolics which regulate religious identities. In dislocating the gender identity of the Christian divinities in Mariology or Christology, we are dislocating and creating chaos in the two areas of Church organisation and theological systems. Therefore, it is not only in the choice of motives that we can criticise a Western male style of theology, as coming always from the same heterosexual matrix, but also the theological logic which considers that theology must be presented systematically, progressively, for instance, instead of disruptively and moment-based. That gender chaos provokes the coming out of other discomforts and areas of tensions such as economics and racial structures of suppression of subjectivities, because heterosexual matrices not only provide us with the master narratives for bedtime, but economic epistemologies and social patterns of organisation. That de-essentialises sexuality and demands from us a located theology. *Santa Librada* is worshipped by the poor and the lower middle class of Argentina. This has economic and social parameters, as *Librada* worship was introduced to Buenos Aires by migrant workers from the north of the country and this needs to be understood in the context of a much damaged country which went through the ordeal of the political repression of the 1970s. During the dictatorial regime, the politics of dressing was severely controlled. In Argentina, decency is closely associated with dress codes which are controlled by the media but also by politics at street level (a woman dressed 'improperly' may be subjected to abuse by men in the streets, for instance). During the dictatorship, leaflets were distributed in public schools teaching adolescents how to dress properly. *Librada* ('Liberated') is the divine transvestite who opens the floodgates of political confinement. Only those of us who have lived under such terrible times of thought control, speech control, dress control, elaborate forms of behavioural regulation and political repression know the truth of resurrection. *Librada* is a testimony to the intelligent deconstruction of the poor people of my country, and their passion for freedom and ambiguity in spite of such controls.

La Difunta Correa (The Deceased Correa) and other loose canons of popular Sexual Theology

> Oh God Almighty, who in Your loving mercy chose the glory of the soul of The Deceased Correa to be the Restorer of the world and comfort of the afflicted invoking Her Name . . .
>
> To You, my God and to the Deceased Correa is the task of deciding upon the fate of all creatures and their actions, and to me, only to seek and follow (Your will) with all compliance.
>
> (Chertudi and Newbery 1978: 161)

If *Librada* leaves us with the aftertaste of a Christ/Mary personality, a Jesus out of the closet with red necklaces and a small waist, the Deceased Correa presents us with another interesting but different challenge. The Deceased

Correa has different religious biographies. The official one can be found in the tourist information booklets of San Juan, the Argentinian state from which her legend originated. It says she was a guerrilla woman called Deolinda Correa, the lover and companion of a man who fought for the independence of Argentina in the middle of the nineteenth century. The man was killed and she escaped with a baby to the desert area of the north of my country, but died of thirst. Miraculously, she kept breast-feeding the baby after her death. The baby survived her. She became an extremely popular virgin/'saint', to the point that the Roman Catholic Church, tired of fighting against her worship, decided to build a little chapel with images of the Virgin Mary and Jesus beside the Deceased Correa's own chapel. In some versions of her biography she is called Deolinda or Dalinda, Antonia, Belinda or even Isabel. Some people think she was married and had three children; for others she was a concubine, or single with a baby boy, or a baby girl. In some versions the baby also died. An old story, narrated in the language of the Gauchos gives us this dialogue between the two *arrieros* (muleteers) who supposedly found her body:

- Cross yourself! Because here we have a dead person and a baby.
- Probably she lost her way on the road, trying to follow her loved one.
- Thirst and heat have killed her, but God gave her the miracle of saving her baby . . .

(Chertudi and Newbury 1978: 98)

However, most people do not know or care for any particular legend at all; her different biographies grow and even contradict each other and yet they seem to be irrelevant to her worship. As with the Virgin Mary's biography, she is what ones wants her to be. This further illustrates the point of how little people care about official divine biographies and their capacity to integrate contradictions and different versions when reflecting theologically on them. Systematic Theology leads us to believe, for instance, that the Christian dogma of the immaculate conception needs to be preserved and hegemonically cited and repeated. Yet, this is not true. Dogmas are dead master narratives, and people's popular theology discards them and modifies them according to time and social problematics. Is the Deceased Correa another Virgin Mary or not? In a country dominated by ambiguous virgins like *Librada*, Correa is an indecent virgin represented as a woman lying down with big, well-shaped breasts and a baby sucking at her. Her white shirt is open to expose her breast which is the most important characteristic of Correa's worship. This undressing is a gross transgression not only for Argentinian decency codes, but also for a religious image. Correa is the patroness of travellers and lorry drivers, and the Virgin Mary of bodily fluids. Milk flows from her breast. She died of thirst so devotees put bottles of water in her chapel. Lorry drivers who cross desert areas looking for *ruteras* (women prostitutes on the roads) carry her picture together with that of the Virgin Mary and other nude women exposing their breasts torn from calendars.

In Argentina, Virgin Marys can only be distinguished by their names and dresses. There are more than a hundred of them: *La Dolorosa* (Virgin of Pain); *la Desatanudos* (the one who unties knots); *la de Luján* (a town); *la de los Angeles* (the one of the Angels). Their names, like *Librada* and the Deceased Correa are only meaningful in relation to their dresses. *La Desatanudos* has a bunch of red ribbons in her hand. *La Dolorosa* has a sword crossing her heart and dresses in dark purple velvet. *La Lujanera* is small, plump and does not have a child. *La Cautiva de Rio Seco* (The Captive of Dry River) has a doll for a Jesus which looks like a baby girl. A single change, such as giving ribbons to *Librada* or putting *la Desatanudos* on a cross, would change their constructed gender and sexualities, from one gender role to another (the Deceased Correa has an overt sexual personality which is the opposite of *La Dolorosa*) and from male to female sexual constructions (the meaning of the cross is male in relation to Jesus but female in relation to *Librada*). The Deceased Correa is a transgressive virgin in whom elements of suffering associated not only with poverty but with the sexual past of a woman are brought meaningfully to the surface of people's popular theology. In the same way that we have the worship of the Bandit Saints, we also have the worship of the prostitute virgin, which reflects the confluence of social class, sexuality and race (Correa is closer to an 'authentically' native Argentinian woman, if such a thing exists in a country made by European immigration and the systematic extermination of the indigenous population). No wonder lorry drivers, who may have prostitute friends on the road, venerate her. Also, in the Deceased Correa the baby Jesus has been obliterated, absorbed into her breasts by an act of permanent, erotic sucking of her splendid nipples. The more elaborate popular prayers present Jesus as an intercessor to Correa, who is the daughter of the Virgin Mary (Chertudi and Newbury 1978: 162), as in the following example. 'Oh, adorable Jesus, of angelic costumes! I, an unworthy sinner, beg you to recommend me to the Deceased Correa and to *Her* pure mother the Virgin Mary.' In this case, *Correa* is the daughter of Mary, sitting at God's side in Heaven, and Jesus has become an auxiliary spirit. *Correa* is the only daughter of Mary; she is Jesus, or at least, another Jesus, or the Jesus of the Other. In another prayer, she is the companion of Jesus created with him for eternity. 'Kind Jesus, centre of all perfections and fountain of grace and infinite mercy, you have taken, oh Lord, this creature [Correa] who was created in your image since before eternity . . .' (Chertudi and Newberry 1978: 162).

The theological cross-dressings keep exchanging Jesus, God and Mary to infinite degrees. The Deceased Correa is an unstable and generous virgin who redistributes wealth and health amongst the poor, but also redistributes the grace of the poor women, the prostitutes, the *mujeres con pasado* (women with a sexual past), and sees the divine in the indecent acts of the everyday struggles of life for bread and for love. There is so much more to Mariology in Latin America than the Virgin of Guadalupe if we do theology with indecent intentions.

3 Talking obscenities to theology

Theology as a sexual act

Perversion means Gender Chaos
(Bright 1997)

Pervert: . . . from Old French *pervertir*, from Latin *pervertere* to turn the wrong way, from *per-* (indicating deviation) + *vertere* to turn.
Perverted: . . . incorrectly interpreted.
(Collins English Dictionary 1979)

Obscenity is another world
(Baudrillard in Gane 1993: 62)

Per/verting Systematic Theology and the case of Vanilla Christianity

I have already said that theology is a sexual act. Theology is a sexual ideology performed in a sacralising pattern: it is a sexual divinised orthodoxy (right sexual dogma) and orthopraxy (right sexual behaviour); theology is a sexual action. Theologians, therefore, are nothing else but sexual performers who need to take many ethical and sometimes partisan sexual decisions when reflecting on God and humanity, because theology is never innocuous or sexually innocent or neutral. Systematic Theology can be considered as the case of an arbitrary sexual theory with divine implications. Gayle Rubin has already clarified the ambiguity of the term 'sex'. By sex we usually mean gender identity, as for example in the case of referring to the 'female sex', but sex also refers to 'sexual activity, lust, intercourse, and arousal' as when we talk of 'to have sex' (Rubin in Abelove *et al.* 1993: 32). Feminist Liberation Theology has mainly focused on sex as gender, and very rarely on sex as 'having sex'. The point is that sex as lust is an important conceptual category which is not new, but has dominated theology for centuries. Denying lust, or the 'lustful desires of the flesh', determines when, how and with whom we go to bed, and as such it has been the issue of main interest in all heterosexually-based theology. All the concepts of sin and grace seem to be unendingly tangled around the theologian's gaze at other people's beds, bathrooms or sofas. Heterosexual theology has found in its development the same problems and difficulties that people usually find in their sexual lives, for instance, issues of hierarchical relations, positioned bodies and monogamic patterns of thought which tend to constrain and de-nurture people's lives. While people struggle to find life and meaning in the relationships of the sofa beds of friends and lovers, Systematic Theology struggles to master and obliterate those meanings. Mary Daly reminds us of Hannah Tillich's memories of her late husband the theologian Paul Tillich, and how he was unable to confront the immediate reality of his life drawn as it was into sadomasochistic practices and bondage and which he replaced by theo-ideological abstractions (Daly 1978: 95). What is to be condemned and regretted is not that Tillich was a sadomasochist, but the fact that he did not find 'the courage to be' out of the closet of his sexuality; a sadomasochist theologian, for instance, reflecting on an issue of importance in his life as in the life of others. Our difficulty with Tillich is his lack of integrity and not necessarily his developed taste for bondage practices, which were probably shared by many other academic colleagues, fellow priests and everyday fellow Christians. Systematic theologians such as Tillich are representative of the millions of Christian people struggling to remain in their own sexual closets and in their own preferential beds while building their identities without sharing their sexual stories and even condemning them in their writings. They keep pretending that friendship is not and cannot ever be a lustful business, and that the chaotic nature of sexuality does not belong to the sphere of interest of theology – except to condemn it.

Writing about Queer Theology, Malcolm Edwards is one of the few theologians who has wondered why so little has been done in the area of the Queering of God (Stuart 1997: 75). My response to this would be that God cannot be Queered unless theologians have the courage to come out from their homosexual, lesbian, bisexual, transgendered, transvestite or (ideal) heterosexual closets. Out-of-the-closet theologians do not leave the personal aside, and that always implies a risk, but neither do the closeted kind. It would be delusory to believe that closeted theologians can compartmentalise their lives so easily. The difference is that the closeted theologians indulge permanently in duplicity between the realms of a public and a private theology. They build schizophrenic spiritualities, those which require to be put aside at meal times, as the late Juan Luis Segundo said. Can we keep carrying the burden of a theology which leaves us alone when having sex? This not only applies to the subject of a sermon preached on Sunday, but more importantly than that, to the choosing of motifs and themes for theology. In the case of Tillich one may reflect on the fact that his concept of love was based on eros more than agape (Thatcher 1978: 47). Therefore, we may end up arguing that Tillich did reflect on his private life in the elliptic, obscure and hypocritical way of heterosexual theology, on issues of his interest which were definitively non-Vanilla. As we noted earlier, in the world of leather practices, 'Vanilla' is a popular term for a lack of sexual options, for the unadventurous and limited. Like Tillich's theology, Vanilla sexuality refers to the scene of the non-radical, non-experimentative side of pleasure (Baldwin 1993: 28). Vanilla Theology is the realm of the decisions made for us by others, like Sexual Systematic Theology.

An out-of-the-closet Tillich may have reflected on 'leather salvation' or at least dreamt of pleasurable options to Vanilla Christianity. His taste for photographs of crucified young naked women tells us so. However, our great theological heroes never left any closet without first trying the compatibility or incompatibility of their patterns of life with current, decent theology. A theologian such as Tillich is an example of what Gramsci calls the intellectual person of the Civil Society (Gramsci 1971: 68). Civil societies are spaces of hegemonic struggle amongst different interests; capitalism, racial and sexual injustices, fighting to determine their power. This may describe the situation of the theologian whose work supports the sexual and political hegemony of the empire, creating a theology which struggles between forces of coercion and consent in the arena of civil societies where theology allies itself to the capitalistic forces of control, together with culture, media and related institutions. We may ask, in the words of Star Trek's Borg, if 'resistance is futile'. The ideological systems in struggle combine themselves and interpellate people, creating subconscious links between their being in the world as their being in the represented world of illusory theo/ideology. It is a fight for representativity, for a person reading theology to be able to be interpellated by the text, that is, by saying 'it is me; I recognise myself in this situation.' Theology has produced a high interpellation power in the area of guilt, but not of acknowledging the sexual lives we have.

Indecent models of God: per/verting interpretations

The God of solidarity

An out-of-the-closet (indecent) theologian may be more aware of what Eve Kosofsky Sedgwick established as the triangular model of male desire, and its use as a point of primary hermeneutical suspicion for analysis (Sedgwick 1985: 1–27). According to Sedgwick, male desire is perpetuated through the interrelation of three elements, mainly by homosocial consent, that is by an allegiance amongst men to perpetuate patriarchy, and also by the regulation of homophobia and misogyny. Male desire circulates in this holy trinity always reflecting two sexual structures of oppression – marriage and hetero-sexuality. Homosocial consent is intrinsic in values such as 'solidarity', which becomes especially evident in Latin American Liberation Theology. Solidarity comes here as a value embedded in that unity of interests and sympathy which comes from an ethics of membership. For instance, solidarity in Liberation Theology is a form of homosocial standing. The fact that it took me three years to be admitted as a student to the leading liberationist theological seminary of Buenos Aires, shows that even at the point of preparing future theologians of solidarity, women in the late 1970s were not allowed to learn together with men. The struggle of lesbigays to study in the same place under threat of expulsion and manufactured administrative difficulties illustrates the same point. Because of the nature of the political and economic situation in my continent, it is easy for Latin American women theologians to accept or to try to work out the border limits of such solidarity constructions. It is easier still for non-Latin American theologians including some feminist theologians, to fall prey to this conceptual trap of 'solidarity', which in its most positive sense of political solidarity is no more subversive to patriarchalism than the right of women today to vote. The social order fundamentally is always untouched, as women in the struggles of many Latin American countries can easily testify.

Homosociability, 'solidarity with the poor', or 'made in His image and likeness' is about constructing God as part of same sex desire; there is *realpolitik* in Systematic Liberation Theology too. Classical theology, the builder of civil society, struggles against the same sex desires which built it, namely male desires. Traditional, old-fashioned theological texts and Bible commentaries were blatantly overt in sexual male feelings and metaphors built around the subjugation of women and men's superiority as part of God's order for society. The fact that we have, for instance, Ruth and Boaz and the *Song of Songs* as non-normative texts strengthens our point. Although these texts are fully praised and male/female relations are elaborated upon in them, we hardly see with Ruth and Boaz that the Christian norm is for a girl to sleep with her boss. Obviously, women are not told either by the Pope or by systematic theologians to go at night and sleep with their bosses (if they are rich and single), and try to get a legal contract from them, as Ruth did with Boaz. In the same way, spending a week making love and describing your sexual experiences as in *the Song of Songs* has not become part of Christian doxology. However, the voices which are heard in these texts are those of the male to male relationship. These are cited, persist, and reorganise people's sexuality in relation to men. Carlos Mesters, in his commentary on the *Book of Ruth*, pointed out, for instance, how Ruth's story needs to be understood in terms of service. In particular, the sexual service she provided to an older man such as Boaz is seen as valuable and commended (Mesters 1960: 66). To resolve this reading we need, as Sedgwick points out, for these relationships to be freed from the web of homophobia and misogyny, and for that, the model of God as a family construction is key as we shall see later in this chapter. Solidarity is the most important value of Latin American societies and the rediscovery of God as in solidarity with people does not stand up to the real test of Indecent Theology. That test needs to be applied as undressing and unmasking the homosocially constructed solidarity. Leonardo Boff's Trinity model, and also Segundo's statement that the Trinity shows that God is society in solidarity relationships, relies mainly on men's perception of social organisations. For instance, consider Boff's understanding of the Trinity as 'the best community' (Sobrino and Ellacuría 1996: 85). That community is made by the God-Father, God-Son and a Holy Spirit which is 'the power of the union' of the male God community, which impregnates the Virgin Mary (Sobrino and Ellacuría 1996: 87–8). To talk about the God of solidarity in these terms of homosolidarity is not novel; the heterosexually constructed God is obviously a God in solidarity with a system to which God belongs. Solidarity with the poor cannot be built around the same parameters. Solidarity requires some unity of interests, as for instance, liberationist interests. If that is curtailed with sexual intolerance towards women and non-heterosexual people in general, then solidarity is bound to be ineffectual, and more a mechanism of ideological reinforcement than a commonality of interest in the struggle for liberation.

The God of imperial sexual acts

The flirtation of Systematic Theology with Liberation Theology may be coming to an end. It may be moving from the liberationist paradigm towards a postcolonial or postmodern perspective, but the point is that the perpetuation of male desire by male theological bonding, and the perpetual creation of sexual boundaries between central models and peripheral realities, give it an imperial characteristic which is bounded by male desire. We may describe an empire as a single politico-economical enterprise of monochromatic characteristics gravitating around a handful of central ideas. It is known that the core of dominating ideas is perpetuated even if the colonies change their political circumstances, for instance, become independent (Loomba 1998: 19). This happens through the internalisation of oppression processes described by the late Paulo Freire in his *Pedagogy of the Oppressed* (Freire 1970) and elaborated from Franz Fanon in *The Wretched of the Earth* (Fanon 1961), and by mechanisms of interpellation such as those analysed by Althusser when considering issues of collective unconsciousness and the mechanisms of ideology. Althusser has argued that ideologies are imaginary constructions which give identity to an individual at the same time as they produce a mechanism of false recognition of the individual in her social position (Althusser 1971: 163). International trade agreements and currency policies, the role of transnational corporations and the media all ensure that political independence does not shake the empire in the least. This is the traditional difference between the politics of development and the politics of liberation. This is High Theology: an imperial enterprise, the art of the android epistemologies but not of humans, and this is one of the factors which allows theology to perpetuate itself (resurrect) through what we have called the decency mechanisms of Black, Liberation, Aboriginal or Feminist theologies alike. Like the parasite in the film *Alien,* interpellation mechanisms provoke identifications and adherences so the alien is nurtured and carried by ourselves, even if in the end, it succeeds in killing us. Few changes and modifications are allowed in order to make possible the historic continuation of ideological institutions of knowledge which, of course, cannot survive historically without a minimum degree of adaptability or 'progress'.

If we want to pursue an Indecent Theology, and to indecent God, we must start first by analysing how theology can perform as an imperial sexual act. There are two aspects to this process. First of all, theology is an art *per se*, that is an aesthetic representation and not a natural but a naturalised way of reflecting/acting on God and people. Second, theology works in a sexual mode, which could do with some per/versity (variations, more versions and positioning of theological acts) introduced into its methodology. For instance, let us consider the double face of the public and sacred manifestation of sexual excitement and desire for non-human objects shown by Systematic Theology. This is a fetishisation process in itself; the reification or 'thingification' of the discourses of enticement towards, for instance, the symbolics of communal eating. In the Eucharist, according to the dogma of transubstantiation, God is what you eat, that fetish of bread and wine. God is what you digest, perspire and excrete from your body. God is the transit of bread and wine in your stomach and bowels. God is the peculiar smell that perspiration takes after drinking the wine of the Mass and the heavy-sweet breath of bread taken on an empty stomach. The supposed sharing nature of the sacraments (solidarity/homosociability) is only the ability to take into yourself and incorporate that fetish thinking. There is no solidarity in holy communion because homosocial solidarity is notoriously non-existent in history, for instance when it comes to forms of the actual production of the bread and the wine. It excludes and exploits others. It is hierarchical and profitable. It does not share but takes. At its best, the sacramental ceremonies in the churches work as acts of exemplary colonial orderings, but not of solidarity. The body gestures of silence, of receiving the bread with cupped hands, and passing to another person on your right or left, can become military operations of precision and discipline not too distant from poorhouse workers at the beginning of the century passing bowls of gruel under the vigilance of the bosses. However, every text carries with it a subversive version, and in communion there is an example of intertextuality or intersexuality with God who becomes (transubstantiation or not) our bodies and shares our complex sexualities. And God becomes chaos: the smell of our bodies when making love, our fluids and excretions, the hardening of muscles and the erectness of nipples.

From that perspective, we may argue that fetishisation is not a bad thing in itself, although I confess that for fetishes, I still prefer motorbike boots standing in my wardrobe to a set of communion cups on my bedside table. It is indeed a question of tradition in fetishism which needs to be explored in an indecent theological way, as we shall do later.

The Soft-Core God

Obviously, it might be simplistic to assume that works of art such as the sacraments may be the only area of fetishisation in Christianity. Theology has also developed an economy of relationships (both internal and external) in which trade patterns can be traced, even historically. Women, men, eunuchs and sodomites fulfilled historically different but mutually dependent functions in the realms of the public and domestic life of theological reflections. This can be identified as part of a Soft-Core Theology, a gentle theological construction where sexual oppression is explicit but kept to what are understood as natural, tolerable limits. As in soft-core pornographic films, there are frontiers to be observed. In Soft-Core Theology, God needs to be boundary marked by, say, sodomites, to express the value that reproduction gives to human relationships and defining God's values too. Without the construction of the sodomites, the heterosexual godly values could not be exalted enough in theology. God's high seminal message would never be shown to the world with such ejaculatory strength if God had competitors. Sodomites are the non-competitors who exalt God's reproductive message to the world. These theological patterns are constitutive of what we can call a Soft-Core Pornographic Theology. Women, and sexual dissidents in general, are merely depicted for the consumption of a constructed male heterosexual reader. Their images may be fixed in situations of pain and sexual torture, but these are acceptable in the history of Christianity. For instance, we may see this as a second-rate porno film where Eve gives birth in pain for ever; Tamar, is raped interminably by her brother in his bedroom; Jesus, hangs naked from a cross, hands nailed, blood coming from a crown of thorns on his head; Mary, says yes to the first angel in her life who appears in her room. What a queer theology this is in the old-fashioned sense of queer! Indecent Theology forces a Soft-Core Porno Theology (namely, Systematic Theology) to assume its real hard-core nature and to come out with the crudeness of its sexual constructions. Sadly, we are so used to Soft-Core Theology we are willing to project these films of Eve and Tamar and the Virgin Mary to children in Sunday School. However, in the strange ways of the world and the present state of theology today, indecenting, that is, denouncing the real hard-core sexual nature of Systematic Theology while announcing gender and sexual deconstructions which could carry precious meaning to our lives in relation to the sacred, and the political implications of theology as ideology, is considered scandalous and immoral.

The God of the colony

It was Julia Kristeva who said that '"art" reveals a specific *practice*, crystallized in a mode of production with highly diversified and multiplied manifestations' (Kristeva 1984: 97). There, according to Kristeva, the complex relations between ideology and tradition, or between desire and law are to be found. The Gospel, the Hebrew Scriptures and the church, including ritual enactments such as the sacraments as we have seen, function as pieces of narratives based on a common Christian symbolic assumption, where tensions in their production (such as desire and law, as mentioned by Kristeva) are present. To unravel this art, which we could call colonial acts, means to unravel a Hard-Core Christianity based on limited desire and non-consensual relationships such as the imposed patterns of what Butler calls the heterosexual matrix (Butler 1990: 151).[1] For instance, in the internal economy of the Bible, historical accounts have been produced in obedience to the matrix of colonial desires which in the name of God justify and legitimise a policy of expansionism, and non-consensual acts of rape and pillage of foreign lands and people's cultures, religions and societal structures. From the perspective of external political economies, there has been a flourishing trade between empires and colonies in the application of biblical texts according to different stages of the political process. Texts favourable towards a consciousness of submission for the colony are drawn upon and used, for instance, to implant a consciousness of the political, religious and moral superiority of the colonising power. Yet, in all this theological trade we always come back to our conceptualisation of God as a work of art, a work of aesthetic and religious applied imagination. Imperial gods became the main characters of colonial sacred novellas, which can be slightly modified through a historical negotiation of interpretation procedures in postcolonial situations but never completely dismissed. That 'God object' of colonial art has become the unique good, and the only object of a desire which participates in a sexual way, since all its internal or external economy is based on a heterosexual structure of desirables and rejectables, in a complex economic and religious interrelation. This takes us to the real point of a negative fetishisation in Christian theology, which is the fetishisation process carried through a historical God/human being, Jesus, performing 'all human being' and 'all God being' culturally, simultaneously and definitively. This is not Soft-Core Theology anymore but Hard-Core Porno/Theology. That kind of porno/theology will always be an imperial grandiose gesture made of universals, essentialism and non-challenged religious and political assumptions. That theology was a melting pot of sexism, homophobia, racism, class assumptions and colonial dreams. That god of the colony, we should like to think, was a colonial master whose crisis point came not as a result of secularisation but a questioning of imperial epistemologies and social and theological struggles for liberation.

The God/Jesus Christ

Let us consider, for instance, the Christological project which achieved the colonisation of souls, a project developed by the Western block of theologians who used to lead the sphere of spiritual production with Jesus as homogenously representing 'all human being' and 'all God being'. Gramsci calls this the phenomena of the Historical Hegemonic Block (Simon 1982:

27). According to Gramsci, hegemony is achieved by a group of individuals or a class, controlling the spheres of production. This has happened in Western/patriarchal theology; Jesus has become a monopoly with strict control on spiritual production of meaning and exchange. However, at the grassroots there is always discontent with the unreality and oppressive powers of these theological meta-productions of God and Jesus. Religions are conflict theories which achieve their best in the struggle for conscientisation and liberation. This has been a crucial aspect of Liberation Theology, for instance, but the monopolistic production of God and Jesus has been done with such authority and for such a long time, that its interpellative strength is difficult to confront. That is the main difference between a liberationist approach to God and an indecent one. As we have said, some Queer liberationists may rightly see in Jesus someone with whom out-of-the-closet lesbians, gays, bisexuals and heterosexuals can identify. That is a very positive step, but an Indecent Theology must go further in its disrespect for the interpellative, normative forces of patriarchal theology. It must go beyond the positive identification with a larger Christ. It must have the right to say not only that a lesbian can identify herself with a liberator Christ but that it must sexually deconstruct Christ too. Then indecent theologians may say: 'God, the Faggot; God, the Drag Queen; God, the Lesbian; God, the heterosexual woman who does not accept the constructions of ideal heterosexuality; God, the ambivalent, not easily classified sexuality.' Indecent theologians should speak clearly for people who like things clear. To say 'God the Faggot' is to claim not only a sexuality which has been marginalised and ridiculed, but a different epistemology and also a challenge to positively appropriate a word which has been used with contempt to humiliate people. Liberationists did that in a way when, during the dictatorial times of the 1970s, the Latin American Bibles had pictures of a Ché Guevara Christ, a Christ with a beret, smoking a Cuban cigar. Christ, the subversive, the terrorist, was at that time a provocative image which was like a slap in the face to state terrorism and the politics of foreign intervention and dictatorial regimes. Those Latin American Bibles were burned in Argentina, together with the books of Foucault and Freire. To be caught with a Latin American Bible or a copy of Paulo Freire's *Pedagogy of the Oppressed*, may have meant confinement in a concentration camp and a death sentence. However, the Ché Christ was still produced out of the pattern of the homosocial solidarity of the poor (although in critical times gender and sexuality productions change). 'God the Faggot' may still be a god of liberation but that God may confront the *Machista* resistance in full, because the challenges presented here are deeper.

The problem we are facing here is that, after all, we still cannot influence imperial theologies, which are based on a kind of inter-temporal interpellative nature, unless we speak clearly, and indecently, queeringly clear. This is why Christology is such an important issue, and not just to debate the maleness of Jesus *per se* as in an old-fashioned style of Feminist Theology. It has to raise doubts, showing in this theological process the construction of this sexual Christology which does not necessarily edify the heterosocial patterns although it fortifies them *ad infinitum* with the institutionalisation of relationships in a society based on the sexual flux of the desired, permitted, repressed, taken, abandoned and so forth. A whole sexual theological performance of dressing and undressing (uncovering), the dis-organisation of bodies and their recasting into naturalised pattern of relationships has been historically materialised into institutions such as the family. God has become the medieval or the capitalist family according to political mores. However, it is not only through the history of theology and ideology that this can be traced. The Gospels present us with an inner structure organised as a family economy which has contributed more to the idea of family in Latin America after the *Conquista* than anything else. But this is not a transcendentalist point. God protect us from transcendentalism! It is rather the acknowledgement of the symbolic of the sacred working as desires looking for their own completion, as in the process of becoming licit desires; as such, in alliance with the licit desires of empires and ideologies they do not experience more struggle than subjugating by displacing and condensing the perceived chaotic and extended sexual life of people and their unlawful experiences. The first step to take then is the indecenting of the production of God and Jesus in order to confront the theological simulation of what we can call the Gospel family.

Pure simulations: terror and obscenity in the Gospel family

> Fundamentally, the scene is arbitrary and that does not make sense from the point of view of conventional space.
>
> (Baudrillard, in Gane 1993: 61)

P

V

(Graffiti: twentieth-century Argentina)

Maria José R de Mangone desaparecida *Julio 1977*
(Graffiti: twentieth-century Argentina)

Let us reflect now on God as a family. The Gospel family might be considered as the scene of a terrible (terror) simulation. It was Baudrillard who elaborated the idea of a postmodern culture where the borders between reality and appearance are systematically blurred as the effect of technology is applied in the media (Gane 1993: 3–5). Simulations or hyper-realities, as Baudrillard also calls them, are cases of cosmetic surgery taking their place as real. But how then do we distinguish between the real and the artificial? We are under the spell of seduction, an erotic style of domination-control that happens to the oppressed. Some forms of oppression are internalised to the point of being desirable (Baudrillard 1990: 174). That is precisely the point of the simulation and the movement of double possibilities of oppression and deliverance, for while simulation is constitutive of the symbolic regimes of our postmodern condition, they also constrain and provide the way for alternatives. We might return here to Paul Ricoeur's concept of the *imaginaire* of rupture which opposes that mixed bag of collective symbolic systems formed through centuries of elite control with people's own internalisations of oppression and expected behaviour. However, Baudrillard's discourse needs to be broad enough to include the technologies of subversion of the poor, that art of resisting dictatorial seductions, such as graffiti. As a Third World theologian, I am not necessarily obliged to elaborate on postmodernism as the cradle of all simulation. Empires excel in the art of blurring the limits of the real and the hyper-real in colonial societies. The actions of the dictatorial regimes in South America during the 1970s in their crusade against overrated Marxist invasions can suffice to illustrate this point. On the day of Pinochet's *coup d'etat* in Chile, he was utterly convinced of the imminence of a Russian invasion of Chile. He said he was expecting Aeroflot airlines carrying thousands of Russian Communist soldiers to invade Chile (Correa and Subercaseaux 1996: 15). In Argentina, children as young as 14 years old who campaigned to reduce the price of the bus tickets for high school students disappeared, considered to be Communists trying to create economic chaos. This military operation was nicknamed by the paramilitaries 'the night of the pencils' (*la noche de los lápices*). Dictatorial regimes carry their own fantasy-land to extremes. Different concepts of media culture, which do not depend on technology, such as graffiti, popular songs improvised at demonstrations or certain fashions (such as carrying a book when walking in the street as a sign of defiance to the military junta), have effectively resisted the seduction of simulations in Argentina. For instance, in Argentina, political graffiti has blurred the limits of the real and the imaginary for decades, including the limits between the so-called secular and theological spheres. As someone who was brought up amidst walls showing the then familiar 'V' with a 'P' on top (meaning 'Perón is alive' or 'Perón will return', depending on the interpretation), that wall narrative of the immediate coming back of Perón who was in exile was not something to argue about. The name of Perón was banned publicly. Nobody could mention it; the government had decided that Perón did not exist. Yet, wall after wall kept proclaiming for years, and with only two signs: 'P/V'; he is alive and he will come back. Graffiti and silhouettes (such as those painted for the disappeared) tend to claim that the dead are back and amongst us. This is not exactly a point about a recurrent resurrection theme in popular culture, but more an affirmation of life through death. That was affirmed years ago in Litto Nebbia's song *Quien quiera oir que oiga* (Who wants to hear, listen), which says that 'To kill is a useless act; death only proves that life does exist'. The silhouettes of the disappeared people during the past decades show this point. A silhouette showing a pregnant woman with long hair and the caption '*Maria José R de Mangone. Desaparecida Junio 1977'* is pasted besides the silhouette corresponding to her husband, '*José Hector Mangone (Pepe) Desaparecido Junio 1977'*, and both were pasted beside the niche of the Virgin Mary at the entrance of the Buenos Aires Roman Catholic Cathedral. The Virgin Mary, with a baby Jesus in her arms and the Cathedral for a husband, contrasted with the two silhouettes of the Mangone family, the wife with her arms cradling her pregnant stomach. Both near each other, yet two different posters, separate but reaching for each other. Which one is the Holy Family? The Virgin Mary and child or the disappeared family of husband and pregnant wife? Fundamentally, as Baudrillard has said, it is 'an effect of perspective' (Baudrillard in Gane 1993: 5).

While in the streets people may not believe in death, and still keep shouting '*Con vida los llevaron, con vida los queremos*' (They were taken away alive, we want them back alive), in the Roman Catholic Cathedral the iconography of the Virgin Mary is a simulation; she is practising cosmetic surgery on the man/woman relationship of a young family. That cosmetic surgery consists in removing them from our society, negating that family while trying to seduce the Cathedral's passer-by into a relationship of simulacra. The disappeared family is then affronted by the simulacra of the Gospel family. Heterosexual theological assumptions may be considered weird sometimes, and the matrix of those simulacras such as the Virgin at the Cathedral. But the whole thing becomes even more surreal (pasted over reality) when applied to the family concept. The Gospel family is a display whose function is put on stage only to perform a showroom for the male body of the baby Jesus, the gender codes of dressing and body postures of the Virgin and the conceptualisation of a God/Christ who embodies a male divinity's behaviour. In Argentina, the showrooms of iconography were used to display to full effect military symbols and imperial crowns. Swords and military honours were displayed beside the Virgin Mary, who received the name of the '*Generala* of the Army'. *Generala* is the female noun for 'general', and although syntactically correct, is a non-existent title. There are no *generalas* in the army: thus the chain of pretences of simulations is endless. That divine simulacra was the one that the popular graffiti challenged. In the same way, the Gospels as art, have displayed for centuries a family simulacra, through oral and written narrative devices, pictures and representations.

The Gospel family is a simulation in two acts, or an artifice which partakes of two orders closely related, sexual and economic. It is not a stable product, and has not produced one definitive simulation model of the family in history, but the primordial family simulacra has that which Baudrillard called 'the dream-like quality' (Gane 1993: 67) which has been addressing and impacting on everyday life through the influence of Christianity. We are not going to talk at this point of the representation of the Holy Family in the Christmas pictures depicting father, mother, shepherd boys and the ubiquitous ass, or worse, go through the nitty-gritty of a historical Joseph, Mary and children, speculating on tales of chastity and divinely justified pregnancy. The point of bringing the work of simulations to this scene has a different, indecent objective. We want to produce a rupture in imaginative identifications. If Jesus can become (and rightly so) a Gay Jesus to be identified with gays, Jesus can also be seen through suppression, by the means of per/verting or finding a different road towards the conceptualisation of the Gospel family.

Per/verse variations: *Un Amor de Chicas Muertas*

> You will never be able to love me
> Only to see me on TV
> I will never be able to tell you how you are
> You will never be able to touch me
> Only to see me on a piece of paper
> Don't stop looking at me on your wall.
> ....
> And you are rubbing your legs,
> crying in the Chapel:
> A love of (for) dead girls
> (Charly García: *Chicas Muertas*, song)

What constitutes the 'aboutness' of the Gospel family? From a liberationist and/or feminist tendency, there are answers to this question from the perspective of class and sexual relationships. However, there are surroundings in Liberation Theology and Feminist Theology which work like the frame of a picture which obscures or allows the viewer to see it. It may be interesting to notice here that not everything can or should be translated. Still following Baudrillard, we can consider that we cannot avoid misunderstanding or misrepresenting reality as it was in the Gospel family, through our perceptions of that saga of infidelity, guilt and illegitimation (of gods, people and angels). Theology has a problem with making compulsory translations of religious symbolic into ordinary life and it does not recognise simulations. Let us go indecent at this point and say that the Gospel family is a simulation in the sense of being 'cut off' (Baudrillard 1990: 75), where the surroundings have become effects of Western patriarchal theology. Back to the issue of translations, I may start a Latin American reading on the mother of the family, Mary, as a dead girl, and Jesus as the son of a dead girl. The question of the Gospel family has a more sombre nature than the liberationist tales of biblical models of equality. What we need to do is a recasting of the fragmented bodies in that family. As in a Gothic tale, the Holy Family holds dismembered creatures and Frankensteins in the making. How do we do this recasting? In two ways. First, by assessing fragments, splits, cracks and brittle elements which are so obvious in their process of having been pulverised and set apart that it is hard to think of them in terms of suspicious hermeneutics. Second, by choosing different actors for this Gospel production. What are the elements that are not obvious for us anymore in this production? The fact that the Gospel family is the location of the primal site of women's disappearance and abortion in Christianity. If it is a man/messiah who is born, this means, in the divine economy, that a woman/messiah is not born; she has been excluded from being born. It is the Virgin Mary (a theological construct) and not a woman who becomes mother. Woman–mother and child, and Holy Family in general are concepts bound to a sacrificial theology. A woman does not become pregnant and give birth, but an illusory virgin has taken her place in simulation. A baby boy Jesus is born, and not a baby girl. In each instance, women have disappeared from the family story and been replaced by, in the case of the virgin, a simulation, an imitation of women which ever since has made difficult the existence of real women in Christianity. Real, conscious, aware women in Christianity, silenced and denied for centuries have been like living graffiti; their presence in churches and factories, with or without children, has been saying, 'we exist', 'we are real'.

The 'aboutness' of the Gospel family lies in the location of this departure of women's bodies in the genesis of the irruption of the Messiah in history, either because they were never born or because they simply *were not*, as in Mary's case. The Gospel family strikes us with that difference which can only be found in the non-obvious, in the site where no search has taken place before: such as the site of women's disappearance. Queer theory has produced a significative change in our paradigm of explanation and under-standing what has existed since the Enlightenment, by the fact of challenging what Donald Morton calls 'the role of the conceptual, rational, systematic, structural, normative, progressive, liberatory, revolutionary, and so forth in social changes' (Jagose 1996: 77). As Jagose says, there is an intellectual model which arises from the privileging of the epistemology of the different, the results of which are to be seen in a new denaturalisation of structures of, for instance, race and sexuality. Therefore, an Indecent Theology needs to denaturalise a 'Camp Christianity' (artificial, mannered and ostentatious in its righteousness) which developed by self-parodying its own sexual ideology to the limits.

The point is that after that Gospel family model, women have dis-appeared in history with tremendous naturality, as if humanity was assuming that the destiny of women is somehow related to a theological erasure. We can indecently frame a theology of the Gospel family with dead girls. Dead girls waiting to be there. If Mary existed historically, then we can say with the Mothers of May Square that 'she was taken into that history alive and we want her back alive'. It is not the question of women simply being resurrected in this story, but re-assembled and localised in spite of the scandalous abortion of their presence in this Holy Family/community tradition. That abortion is a pronouncement which mimics the Christian ideal of the impossible woman: the mother–virgin of divine sons, protagonist of history and maker of economy and theology.

Taking the bias towards the dead girls of this story, and making of them authoritative sources of indecent Birth Narratives seems too much, too excessive. Instead of that, we are accustomed to being radical translators of theology, permanently seduced by this simulacra. It is just a question of calling 'Mary', 'Miriam' and 'María', or the more popular *la María,* and dressing her as a Latin American peasant in traditional costume (with underwear). Liberationist and feminist theological exercises of translation are famous for trying to translate the Gospel family for our times. It is futile. They are only exercises of translating, and translating simulations. The point some feminist liberationists are failing to contemplate is that there is no such a thing as an 'original' which only needs to be translated for our times and culture or present moment of consciousness. This idea of an original excludes the conditions of production from which texts and religious constructions come, including the pre-texts of the sexual conditions of the construction of Christianity (Humm 1991). The genderisation of translation rules by virtue of faithfulness, mimesis and obedience to the normative male discourse. One can also add, ruled by norms of that theological category, which we shall analyse later, called 'purity'. The cover up of women's disappearances in theology has been partially done by resurrecting women in the Scriptures, sometimes in a quest to know their names. Their stories and their relation with God is then re-evaluated in terms of their life's fruitfulness, that is, the reproduction of Christianity amongst women or their degree of theological productivity. The shortcomings of this theological strategy of translation are self-evident. Faithfulness is proven by inerrancy and literality. Women are the flat characters of theology, which is accompanied by the predictability of their movements. They are corpses floating in the texts of the Bible and Systematic Theology. It is not that women characters in feminist biblical hermeneutics are not read without challenge and disobedience; on the contrary. The question is that the hermeneutical principle of inerrancy is given not merely by how static the biblical text remains as the implied author of Christianity, but by excluding indecency. For instance, recognising abortion as a theo-logical prerequisite for the Holy Family (women prevented from life; not born into that family) means that we are recognising the use of different Queer categories for doing Christology.

It is sad to say that theology as a text is a deathbed where the woman author has never existed, and has been aborted. Indecent theologians are usually found glancing at these deathbeds, pondering what to do with the remains. Shall the corpse be buried or preserved in alcohol? It is from there that methodological problems arise such as the question of women's silence as a hermeneutical challenge. However, feminist methodology has a tendency to obscure the point that women in Christian theology are 'dead girls'. Women are dead because the symbolic patriarchal theological text always precedes them and constructs their meaning as an interplay of manifestations within the limits of the text. Death is part of the aboutness of Feminist Theology, and its understandable obsession. This obsession is manifested, for instance, in the studies of women in the primitive church, assessing their supposed equality with men. This position is the liberal and early radical feminist one on 'sameness equality' which denies difference and therefore supports by default the patriarchal system (Evans 1996:14). Thus an important issue in the debate about the ordination of women in the Anglican Church (in England), was whether the Phoebe of Romans 16 was to be 'accounted "a deacon" and not simply "deaconess"' (Hampson 1990: 31). However, it is the death of probabilities that we are talking about here, and therefore, a theology of women's resurrection in the Scripture cannot be satisfactory from our indecent perspective. How do we resurrect women in the Gospel family? Christology needs to consider that Jesus Christ came from a heterosexual matrix, probably different from ours but a sexual male dominant intellectual model of relating, loving and knowing. It is the coherence of life shown in heterosexual Christology which takes the role of legislating the symmetry of theology. Such symmetry always rules out indecent corners. Resurrections re-accommodate the order of symmetries when lost in theological crises around issues of race, sexuality, culture or politics. Instead of that, dissent and distrust in theology destroys built coherence and symmetrical (dualistic) patterns of thought. This is true for theology and also for politics.

By purity and by viscosity: obscene thoughts of the Single-God

Is resurrection a reproduction case study on male envy? Is resurrection rooted in purity, as reproduction comes from blood? The purity of the white garments and the 'don't touch me' of Jesus to a woman may be part of this *virginal* childbearing act, this clean parturition without screams, smells, blood, sweat and urine. Who was the parturient subject there? God? Jesus? Purity is, like the Western whiteness which represents it, a single-frequency thought. The myth of the virginal conception of Mary is the myth of the internalisation of the divine phallus, characterised by singleness of mind and obsession. The text of Luke does not even make clear who was the owner of the inevitable phallus which started its appearance in the Gospel narratives by reproducing itself and finished by resurrecting itself. There is intermediacy. In the Gospel narrative, someone (a man of God or 'Angel') speaks *in the name* of God to Mary. It is not a direct dialogue with the divine phallus. Similar to the old Boys Brigade dictum of 'always a cloth' at night in order to at least obstruct masturbation during the small hours, God's phallus comes to Christianity wrapped and invisible, as an intermediate but forcefully enough to be eaten by the primordial Mary. The resurrection of Jesus has been described as a singular event, precisely because it is a duplication without dissent; the phallus that Mary ate comes back to be eaten by every Christian woman. We are all Marys with gigantic divine phalluses stuffing our mouths, and not necessarily by our own will. That is purity in Christianity: hegemony, singleness and obsessive cloning desires. Theology has developed into a gigantic *Chupadero* ('sucker') where you either commit ontological suicide, as for instance a woman, or you became absorbed, sucked up. *Chupadero* was the name for the concentration camps in Argentina from the years 1975 to 1981. They were places of abduction, where a person was sucked into torture, oblivion and death. Only the ones who were 'redeemed' by repentance of their political standpoint against the military regime were able to leave. It is interesting to remember here that the Military Junta described itself in terms of the Holy Trinity: 'Three different responsibilities, and only one goal. Three military powers, and one indivisible political national power, embodied in the Military Junta' (Verbitsky 1987: 95).

Has Liberation Feminist Theology stopped eating divine phalluses? How do we position ourselves in South America in relation to theological *Chupaderos?* Does Feminist Theology have a quest for purity still, for singleness of desire and hegemonic resurrections? The quest for transcendence in Feminist Theology, even in the context of political theologies, is still a quest for an out-of-body experience of purity. Purity contradicts materiality, and therefore the transcendental phallus needs to be conceived outside sensuality. Although Jesus' resurrection is a coming back from torture, and therefore cannot be conceived outside sensual realms, Jesus' coming back belongs to the realms of forensic science, because it serves the purpose of reifying an order of things which by being 'risen' is made exemplary. The purity of the aboutness of resurrection is manifested in its singularity: it is an idealist dimorphic experience, and it is not historical. One can only pair that experience outside the realms of the body. A sexual dimorphic experience of resurrection has contributed to fix geographical and biological spaces of destiny. It has worked as a utopia of transcendental sex assignment which translates literally into a theological functionalism, where people respond to the call to purity by abnormally resurrecting the parody of heterosexualism (since resurrection is not a historical sensual experience). Butler's concept of citation or repetition (Butler 1990, 31) is at the core of the concept of Christian resurrection. This resurrection is materialised in both the private and public spheres of life, and its multiple links can be discovered between singular knowledge of reproduction, political and social theories as well as theology. People may delude themselves, equating resurrection with hopes of a form of eternal life (in real life nobody resurrects), but resurrection is that repetition or vicious circle of sexual ideologies. Is it because resurrection is not based on a historical experience that real sexual experiences of people beyond dimorphism have never been taken into account for *resurrection* theology? We are always moving in the realms of idealism, ignoring the links between making love on our neighbour's sofa and being justified in the legal order of purity. That is the disruption of resurrection, historical experiences of love and relationships.

If purity is a common base for Liberation Feminist Theologies, or to put it differently, if purity is to Liberation Feminist Theologies as colonial thought is to Christianity, the frame we are dealing with is indeed very limited. Sooner or later, as a faithful translator of a singular text, struggling to be left on its own and to be taken at the same time, the theological *recit* will end betraying those outside the heterosexual matrix. That is related to what Derrida calls the double bind of translation. The betrayal is that if a theological *recit* cannot be translated into reality, neither can *las chicas muertas* ('the dead girls') of theology. But not only girls are dead or never born in theology. There are homosexuals 'entombed in us' (Shelley, in Jagose 1996: 42) and aborted identities from unrecognised desires which cannot find their name when reflecting about Jesus, because there is nothing translatable there.

The problem with translation starts when we make of it a mechanical art. In theology, purity is a mechanical art too, and pretends to do a direct translation of certain relationships between men, God and women in the New Testament into our lives. Defiance becomes indecent, since it complicates and rarefies the presented coherent system. Defiance is the path of the obscene. The obscene is the category of the indecent, and the subversion of forensic theology and common order. Obscenity is a sign of presences to come which are inauspicious, thus the frame of threats and destabilisation of disclosure that is dreaded. In his discussion on sadism, Sartre has seen obscenity as a category of body visibility, an exposure of the flesh without means of control, such as jiggling or body postures outside the law (Danto 1975: 123). For instance, it may be acceptable to look at a nude Jesus hanging tortured on the cross as long as he doesn't have an erect penis. Of course, we do not know if Jesus had an erect penis at his death; for all we know, we cannot even take for granted that he had a penis at all, for the narrative testimony of his supposed existence only tells us that he was considered biologically male at birth. The rest is a question of gender status: the promissory baby boy born to be God/man. We read that Jesus had a penis when he was taken to be circumcised (Luke 2:21), but we don't know if it developed, if he had an accident, three testicles or grew up with what might be considered a socially underdeveloped penis, and so forth. In other worlds, we know more about the process of gender making of the man Jesus than of his biological status or, what is more important, his sexuality.

If theology was written by women in a patriarchal fashion, but objectifying men's bodies as we women have been objectified, a whole biological theology may have developed from the single question about Jesus' elusive penis, that sexual promise never (narratively) fulfilled. The authors of the Gospel wrote from the perspective of purity and resurrection: in this way, sexual and gender construction have more reality than the actual sexuality of Jesus, that is, the only certainty we have in relation to his apparent masculinity is a gigantic communal quasi-memory of Jesus' malehood. This quasi-memory refers to the fact that we have images of Jesus but not a memory, because we have nothing to remember except the Gospels which constitute themselves in the imagining of Jesus. That quasi-memory, which may be real in the historical sense, is built upon a trace, a footprint or outline which has the characteristic of being present in the text only by denoting an absence or otherness. When Derrida uses the French word *trace,* he is using other meaningful implications of the word as trail, slot, mark and impression. In Spanish, *traza* (trace) has strong connotations of appearance, of codes of dressing decently or indecently. *Mal entrazado* is a person who is badly dressed in the sense of careless or disrespectful to such codes, which make us perceive the person as a menace: a woman using short trousers at Mass, or a judge with socks and sandals. During the military dictatorial regime in Argentina, it was unlawful for men to have their hair longer than a man in the military, and women were arrested if their skirt length was above the knee. Not only that, but men with long hair were taken to jail and had their heads shaved, and women with short skirts would have their legs smeared with mud. To be defined as *mal entrazado* was a political subversive act (Caraballo *et al.* 1998: 105). There is a link between *la traza* of a person and her criminal potential, and the uncertainty of being respected or not. That is the menacing aspect of a religious quasi-memory such as the Christian one, which works as the text of a logocentric faith. Which is the obscene *traza* that can be found in the quasi-memory of Jesus? What disconcerts us if it is not the disappearance of the heterosexual male and the surplus value of parthenogenesis, to the point that parthenogenesis subsumes several religious discourses in the Gospel? The difficulty with the Gospel narratives is that they are built to produce a distressing effect on readers. Such distress is of a sexual nature. What we find in the Gospels are different layers of sexual forensic laws in permanent deterioration, superimposed by a retroactive technique. Centuries of projecting modern and traditional patriarchal ideologies backwards and constructing a history based on the chronologies of male power urgencies have produced layer upon layer of confusion. This is why recasting more than resurrection might be the crucial hermeneutical clue to understanding the Gospels. The casting of Jesus in the quasi-memory of Christian people is made up of material superimposed on the surface of gender and (hetero)sexuality, internal and external aspects of sexual control (forensic law), health control (safe and unsafe sex, for instance, for purposes of eternal life), abortion (women are not born; if born, they never fully develop as narrative characters; only certain types of women are born, for instance, not messianic types) and harassment as a method to institutionalise heteronormativity. Harassment is a way to keep people in their place, in a certain sexual style and in a dynamic of compulsory heterosexuality regulated by norms of activity and passivity and regularisation of desires. The regularisation of desire in the Gospel is effective harassment. However, distressing effects in the Gospels are not negative in themselves, and allow us to find unpainted and uncovered colours in forgotten corners and odd places. For instance, the Gospels never tell us anything about Jesus' sexual identity and performance. That sexuality is assumed, because we read through the lenses of normative sexual conduct, through the lenses of the Gospel family story as we have analysed it already. In all the relatively recent discourses of 'Jesus had a penis', which became fashionable especially in Black Theology (Beckford 1998) and in some forms of European liturgy addressed to young men, heteronormativity is highlighted, although this discourse borders on the ridiculous. It is a completely irrelevant discourse because having a penis, a vagina or breasts does not say anything about the sexual identity of a person. The 'Jesus = Penis' discourse is part of a homophobic discourse, which homologises heterosexuality and normativity through a discourse of biology and (selective) penile penetration. Even so, if Jesus had a penis, we are not told what sort of penetrative activity this phallus had. The heteronormative discourse of Jesus is not set against particular acts which define what the being of heterosexuality is. There are, for example, no instances of explicit sodomy in the Gospel against which some sexual heteronormativity could have been inscribed in Jesus. Also, we find very few sexually deviant and risqué characters to define heterosexuality by default and bordering of limits. There are no gay, lesbian or bisexual characters, although promiscuous women and proud men are portrayed. These women are the only ones to suggest a counter-definition of what is not religiously sexually accepted, yet it is done within the legal limits of heterosexuality. These women are part of a heterosexual definition in the system of purity/impurity.

And how about Aids in the time of the New Testament? As health issues are associated with religious obedience, there is also another border to be considered. Jesus' apparent good health is constructed around the ideal of his clean lifestyle. We do not need to project the tragedy of Aids retrospectively into the Gospels, but there is a relation. Jesus' health is a paradigm of the innocent, built around sexual conduct. This is a heterosexually constructed behaviour, namely vaginal penetration or at least the presumed desire and/or capacity to do so. However, the disappearance of the heterosexual man is also obvious. As we have already said, there are no border limits of counter-sexuality which might have defined (hetero)sexual normativity in Jesus. Neither are there elements of parody, which define constructed heteronormativity by exaggeration (Butler 1990: 51). The obscene is to be found in this dis-order characteristic of processes of sexual theological naturalisation. Not having been set between limits in the sense of prohibitions by contrasts or by exaggerations, Jesus' sexuality belongs to something intuitively recognised in him by Queer people: a dis-order, a Christ painted in the permanent exposure outside the normative borders, and a Jesus of a corruptible nature. The point is that in the self-preservation of a systematic confinement of heterosexuality, corruption is the only hope for breaking free, for allowing the integrity of heteronormativity to dissolve. Corruption like alterity spoils heterosexuality and breaks it into little pieces. The 'Jesus had a penis' discourse tries to correct the distressing effect of the

Gospels by establishing that potentially Jesus was ready to fuck only the women in his life, according to an internalised sexual behaviour imposed by heterosexuality. This style of thinking fails though, because the penis discourse would only have validity if immersed in a counter-discourse of castrated men, because we only have hints of Jesus' maleness through the brief biological descriptions, such as circumcision. Since we can assume that all men in the Gospel narratives urinated by means of holding their penises in one of their hands, such an affirmation that 'Jesus had a penis' is no more intriguing than affirming the presence of pubic hair in the women of the Gospels. It does not add to any critical discourse on the Gospel.

The question is 'Why does Jesus not speak out?' We have found an obscene trace, a *marca mal entrazada* (badly traced mark) in Jesus' disorderly produced sexuality, which is corrupted. Why? Because in it lies the quality of being potentially capable of altering heterosexuality. However, the trace has a fleeting presence, an obscure implication but not a voice. Why does Jesus not speak? In Chapter 1, we suggested that the silencing of Latin America during the *Conquista* was similar to the analysis of Lacan with reference to silence and symbolic knowledge. The Lacanian argument is that language (Sauval 1998) is not an element for processes of communication, but rather a determining *habitat*, a *natural oikumene* or common house of geographically reduced and naturalised realities. Unless realities can manage to escape from a unified field of symbolic knowledge, they cannot speak. Lacan has called the unified field theory that which subjects reality to an orchestrated dialectic of harmony between the real and the symbolic. That 'unified field' theory is the dream of expressing in only one set of equations the certainty of the movements of the planets and subatomic particles (Sauval 1998). The point is that certainties immobilise; certainties have already spoken 'all' and there is no more room to speak. Paraphrasing Lacan, one may say that the *oikumene* of certainty silences everybody and everything, and it is only by opening the relation between the real and the symbolic that one can envisage the return of the excluded. The planets will speak again when we discover that truth is brought about by the discordant presence of certain knowledge which is not coincident with, for instance, the symbolics of Christianity.

Can we talk about Jesus-the-Moon? Following from what we have already said, we may ask if Jesus is like a silent planet, or a moon. If Jesus were the moon of Jupiter, this would be obscene in the sense of being ominous, of threatening adversity to the basic sexual constructions of the Christian faith. Jesus the moon acts as a mirror of imperial light, and is the reflection of transient naturalised human concepts. Would this explain the almost ritual silence of Jesus' sexuality? Jesus was constructed in a way such that he was born to speak and to be silent at the same time. We may just quote Lacan at this point: 'Is this our goal? To reach the unified field and to convert men into moons? Are we not making them speak a lot just in order to silence them better?' (Sauval 1998). There are disjunctions happening in the use of distressing techniques, which occur because our symbolic knowledge and our reality do not coincide. Neither should they. Jesus *is* a moon because he has been inscribed in a symbolic theological system which is closed, predetermined and stubborn. How could we have so many paintings and icons over the centuries, showing a Jesus child with a substantially developed penis if it was not the case that, as we have said, there were no parameters of heterosexual constructions in the Gospel, apart from a few over-quoted biological references (concretely, to be called 'son', 'man', 'son of man') and one episode of (male) circumcision? There are two things to remember here. First, that theology tries to translate symbolic systems, but cannot translate reality. This means that Jesus is not about Jesus, but a religious system organised as a projected sexual utopia of the origins of heterosexuality. Second, that we do not reflect frequently on the phases of Jupiter. Life is less static than theological systems. Before his death, Copernicus was told that if his doctrines were true, Venus would show phases like the moon. Copernicus replied: 'You are right; I don't know what to say but God is good and will in time find an answer to this objection' (White 1960: 130). That came years later with the invention of the telescope. Jesus does not speak, apparently, because Christology is usually based on immobile notions and theology does not have a further vision, but only a sense of the immediacy of the preservation of dogma. Men might have been moons, and Jesus as a planet without phases, constructed in unity, irrupts with traces of the obscene, the corrupter of the system who forgot to set its boundaries around him. In fact, the only physical boundaries constructed around his identity are those of pain: physical pain at his death and vague emotional pain during his life. He is the man of pain. Pain distinguishes him, frames him. This is a pain reminiscent of the plot found in back issues of the *Good Housekeeping* magazine, as it tries to sell comfort to indecent people struggling with their life of confinements, to poor women setting their domestic lives against a wordly (public) but undesirable one. Power then is symbolically bestowed on the woman at home; the Christ, of the Marginalised, the Queer, the Indecent. Who would like the power of the world of men? It is not good enough. Jesus' story is set in this romantic frame of a man whose access to public power is unsuccessful. Jesus presents a case of chronic, terminal pain, objectified as a way to produce an illusion of Jesus having some control to assert on the realms of emotional/body pain (sin; demons, enemies in this world and in the 'other', these are some of the possible objectifications of Jesus' pain). That pain has socially informed Christianity but the question remains of how the pain was produced. About his sexual life, the only thing we know is that, as with most of us, he is not what we think he *should* be. Pain as a fundamental experience in Jesus' life may have been a sexual experience too. That is the main reason why theology speaks so much, and Jesus is a silent moon. That is the reason why theology has been *systematically* silencing the Moon.

Is Jesus a sex symbol? While women have an ambiguous relation to the normativity of the past in the construction of their Christian identities, it is important to acknowledge that the aboutness of Christianity is produced through sexual fixation. This is not a past, but a permanent present; sexuality is diachronic, not punctual in Christian history. What the Bible says, or how political theory and ideology intercept Systematic Theology, masks any trace of the different in Jesus. Jesus is a sign *sous rature*,[2] unfulfilled, suspended and carrying the trace of unbounded sexuality. It is interesting to notice the connection between these two gods, that Metaphysics of Presence who is YHWH and his 'son'. In the Hebrew Scriptures, YHWH was constructed not so much in opposition to as in excess of patriarchal heterosexuality. Who subjugates women as He does? Who undertakes sex and war in the name of destiny as does the God of Israel? These seem to be statements which recur throughout the whole of the Scriptures. In the New Testament, the sexual harassment of a child, Mary, and the torture of Jesus are His main attributable actions. There is even certainty about YHWH's preferences: He prefers young girls. He did not choose Joseph, or a Prophet for instance and make him reproduce in this 'everything is possible' universe of the Bible: only the young Mary. Admittedly God could have decided to reproduce the God-self through a man instead of a woman. It is true though that according to the Hebrew understanding of reproduction only men carried the reproductive force, while women were only the 'space' to carry the life till the person was born – but the narrative could have privileged a man as the space for the Son of God. If Jesus is built as a character in opposition to YHWH (in the sense of defining his identity by a process of contrasts, by lack or excess), then there are possibilities of finding here a different gender and sexual construction, perhaps one associated with pain. Or can we disassociate, in a Cartesian fashion, the emotional pain which comes from the Gospel from a physical experience of pain? Pain is an experience of limits and mobilises dependence or independence from pain's habits. The narratives of 'the struggle of the soul' of Jesus, with conflicting emotions such as the scene at Lazarus' death, the sighs, tears, weariness and temptations of denying death, plus agonising feelings and frequent talks about anxiety – is a narrative of sexuality in itself. By sexuality we mean a site of bodily and emotional preferences which defines a sexual and/or gender identity. Although we are going to develop this point in full in our next chapter, current associations at grassroots level between Jesus and leather S/M practices may have deeper roots here than previously thought. Jesus is a site of pain and pleasure, in the ambiguity of what is consensual and what is not. This happens because the relationship between Jesus and God is the relation between person and potential. God is always potential. How do people deal with authoritative potentials? According to *Vanilla* theologians, by behaving as bottoms (slaves, subservients), that is, by being dominated and obtaining our pleasure from that. However, consent is here ruled out, and it is assumed that Jesus took his pleasure from his dominant potential God.

In all these discussions, it is interesting to notice that Systematic Theology is still a major stumbling block in Liberation Feminist Theology and a re/source of obscurity in the praxis of women's theology. Although Systematic Theology has been thematically contested, even if partially, the assumptions of theology as part of a methodological knowledge persist. Indecent hermeneutics is not about tracing the path of methodological progress in our theological constructions. On the contrary, it is the art of pinpointing obscurities, twisted categories and queer details which appear in disorder, and with or without apparent continuation. Traces of the obscene in Jesus act as exemplary measures to prevent us from falling into what Butler calls 'the illusion of the true body beyond the law' (Butler 1990: 93). There is no pure, incorruptible and unique, coherent Jesus beyond the law of sexual regulation of heterosexual Systematic Theology. The extraordinary consequence of this is that God cannot be considered one body only beyond the law. God appears indecent. If, as we have already suggested, obscenity is the aboutness of Indecent Theology then this theology participates in and is participated in by that sense of transcendental viscosity which is determined to stick in any reference to out-of-body defined transcendental revelation. In this we are referring to that element called 'viscosity' by Sartre, which refers to the slime quality, or *le visqueaux*, as constitutive of Being (Sartre 1956: 604). Viscosity is here an affective characteristic of Being, a mantle or cloth which covers Being, which Sartre basically organises in a dualistic form of *Being In-and-For-Itself.* Viscosity is this gelatine quality of the For-itself (*Pour Soi*). Any sense of transcendence is marked with this gelatinous, viscous condition, this fluidity which seems to taint and wet transcendental conceptions which want to deny the body. Theology cannot clean itself enough of *le visqueaux*, and from here, it fails to understand the need for obscenity in its analysis.

Obscenity as the way to avoid unnecessary transcendence

We are going to use Sartre's concept of obscenity, although in reverse. Sartre has worked out in a theological fashion an oppositional pair consisting of 'Obscenity' and 'Grace' (Sartre 1956: 401). This is done in the context of Sartre's comments on sadism. The example which Sartre brings before us is that of a dancer who dances without clothes, but with such 'grace' that in a way, the dancer covers her own body and inhibits lust from the viewers. Grace here is described in terms of a cover-up, an emotional make-up and a form of metaphysical underwear, a spiritual cold shower which controls lust, and controls the body. Returning to the narrative of the Gospel family, it is tempting to identify God with Sartrean grace, for God controls the body and the lust of Mary at the same time. From an indecent perspective, then, Mary becomes the symbol of grace for women, who are called ontologically and materially to cover themselves up and metaphysically speaking to take a cold shower to inhibit lust. Meanwhile, obscenity is the opposite concept. The obscene is, in Sartre's own words, that which renders visible the flesh as flesh, or in the case of the nude dancer, the kinds of movements which do not cover the dancer's nudity but expose it and add the element of the uncontrollable body to the scene (Sartre 1957: 141). Following this argument, then, we may say that grace is destroyed by obscenity. Obscenity appears now to us as the *dis-covering* of grace, and the way to transcendence. Obscenity does not renounce the viscosity of materiality but sets it free by exposing it. Obscenity leads us towards a theology of exhibitionism, which is a very encouraging sign for the task of affirming reality and the suppressed aesthetics of Christianity. Theology as a classic systematic sexual act is in need of exposure and grace dis-covering obscenity.

The quest for the obscene Jesus is neither new nor restricted to a liberationist feminist enterprise. Historically, obscene Christs have appeared when people wanted to uncover the graceful pretences of current Christologies. The Black Christ of Black Theology was obscene because it uncovered racism under the guise of a white Jesus. I was told by a student that in Jamaica when, several years ago, some people threw black paint over the white statues of Christ in a gesture of defiance, to show that a Jamaican Christ could also be represented as black, even black people were horrified and saw it as blasphemous and obscene. What was obscene was the uncovering, the racial kind of nudity produced, that striptease performed before the reality of a Christ that even amongst black people needed to be represented as white and Caucasian. The *Christa* is another example of obscenity. It undresses the masculinity of God and produces feelings and questionings which were suppressed by centuries of identificatory masculine processes with God. Why, for instance, is the tortured male body of Christ less offensive and infinitely more divine than a woman's tortured body? Or why does a woman's tortured body become sexy, as in the images of dismembered women found in some pornographic magazines? MacKinnon gives the examples of images of women hanging from trees or with severed limbs, which are portrayed as sexy even if their genitalia are not exposed (MacKinnon quoted in Easton 1994: xii). Why is it that, confronted by the naked body of a female Christ, the heterosexual gaze is still fixed on the shape of breasts, the youth of the body and its sexual desirability? The *Christa* is significative, then, not as the female parallel version of Christ, but only when she uncovers the contradiction and difficulties of a female Christ if construed as 'the other side of the coin' of Christ.[3] The undeniable fact is that the existence of some Christ of history has been superseded by the symbolic construction of reality based on sexual and racial grounds. Therefore, any uncovering of Christ needs to follow that pattern of obscenity as disruptive and illuminating at the same time, because Christ and his symbolic construction continue in our history, according to our own moment of historical consciousness. In a way, all Christologies are limited by the frontiers created by our lack of questionings and suspicion. Only recently have our sexual suspicions come to the fore to question the construction of human beings in their relationships. The consequences of this are vast, including economic theory because economics like theology is the old science of human relationships.

Some theological per/versions

Obscenity no. 1: Bi/Christ

Queer theory claims the use of what has been called, after Henry Jenkins, 'textual poaching'(Jenkins 1992). The theory behind this term is that readers 'poach', choose those elements, in the readings which relate to them and give them some meaningful insights into their existence. The 'poacher' is not an expert but an individual or a community which relates to elements which have been obscured or disregarded by others as of lesser importance, yet which are appropriated by those who recognise them as meaningful. In Christology, one element which people at the margins usually 'poach' is that elusive fluidity of Jesus: that fluidity which eludes, presents round edges and becomes ambiguous, in contrast to the legalistic Christ of definitive answers to everything from the book of the law and the regulations of God. For Robert Goss this is something like a divine coming out of God in Jesus, shown by Jesus' defiance of oppressive laws and structures of his time (Goss 1993: 76). This statement is somehow exaggerated (Jesus did not stand up against the forces who occupied his country, as Palestinians do today) and it is a fact that his historical consciousness, seen from our perspective, is found lacking. However, there seems to be a destabilising element in Christ, even if it is not much more than the contradictory images of Christ presented in the Gospel: the Christ of Peace, and the Christ of the whip, against the poor people who traded their humble merchandise in an authorised space of the temple; the Christ who defied social conventions meeting a lonely woman at a well, and the Christ who did not dare to challenge impurity laws against women concerning menstruation (Althaus-Reid 1995: 149). This Queer indecency leads us to take the path of obscenity, as a methodology, to find more radical per/versions of Christ. Following the Sartrean metaphor of obscenity, the garment which covers the dancer swirls around, uncovering the dancer's nudity, but it does so by a series of unpredictable movements, folds and creases, in a fluid movement. To challenge the cartography of heterosexuality we need to follow fluid movements in Christology.

We are talking here about a systematically deviant Jesus. Let us use this last metaphor of clothes and nudity to ask ourselves how is Christ currently dressed in Christology, and if we ever pay attention to that. The dressing of Jesus may be critical here, because in reality the only thing that we know about Jesus is that he has been dressed as a heterosexual man by hetero-sexual theology. Even if we accept that Jesus was biologically a man, his sexuality has been put together by argumentative cover-ups, elusive stories of real manhood, yet nothing seems to be quite so clear as heterosexual patriarchal theologians would like us to believe. Take for instance the claim that Jesus was a 'friend of sinners and prostitutes'. Does this statement not imply then that he shared his life with sinners and prostitutes? What sort of sinners: men who lied to their neighbours, slept in the synagogue, shared bacon rolls with Romans or sexual deviants? A friend usually has things in common with her friends, beyond compassion. Jesus must have had something of the sinner and the prostitute too within himself if he enjoyed their company. At least he must have felt that they had things in common, ways of thinking or laughing or befriending. The assumption that Jesus went to those circles of vice in his society to preach and show his compassion in a detached old-fashioned teaching mode cannot be completely true. 'Sinners' and prostitutes are human beings like anyone else. Like anybody else they may at times need compassion for their troubles, and at other times just friends for an intimate encounter, conversation and laughter. Jesus kept going to them, with the obstinacy of the Argentinian gays who kept going to the few gay clubs in Buenos Aires during the years of the dictatorship. The call of love and intimacy is always stronger than anything else. Jesus' friends were not the *tabula rasa* of God (that colonial concept used in Christology when referring to conversion). They must have also had their opinions on religion, politics and life and they may have taught Jesus a couple of truths too. We all learn in community, even god/men. It is a historical law. However, Jesus' strong attachment to deviant people is preserved in collected stories which are capable of more than one reading into his sexuality – per/verted readings, options along the road of interpretation. The hermeneutical clue that we are missing is concealed under Christological 'coverings' which produce that effect of citationality around the sexuality of Jesus in theology. To pursue this point let us consider the following comment by Judith Halberstam on watching the movie *Batman Returns*:

> When Batman and Catwoman try to get it on sexually, it only works when they are both in their caped crusader outfits . . . [T]heir flirtation in capes looks queer precisely because it was not heterosexual, they were not man and woman, they were bat and cat, or latex and rubber, or feminist and vigilante; gender became irrelevant and sexuality was dependent on many other factors . . . [I]n other words, the sexual encounter is queer because the gender of the partners is less relevant. Just because Batman is male and Catwoman is female does not make their interactions heterosexual – think about it, there is nothing straight about two people getting it on in rubber and latex costumes . . .
>
> (Halberstam quoted in Hall and Pramaggiore 1996: 57)

This statement, as part of an interesting Queer film analysis, focuses on sexuality and leaves gender as a cover-up, a dressing-up which shows something trying to determine it, but able to do so only at the surface level. This makes us wonder up to what point can the dressing of Jesus determine his sexuality, to the point that even radical Liberation Theologies have been unable to challenge. It is obvious that Jesus did not dress as Batman, neither has Christology represented him as a leather man, even though leather people may sometimes entertain theological fantasies on that point (Baldwin 1993:35). Jesus has been represented in art as nude, half nude, or dressed according to the fashion of Palestine at his time, but this is not all the dressing to which we are referring here. He has been dressed theologically as a heterosexually orientated (celibate) man. Jesus with erased genitalia; Jesus minus erotic body. When we think about Christ, we do not think about a man, we think about a God/man, a celibate batman, batteries included to supply his head with that halo of light which we frequently see in paintings. Theology has made of Jesus the 'Systematic Messiah', and this means that he comes wrapped up in male heterosexual masculinity so obsessively as to reach the point that it does not allow us to see his relationship with his community or with us as instances of the way that human beings relate to each other and have done so for centuries. Jesus is then somehow Batman, and the way people are asked to dress up (cover) their sexual identities when relating to him is what we may call queer (strange). On a positive note, our theological dealings with Jesus are queer, of an indecent nature, precisely because Jesus' gender performance is blurred with a sexuality which depends on a subtle divinity consciousness (his own, and that projected on him by friends, family, enemies and admirers) and on location. These locations are not the historical ones, but the narrative ones. For instance, the account of Lazarus' death and return at the call of a Jesus, who could not stand life without him, is reminiscent of those love affairs between two men which are tempestuous, with one abandoning the other even if still in love, yet coming back at the sight of his desperate lover, who 'comes out' to shout his love before the community at that moment.[4]

The question of a Bi/Christ is related not to the sexual performances of Jesus, which we ignore. As far we are concerned, Jesus may have been a transvestite, a butch lesbian, a gay or a heterosexual person. Heterosexual patterns of thought prevail in the narratives, and this is easy to identify not by the 'girl meets boy' model (or girl meets God), but by patterns of hierarchical, binary constructive organised thought. The Systematic Messiah is a Christ of clear limits and boundaries, a compromise found amongst the ambiguities of his character and the almost military precision and clear planning of his life which heterosexual thought requires. This is a Messiah whose Messianic project seems to be 'about heterosexuality' in a deep way, because it goes down to issues of power and ways of thinking theologically – to which we should like to add, ways of organising the church too (Stuart 1997: 7). Heterosexuality is an economy, an administrative pattern which is sacralised in our churches even in the way they organise themselves. However, Queer theologians like Goss and Stuart, amongst others, have been focussing on a Christ who is neither this nor that, a Christ who embraces and shows life as fluid, changing, outside the reductionist patterns which confront people with irrelevant options. For instance, browsing on a website,

I recently found a discussion group about Christian women. They were exchanging opinions about women's limits in society. They asked if a woman can be a Christian and work outside the home or not? The whole matter does not deserve much attention except for the fact that it is an extreme example of how heterosexual patriarchal systems work, by either/or categories. Either Christian at home, or non-Christian working in a public office. New opportunities in the market place for women are not analysed in terms of the conditions of labour, but from patriarchal Christian assumptions of the legitimation of womanhood by their activities in the private sphere of work. This pattern of thought has spatial indications (home or work) and temporal rules (the codification of women according to ages), based on heterosexual practices. The term heterosexual here is used according to that certain construction of heterosexuality which positions heterosexuality (the assumed women's sexual preference for men and vice-versa), in terms of reproductive and monogamous relations. However, heterosexuality cannot be confined to these limits. In the historical experience of human beings, relations are seldom monogamous nor simply reproductive. People at different times have had to pay a high price for contravening legislation which taxes sex in our societies.

A Bi/Christ has been coming out for a long time, especially in Liberation and Feminist Theologies, because implicitly they have consistently refused to consider Christ as limited to the boundaries of ideological dichotomies. For instance, the theological debate in some (wealthy) circles about the option for the poor in Liberation Theology and in Freirean conscientisation processes has developed along lines of thinking that Christ can only be the Christ of the poor. European theologians have often asked me 'What about the rich in Liberation Theology?' and 'What about the middle-class people?' Christian people who do not have a clear point of solidarity with fellow human beings who live under extremes of poverty and deprivation feel threatened and excluded by the option for the poor. During my courses on 'Ethics of Liberation Theology' in the University of Edinburgh I have found this issue constantly arising. The students are troubled by the thought that a middle class person will be automatically excluded from participation in Base Christian Communities or popular Bible studies at parish level. The reasoning behind this is simple: it is assumed that once the poor are given their place of decision-making responsibility in church and theology, they will oppress the rest. This will be then, the theological 'dictatorship of the masses'. At this point it needs to be explained to them that the option for the poor has never operated amongst liberationists as a new category of exclusion. On the contrary, a basic point of Liberation Theology (and Feminist Liberation Theology) has been to say that the non-poor are also oppressed by the categories of structural sin which are economic, sexist and racist. To liberate the oppressed means also to liberate the oppressors from the sin of oppression which engulfs their lives. Therefore, we do not have an 'either/or' category here. This understanding of the option for the poor

carries in itself a latent bisexual pattern of thought, as it moves away from
the dichotomies presented in current epistemologies which come from that
very basic structure of sex opposition. It is not 'poor vs. rich', but poor *and*
rich immersed in the same structure of oppression although with different
results. This is why we can say that in the liberationist movement there was a
seed of a larger Christ, a Christ who would come out of the closet without
sitting on the fence and constricting the Christself, in a dialogue between
overlapping sexual spaces (Hall and Pramaggiore: 1996: 4). That image of
the fence, which Pramaggiore uses in her analysis of 'Epistemologies on the
Fence', is one which we can aptly use for constructing a Bi/Christ. The
Heterosexual Christ, or the Gay Christ or the Lesbian Christ, the Transgendered Christ and so on, do not need to be exclusive but located in the
space/time of a community's experience. While Queer theory has a point in
not wanting theoretical analysis producing a *coup d'etat* in sexual identities,
thus diluting them in an abstract discourse of Queerness in a sort of
universalising perspective, what is at stake here is the basic dual epistemology which organises theological thought and Christology. Christ can be
represented very movingly as a young woman holding another woman
tightly, as they stand at the closed door of a church amidst voices from
within the church shouting 'stay out' to the young lesbian (Stuart 1997: 23).
For many people (including myself) who have suffered the experience of
being locked out of a church, for whatever reason, that image of the Christ
Woman crying with the excluded woman at the door of the church
represents exactly what they suffered then. But even more important than
that, it shows the Christ whom they needed at the time: a Christ outside the
gates. Curiously, some people have told me that even if the church changed
its attitude and welcomed them, they still need that Christ locked out from
the church. It is as if Christ may refuse to come back to worship because of
the tragic exclusion experiences suffered by many Christians. In the same
way, an old gay friend of mine in Argentina used to say that for him Christ
was the gay companion of an old man like himself, suffering from the forms
of social and economic exclusion, and the degree of loneliness of old poor
gays which few other people may experience in their lives. Or we can envisage
a transgendered Christ, taking on the Christself the oppression and injustice
that a person suffers when gender and sexuality are bodily dislocated. The
Bi/Christ takes it all into his life: economic deprivation and social marginalisation, exacerbated by a kind of heterosexual excommunication from God
with which people who happen to be sexual political dissenters are confronted. Excommunicated from love, not only the divine, but the love-
solidarity of communities and neighbours, this larger Christ goes beyond
'either this or that', because there are so many sexual identities to which we
do not have names to give. This is what Biddy Martin refers to when she says
that heterosexuality is obsessed in its efforts for boundary controls of the
kind of 'who is what' style of argument (Barrett and Phillips 1992: 97–8).
Martin sees here the threat of coming out as disintegrative of heterosexual

culture, by highlighting what Sedgwick calls the 'conceptually intractable' contradictions of a sexual system which is a servant of established power and knowledge (Barrett and Phillips 1992: 100). Heterosexuality preserves its colonial space of defining reality by sorting out its own heterosexual categories when addressing non-heterosexuals. The stereotype of the homosexual man as feminine and the lesbian as masculine, and the butch and femme typology are just an example of this. The same can be said of the bisexual as the woman who likes women and men. This makes us question what sort of women, and what sort of men are we talking about here? Straight men? Does this cover women who live with gays? Straight men, mostly married who enjoy what is called 'rough trade' (sporadic sexual encounters with men)? Lesbians trapped in male transvestite bodies? The point here seems to be one of creating a stable heterosexual subject even amongst non-heterosexual people.

In a Christology of a Bi/Christ we are considering two things. First, the reality of people's identity outside heterosexualism, and second, a pattern of thought for a larger Christ outside binary boundaries. My old gay friend was wise enough to think that Christ is a gay companion who knows his sufferings and is in solidarity with him. But this is also the Christ that Carter Heyward's Lesbian Christology elaborates, the She who is amongst us. Carter Heyward's way of trying to escape from the theological trap of either divine or human for Jesus Christ goes beyond heterosexual readings in theology (Heyward 1989). In Christ there is a conjunction of divinity and humanity, and there is not just *The Christ* but a diverse Ultra-Christ, incarnated (located) in our specific time and communities. And there are old gays and young transgendered, and many dissenting heterosexuals in those communities, and, yes, in the communities of the poor, of course. This is what we could call an indecent Christology where a Bi/Christ is important if bisexuality is the sexual thinking which works by refusing to take into account the perpetuation of heterosexual categories in theology. Liberation Theology did not use general principles, or universal types of moral discourses but went to find 'what was there', in the communities of resistance. Richard Rorty also asserts that this aspect is relevant in his development of the notion of solidarity, not as part of a metaphysical programme but a sympathy which refuses to marginalise the different (Barret and Phillips 1992: 14). How do we find 'the Christ' who is there, and reflect on it in a structural theological way? Bisexuality has been classified as a confusion and a lack of commitment, the latter being a typical heterosexual (theoretical) obsession of marking clear (universal) sexual spaces. As a theological category bisexuality erases what Brian Loftus calls 'the sexual marking in the establishment of hierarchy and power distribution' (Hall and Pramaggiore 1992: 217). What it interesting is that in his article, Loftus refuses to consider bisexuality as made into yet another sexual category under risk of repeating the heterosexual ideological mechanisms of ordering and limiting sexualities. Instead of that, he speaks of bisexualities as invisible desires contravening the 'normative vision' of heterosexual difference (Hall and Pramaggiore 1992: 210). This point has been very well developed in Elizabeth Daumer's article 'Queer Ethics'. According to Daumer, bisexuality brings to the surface the difficulties in organising sexual identities and that discontinuity, more than coherence which is basic to an individual sexual act, the affection of that individual and his/her own political commitment and, we may add, theological options (Daumer 1992: 98).

The reality is that Bi/Christ is the Christ who 'gives us something to think about'. Paul Ricoeur defined the symbol as a structure of signification which gives rise to thought. He said that *'le symbole donne a penser'* (the symbol gives us something to think about). Human thought has deciphering modes, hermeneutical vocations trying to locate the different hidden meanings of those structures of signification which Ricoeur calls symbols (Ricoeur 1974: 13) This is a hermeneutical task, and a work of interpretation which symbols demand from us, by unfolding several levels of superimposed meanings which, like peeling an onion, always directs us to another hidden meaning we have not seen before. Jesus Christ's true life is hidden in the historical theological interpretation narratives. Its meaning can only be peeled off in our creative religious imagination. There, we find a Christ 'who gives us something to think about'. Christ's historical deeds are too brief, distant and too heavily mediated from us. His resurrection is totally elusive, outside the boundaries of our religious imagination, but it need not for that reason be less effective. On the contrary, there is more possibility to produce an efficacious Christology with our creative imagination, nurtured by our own historical experiences, than by just following thirty something years of his life which have been reduced to less than thirty something minutes of reading in the Gospels. The symbolic construction of Christ, as in Ricoeur's symbol, can also be characterised by this food for thought process. A Christ who gives us something to think about, who is not a closed discourse and premature death without resurrection, because resurrection has become a mere reproduction or continuous videotape of definitions and regulations. Such death by closure of the symbolic dimension of Christ is in the end a monosexual project, born from the monosexual empire of current theologies. This is the Christ of mono-relation, Monotonous Mono/Christ. To think Bi/Christ is to dismantle the foundations of these sexual monopolistic claims of naming reality but also of organising it. Goss speculates on how Basic Christian Communities could be organised on Queer principles (Goss 1993: 140). His position, which is a Queer re-reading of Liberation Theology, is that such communities are meant to be built away from homophobic theological principles and compulsory patterns of relationships. Traditionally, Christian Basic Communities have been built around the best principles of (homo)-solidarity's forms which can be found in heterosexuality: protection for women and children and female leadership only when men are unavailable and with limited recognition. There are even dual patterns of public (community-based) recognition of leadership simultaneous with women's domestic abuse in BECs. They go unchallenged because Christian theology re-enforces sexual stereotypes of control and submission.

Therefore, Goss's project touches deeply the roots of the problem. Deep changes in community and in nations are bound to be challenges in people's consciousness to be effective. In this way, a Bi/Christ gives us food for thought in terms of church organisation and strategies for community transformation, breaking down monopolistic economic and affective relationships. The 'either this or that' is problematised. The imprecision of a Bi/Christ may give way to new perceptions of coherence, outside the coherence of binarism: good faithful women in Latin America are basically mothers; men are *macho* but good, and the rest are perverts. But per/version is just the name for another interpretation, more rooted in reality than these representations and parodies of people's lives, which seem to come from vignettes of colonial textbooks. Consider, for instance, the following extract from *Aunt Africa*, a book from the beginning of the twentieth century addressed to British children:

> Some would be wild and ignorant savages, not wearing even a blue stripped shirt . . . But what you called a tame Negro may still have his diamond undiscovered and uncut.
>
> You mean that a civilised and educated Negro may still have a soul that is not found? – said Miss Brown.
>
> Like an educated Englishman, said Aunt Africa . . . It is hard to feel that (Negroes) really belong to (the family of humankind). Yet there is only one great Father.
>
> (Gollock 1909: 206)

This description of Africans belongs to the realm of Colonial Theology, but what I should like to highlight in it is the mono-relational pattern of heterosexuality present in these words. 'The Negro' is human if he submits to 'God the Father': a one to one relationship without possibilities of constituting Africans as diverse as God, Godself. The postcolonial construction of the narrative of 'poor Christians' goes somehow hand in hand with Aunt Africa's Christology, and its characteristic mono-relational patterns in society and in the church. In this sexual economy, African souls are diamonds, like the diamonds the Empire was taking from African soil for its profit. This is the reproductive pattern of the one to one relationship; almost a marriage contract. 'One Father' implies one humanity, not for ideals of solidarity but in order to simplify the formula of dualistic submission. Which other category, apart from a bisexual one, can contradict this economic, sexual and theological monotony? Only a Bi/Christ category which happens to be so unsettled, that no mono-relationship could have been so easily constructed with it. Bi/Christology walks like a nomad in lands of opposition and exclusive identities, and does not pitch its tent for ever in the same place. If we consider that in the Gospel of John 1:14, the

Verb is said to have 'dwelt among us' as in *a tabernacle* (a tent) or 'put his tent amongst us', the image conveys Christ's high mobility and lack of fixed spaces or definitive frontiers. Tents are easily dismantled overnight and do not become ruins or monuments; they are rather folded and stored or reused for another purpose when old. Tents change shape in strong winds, and their adaptability rather than their stubbornness is one of their greatest assets. The beauty of this God/tent symbolic is that it can help us to discover Christ in our processes of growth, the eventual transformations through unstable categories to be, more than anything else, a Christ of surprises.

Obscenity no. 2: the resurrection of lust

> Only women know, as the organisers of *las costumbres* [social custom, family habits], which sort of abyss, which terrors, which obsessions, which mad pleasures are hidden behind this tranquil word *[las costumbres]*.
>
> (Bocchetti 1993: 230)

Born out of a split relationship between *eros* and agapian love, Christ has become the lustless messiah of systematic theologians. Why 'either/or'? Why choose between agapian and erotic love? Why these two separate concepts and a fence between them, ordering them by alphabetical categories? What sordid or brilliantly passionate stories are hidden behind the love which is constructed as de-eroticised? According to Mary Daly, lust has always been an obsession of patriarchal theology (Daly 1984: 2). Equated with malevolence, phallic lust's destructive forces have been formally rejected from the by-products of theology such as Christian treatises and sermons. However, lust has always been alive and kicking, even if by rejecting it, they were killing to prove that life still exists. For instance, in the several volumes of Barthian theology, which Daly sees as destructive of female be-ings, there is lust which needs to be frantically controlled by gendering, by family structures and so forth. Meanwhile, Barth's lustful passion for his lover was present during his writing. And the theologian is never so detached from his life's experiences as s/he would like to be. We may add to what Daly says on lust, that this dismembering of being in patriarchal lust may have also consumed Barth's own life. This is the bi/liberationist standpoint: the oppressors are engulfed by their own oppression too. Therefore, it is not phallic lust which destroys a group of Queer or indecent people, for we must remember that in reality, heterosexuality makes of every courageous human being a Queer, indecent person. Only very hypocritical people may claim to live according to the rules, *contra natura,* of heterosexual politics and theology. Deep in our hearts, we are all 'Queer Nation' needing to come out and denounce that human beings live and love according to reality, and not Christian indexes on morals. The important contribution of Daly is that she does not only denounce patriarchal lust, but also recaptures the concept of lust as a living force, and a material spirituality.

This may motivate us to ask some further questions. For instance: Which Christ resurrected? The phallocentric heterosexual Christ found in Edwardian biblical commentaries, from the time when *Aunt Africa* was written? Moreover, we may like to ask: Where is love in the resurrection of Christ, if there is no lust?

Obscenity no. 3: the resurrection from below

> Negro, animal de trabajo,
> clamo la luna por vos.
> (Black man, a beast of burden,
> I claim the moon in your name)
> (Fito Páez: *Apocalipsis de Abajo*, song)

Having been educated as an Argentinian woman in Liberation Theology, I must confess that resurrection was not a theme for my generation. We seldom discussed it in my years of theological studies, at least in its over-spiritualised classical form. *Los desaparecidos* (the disappeared) was our theme, not illusory tales of leaving graves. We did not even know the graves of the disappeared! At that time, people were disappearing daily without leaving a trace behind, as if people could evaporate into thin air without leaving a body behind. The *Madres de Plaza de Mayo* went around the *Plaza* every Thursday, walking in a circle and asking for the return of their children in what, somehow, we knew was a plea for a different kind of resurrection (Althaus-Reid 1998: 397–9). It was a resurrection of justice, of those declared 'vanished', to say that they had bodies, corpses, and these needed to be found. It was resurrection with a strategy and time limits. It was a Resurrection Theology asking when and how and why. This was the theme of life at that time in the circles of Liberation Theology in Argentina. It was resurrection of the people, or what a popular song from Fito Páez called 'resurrection from below' *(Apocalipsis de abajo*, in the sense of the physical uprising of the humble ones, the poor, the oppressed, from below as opposed to heaven). In Nicaragua, peasant paintings depicted the open tombs and the resurrections of Ché Guevara and the Sandinistas killed during the revolution, coming to life again together with Jesus. Liberationists always emphasised the materiality of resurrection acts, but also their consequences, because in Material Theology one always assumes that apart from thoughts, things happen. J. Michael Clark, in his book *A Place to Start: Towards an Unapologetic Gay Liberation Theology*, has taken the liberationist way of de-emphasising resurrection because it carries the risk of carrying with it the dichotomy of spiritual life versus material life. Still, the road is broad and needs to be per/verted (given another interpretation), twisted in a forbidden direction, the way of lust. As I write these words in América, in the summer of 1998, the news is of a young university student from the United States, who has been tortured and killed because he was not heterosexual. He was gay. As I look at his picture in the newspaper, the face of an intelligent, handsome young man smiling, I wonder if he is going to resurrect, and when, and how? Perhaps only when we acknowledge that Christ's resurrection is part of our common business, that somehow we must work for that student's resurrection by acting in the denunciation of the roots of homophobia. Of course, this not about the resurrection of the dead from tombs and ashes, but the resurrection *de abajo*, of the people who are oppressed and die different sort of deaths every day: the death of hopes and dreams, and of rights and love and lust. I have said elsewhere that people live and die in community, but also resurrect in community (Althaus-Reid 1996: 194–206). When Jesus died, in a sense a whole community died with him; with the death of the presence of that friend amongst them, of intimate relations with Jesus which were now gone, death took from them someone who was the witness of their lives. Or again, following that Gay Bible study in Buenos Aires, we can say that Jesus resurrected Lazarus because with Lazarus' death Jesus himself died of abandoned love and terminal anguish. And a man who cried as Jesus did according to the text, and shouted to his beloved to come back from death, must have given so many kisses and cuddles to that beloved when he returned that it makes me sigh with envy just to think about it. That episode of Lazarus is nothing else but a scene of a physical resurrection in lust. Where was Lazarus when Jesus died? That may be a crucial factor. We do not know. Was their love finished? Yet, with Lazarus or any other scandalous beloved around him, Jesus'resurrection could have had the possibility of lustful resurrection or at least the indeterminacy of criss-crossing love/agape and eros, instead of the 'do not touch me' directed to Mary Magdalene. It was Gillian Rose who wrote that

> To spend the night with someone is agape: it is ethical. For you must move with him [sic] and with yourself from the arms of the one twin to the abyss of the other . . . It may not be a marriage, but it will be sacramental.
>
> (Rose 1997: 65)

Where does resurrection intercept an intimate relationship? The over-spiritualising of resurrection that Clark has criticised has produced this outcome, that resurrections seem not to be about relationships, for the resurrected Christ is present only in some departure mode, the end of the lusty body and the beginning of an 'angelic body'. The sacrament of lust and intimacy is not present, it is lost. In the end, Resurrection Theology ends up achieving the contrary to life: it ends negating it.

I have said elsewhere that I can see Christ as a poor prostitute (Althaus-Reid 1999: 39–51). People who cannot see Jesus as a prostitute refuse to consider seriously the web of sex and oppression which exists in our societies. Technically, there is no difference between seeing Christ as, say, a poor miner covered in sweat and broken down by tiredness (as I have seen in some representations of Christ in Latin America) and a young girl kept against her will in a Sauna. Or as Mary, a young prostitute from Edinburgh, told me once, she goes to the street 'to keep the children till they finish school', but she is a Christian woman, in her way. Poverty does not always allow people choices. Yet Christ embraces sexual oppression but also intimacy and good love. This Christ gives us food for thought if we consider resurrection as a coming out experience. Christ came back to life because he loved life. A person comes out as a human being, because that person loves life so much that she has decided to come out from structures of death and oppression. T., a gay man from my church, came out in Latin America, when, surrounded by a loving community, he decided that he had been dead for far too long. Significatively he changed his name to 'Renato', which in Spanish means 'reborn' and he felt that it was his moment of resurrection from death to what Mary Daly has called lust as 'an intense longing: craving.... Eagerness and enthusiasm' for life (Daly 1984: 2–3). Following Daly, the resurrection of Christ can only be understood as part of Christ's unsettledness, this 'wonderlust' which cannot be confined to a tomb, not even to the tombs/tomes of heterosexual Systematic Theology. Christ's resurrected presence can only be seen then as a craving, an enthusiastic passion for life and justice, in the diversity and unfenced identity which is searching for that land called *Basileia* by European theologians and 'the project of liberation of the Kingdom' by Latin Americans, in which we are all called to be co-workers. We join then Christ's resurrection with our own coming out for the obscene Christ in a per/verted Christology which reminds us of the ethical need for resurrection. People do not disappear: the *desaparecidos* were killed, but we all learned their names and saw their silhouettes pasted at the doors of the cathedrals and beside the supermarkets. In South Africa, black people see their own disappeared people coming back to them in dreams, demanding to be buried in their land so that their spirits can rest (Vika 1998: 16–30). In the north of Argentina some indigenous people devised forms of funeral rites without the bodies of the deceased, by gathering together what belonged to the *desaparecido*: a poncho, a hat, a pair of sandals, an opened tin of milk powder if they were babies (Althaus-Reid 1998: 397). They all come back because their memories keep coming back to people who remember them in the struggle, and sometimes even their bodies return: the body of Ché Guevara and his companions, the body of Evita. Resurrections, we have said before, carry some consequences, for instance, the continuous struggle for justice and truth.

The Queer are not *desaparecidos*. Indecent Christians are not disappeared. They lived and are still around and leave their traces in history. They are multitudes. People leave traces of their lives and everyday little deaths, the frustrations and pains of everyday life, in their communities, in their neighbourhoods and workplaces. They live and resurrect in lust every day: Ché's lustful wondering passion for life and human dignity; Tania, his guerrilla *compañera* who died with him; Monseñor Romero's passion for the life of his country. And so also the lustful love of those people who during the 1980s distributed home-made photocopies around gay bars in Buenos Aires and started the work of the Metropolitan Church in Argentina. The gay minister who took a train to cross my vast country to visit the family of a gay man killed during a massacre of gays and transgendered people in Argentina acted up for resurrection. He was on his own and very fearful too, as he told me, but he went to offer that family legal help and Christian support. He said to me that he just went to say to this family, who were afraid to present a denunciation to the police: 'We are here with you. Your son has been killed, but we do not accept that. No other sons will be killed. In their lives your son will come back.'

It is in vain that theological per/versions are condemned and prevented in Christianity. The obscene (re-discovery) of God in Indecent Theology may prove that perhaps God still exists, but for that we shall need to have a sexual-story case style of doing theology from people's sexual experiences.

4   The theology of sexual stories

What do you suppose it would be like to kiss God?
Would it be a rush,
Like sticking your tongue in a wall socket?
Would you survive the experience?
And if not,
Would it be worth it?

(Poe 1998)

French kissing God: the sexual hermeneutic circle of interpretation

Is the idea of French-kissing God a theological novelty? I have argued elsewhere that theology is a passionate and dangerous business, a *laberinto de pasiones* (a labyrinth of passions) of historical struggles between blind, consuming desires.[1] It would be difficult to ignore the fact that the methodology of Liberation Theology has been the product of a passionate, risky affair with God. If that were not the case, Latin American Christians would not have so many names amongst the lists of the murdered and disappeared. Their passion for an orthopraxis theology took them into jails and torture chambers. There were other consequences of an engaged theology (*teología comprometida*), such as losing jobs or working for very little money in jobs not related to the church or to theology, and all this was done in anonymity without the comforts of recognition for their action or widespread support apart from their immediate communities. We could use a sexual metaphor to describe that passionate commitment which risked so much for the love of a God of Justice: the illicit lovers who risk everything for a furtive embrace, not because they do not value the opinions of co-workers or family and friends, but because their desire is intense, and carries that of life in itself. Moreover, because their passion for a committed theology was driven by the very nature of desire, it carries within itself the duplicity of creation and chaos. For instance, the search for intimacy with the sufferings of the poor meant that many times the traditional borders between violent and peaceful actions were blurred. Let us say then that liberationists had something of that lusty love for God manifested in their option for the poor. Many of them had probably put their tongue in the wall socket to kiss God, and most probably it was worth it.

The methodology of Liberation Theology should always be worked around elements of a passion-arousing style. It was originally developed as a 'see–judge–act' type of work, or 'see, discern and act'. The 'seeing moment' was always very important, and very sensual, that is informed by the concreteness of the conditions of life amongst the poor. At a community level, this meant that people's starting point has always been their own experiences. Could it be that the moment of seeing is also the moment of kissing? That border limit of love and something like bursting anger which constitutes passion and makes the lover's lips twist before she kisses you is what allows people to name their reality. This is what moves them to feel a loving commitment to their lives and a strong passion for destruction of the oppressive structures, for change does not always involve reconciliation, or at least reconciliation processes without a sense of justice in life. However, the first moment of seeing or ad-miring[2] reality does not come easily. We all need to learn to see, that is to name our experiences. This moment corresponds to what has been called the popular conscientisation process, which has been loosely based on the seminal work of Paulo Freire's *Pedagogy of the Oppressed*. The fact is that we all need to learn and discern our lives and circumstances, a task which most of the time is achieved by a gradual work of unmasking ideological constraints and deeply ingrained beliefs. For instance, in Latin America poor Christian people have traditionally 'seen' poverty as God's will, a sort of divine fate where some people are born poor and others rich. The sometimes catastrophic famines involving whole towns and regions have been theologically perceived by the people as a form of God's punishment. For centuries they have embarked on the organisation of religious processions, and paying for masses and promises to God and the Virgin Mary. This has been for the forgiveness of the gods, and not the changing of the conditions of international trade. Jubilee was requested from the deities, to stop the economic crises which were destroying the lives of whole communities, but nobody thought about organising a Jubilee campaign for the lesser gods of the International Monetary Fund to cancel the external debt of the Latin American countries. The same can be applied to the pervasive gender-making structures of our *machista* Latin American society. It is difficult for people to see the sacred in their lives outside heterosexual parodies, repeated endlessly in the authoritarian structures of Latin American governments and societal patterns. The Virgin Mary was a girl, the angel was a boy and God the father, a father. The role of sexual stories in theology has been to repeat and reinforce (hetero)sexual imaginations beyond naturalisation processes by divinising them, but also by concealing the questioning of reality and obstructing the creative imagination to find alternative ways of life.

'Seeing' as a sexual challenge

Learning to see, as a methodological step, is in itself a sexual challenge for Christianity. Theology, through influential systems including liturgies, hymns and prayers, powerfully maintains the sexual metaphors of heterosexuality in their conditions of invisibility and pervasiveness. This invisibility is what stops us from questioning. This works in a similar way to recent efforts by scientists in the United States to research the possibility of other forms of life based not on carbon but on silicon. They have declared that some different life forms may not have been recognised simply because scientists were only looking for carbon-based life. Little has been done for instance in Latin American theology to consider the role of sexual prayers amongst and from the poor. By sexual prayers we mean the prayer which fulfils the role of gender repetition and re-linking of sexual stereotypes with divine categories. How have these prayers been performed in the lives of poor communities? Which consequences in relation to oppression and liberation can be drawn from them? Reading a book recently published by the Institute of Pastoral Studies amongst Indigenous People (INPPI) (Carrasco 1995), reflecting on the work of a Base Ecclesial Community in an Andean Quechua population and the Shuar tribe, we find a striking contrast between sexual and political prayers. The genderisation of God in their popular theology through sexual prayers seems disproportionate in relation to their political consciousness. They are able to criticise modernisation processes, and pinpoint sophisticated relationships between idolatry and the total market theology and yet God is still male, and He is a chief. Taking some examples from the written prayers of this particular community, we find abundant male metaphors of hierarchical gender characteristics. For instance, in a prayer called 'Dear *Taitien*,[3] protect us', the adjectives used to describe God are: protector, powerful, the giver of strength, good, *conocedor* (erudite) and *dueño* (owner). In 'God *Pachacamac*, the liberator', the adjectives are *dueño,* powerful, present in the struggle, a presence of strength/ power, chief, and the conqueror of the capitalist system, the market economy, modernisation and militarisation. In 'God-Community', God is described as 'the one who gives his spirit to a man [sic], creator, strength, a presence (in Basic Ecclesial Communities, families, popular organisations)' (Carrasco 1995: 17–20)

The peasant women's role is obviously emphasised only in prayers to the Virgin Mary. With admirable candour, one of the so-called community-written prayers of the Shuar speaks about women in the third person: 'Wives represent the Virgin Mary at home; they must organise the home with joy, although they frequently have so many sufferings' (Carrasco 1995: 88). Women's prayers repeat the following elements: women as mothers, carers of the community (looking after the sick) and women as educators of children. At the end of the reflections there is a community reflection on structures of sin based on their understanding of Liberation Theology:

> There is sin in every culture and *pueblo*. The problems (*fallas*: failures) are to be found in thinking, words and actions manifested politically, religiously and in economic systems . . . These sins are the idolatry of power; adultery . . . false gods.
>
> (Carrasco 1995: 229)

We may well ask ourselves why adultery is mentioned here together with power-idolatry concepts, and how it further relates to the sexual stabilising prayers of God as chief and woman as mother/seductress. Traditionally, in Latin American cultures, women are the ones punished for adultery, and not men. Male adultery is an institution in Latin America, and women are supposed to be responsible for that at many levels, by tempting men, or by not taking proper care of their husbands. The prayer adds a sexual link to sinful actions of the economic system, women unable to fulfil some traditional expectations or vague assumptions about their behaviour. At the end, that sexual prayer organises the defiance of men in the struggle for liberation and the unchanging role of women and not defiance of sexual structures in Latin America.

There is a disparity of moments of critical consciousness when political prayers meet their counterparts, which are the sexual prayers of no change and, moreover, of opposing changes in sexual perceptions which may exist in the community. Meanwhile, other indigenous groups in the struggle, such as the Chiapas women, present us with a counter-vision to these prayers. They claim that in the indigenous community there are some forms of gender sabotage presented through indigenous perceptions and discourses, but they have not been systematically taken on board (Pérez and Castellanos 1994). In the words of Major Ana Maria, who was in charge of the occupation of the town San Cristóbal de las Casas, women's engagement in critical consciousness processes was crucial for the Chiapas insurgency. So Major Ana Maria claims that 'Women from the towns were instructing their own daughters, sisters and nieces and told them "it is better to get a gun and to fight!"' The democratisation of the life of the Indian communities came together with the political struggle, but went as far as to challenge cultural traditions of women's oppression which had been part of that community even before the *Conquista* of the Americas. Marcela Lagarde, commenting on the work which has been diminishing or erasing the gender subordination structures in Chiapas, says,

> Any (political) summons... must have a call to a political change of gender structures. If not, it is just what we already know: other voices and other faces, but the same old mentality. If we do not deconstruct patriarchy, we recreate it.
>
> (Lagarde 1994)

Liberationists could not have said it better: there is no neutrality in the fight for social justice, nor in theology. Indigenous women in Latin America may

be fighting the same political struggles as men but, at the same time, they
have additional battles, of gender and sexuality. It is not true that poor
women – if conscientised – only care about fighting for economic and
political liberation. Some of them have gone further, claiming that both
struggles need to be simultaneous. Unfortunately, women from the BECs
seem to be losing this vision, since Christian theology tends to sexually dis-
organise them in their political struggles.

Reading the Bible sexually

The moment of 'seeing' always requires some critical tools of analysis and
reflection, and this was the goal of popular conscientisation work. The
second moment (judging) requires discernment. It consists in critical
appraisal of the situation and strategic planning for further action on the
problems which afflict the community. This is the moment when the popular
study of the Bible is supposed to come in. The whole methodology or style
of working is, of course, not progressive but circular and fluid. As Gustavo
Gutiérrez commented in a conversation about the work of Basic Ecclesial
Communities, people can even start by reading the Bible (and seeing their
situation by analogy) or not read the Bible at all (Gibbs 1996: 365–70). It is a
fluid, dynamic, real process not something taken from the pages of an
academic 'do-it-yourself theology' manual, or a formal meeting of a church
committee. We can take our draft exegesis for a gay Lazarus from the last
chapter as an example of this process. Only a man whose life experience had
been made up of ruptures from and departures of lovers, in the tension of
keeping the heterosexual masked ball going, in his job and family, is able to
see a dramatic love story between Jesus and his intimate friend. The moment
to judge comes in analysing that situation and not in proving with the
mediation of biblical commentaries, what was historically right or wrong (as
if anybody could know, after twenty centuries and with a scant Gospel
narrative which falls short of a biography of Jesus). After a comment made
by one person, we may then have the sharing of other people's experience
and some form of affirmation of love shown by Jesus in defiance of conventions. For instance, making a public scandal at a funeral and resurrecting a
friend is not, by any means, a decent or conventional thing to do. The third
moment, then, is to act, but action comes after some strategy has been
worked out as to what the community may feel capable of doing within the
lines of people's usual limitations, in a society which denies them access to
responsibility and decision-making. A whole debate on 'coming out' from a
political, legal and affective perspective can take a privileged place here.
Perhaps a simple public demonstration for some important issue can take
place, although it is important to acknowledge that demonstrations are not
simple things to do. In Latin America they are complicated by the innumerable dangers of political persecution, loss of jobs and even death. Perhaps
the community may think about something else to do. People are very

creative. In fact, a second reading of the Lazarus story, perhaps from a transvestite in the community, may create different relationship patterns in the reading and in action. That is the point of telling sexual stories: they are always tentative, unfinished, as is a sexual Jesus. They open our eyes to different networking strategies and also to sources of empowerment.

On other occasions, liberationists may find that the Bible also needs to be redefined. Amongst the people at the margins, for instance amongst the urban outcasts of our big cities, the Bible is not a book, but a collection of sayings and vague moral prescriptions which people remember from the media or political discourse, but not from an actual reading of the text. In the 1980s I used to work in a popular project of a church in Buenos Aires which fed five hundred beggars per day. For a time, I was in charge of the Friday Bible study, but I have never seen beggars carrying Bibles in their bags or pockets. Most of them did not even know how to read. However, there is another Bible, that which has been created by five hundred years of Christianity in the continent. This is the Bible of popular proverbs and selected images. Many poor people at the margins in Buenos Aires know the story of Samson (in Spanish, Sansón). They have recreated it in their lives, re-read it and it works as a biblical paradigm, more effective than Exodus. They pray to *San Son* ('Saint Son'), because he was a man of physical strength, and that is something people need in their lives. The Bible can also be read through the legal and political traditions of the country, and in the engendering of political debates too. After all, for the debates on women's votes in Argentina, the Congress made allusion to Genesis to put arguments about women's subordination to men. Women facing crisis in patriarchal homes, or men with broken hearts who lose their jobs because they are gay, need to find a different dialogue with the Bible, outside the familiar realms of Scripture-proving methods. The Bible does not mention Aids, but it mentions justice. Justice as integral to our conception of God forms a community dialogue with the Bible, outside the printed word.

I have found that the key to working in this popular style, is to let life circulate and only hang on to the radical principles in the Bible which subsume the rest: justice, peace and love/solidarity. Of course, these principles need to be enlightened and redefined by the community, as in the case of solidarity, in order to advance beyond homo-solidarity for instance. Then, the community reflection tends to float free, finding new elements, arguing against others and enriching their lives outside the narrow confines of texts which were written two millennia ago, in a different setting and moment of humanity's historical consciousness. Obviously a key for any kind of success in this style of work is the support of the community who are working together. Individuals get crushed easily. The community's support and sustaining is crucial. The community carries the task of resurrection of crushed individuals all the time. The point is that sexual readings of the Bible have not been done seriously outside the borders of the sexual traditions of the church, conceding that they may provide some room for heterosexual egalitarianism but the radical principles get diluted in the heterosexual patriarchal setting of the Bible. If this is all part of what has been called 'the theology of our own stories', this part has been touched most by the work of feminist Latin American women. Liberationists also did so, but patriarchally delimiting our stories, and not allowing any Queer voice which did not fit the ideal of a Christian community to come to the fore. There were many tensions in that process, but heterosexuality is inflexible. A poor, honest, devoted Christian man, apparently, cannot be a transvestite, and lesbian women do not fit the mother orientated family pattern of Liberation Theology. At best, they will encourage people not to be judgemental, but the situation would be one of abnormality. This is *accepted* (tolerated) in Liberation Theology with a spirit of love.. The point is that toleration is a category based on certain normative principles (Laclau 1996: 50). That normativity is what decides what should or should not be tolerated. According to Laclau then, toleration 'fails to deliver the goods' because in the end it consolidates the limit between the tolerable and intolerable. Only by dissolving those frontiers (and therefore dissolving the concept of toleration) may we be in a position to find a society where internal differentiation and not toleration can be the ethical value (Laclau 1996: 51). The heterosexual foundation of Liberation Theology can claim for toleration of the abnormal in its communities, but it is heterosexuality as a compulsory system in itself which is abnormal, not Queer, indecent people. Indecent people challenge precisely the unnaturality and abnormality of the present sexual ideology, in all the consequences of this sexual and political theology. The fact is that our lives as heterosexuals, gays or lesbians are always abnormal, that is, managed by remote control from idealism. Therefore, liberationists or not, we are always called to confess and repent from normality and its policy of toleration, and we need to stop the circle of the life-energy wasting process of trying to fit into that ideal heterosexual being we should be. This goes for gender roles in society, sexual organisation of relationships but also our way of being society.

Why do a theology of sexual stories? Is that not too particular, or too concerned with the 'private realm' of a person? The answer is no, because sexuality does not stay at home, or in a friend's bedroom, but permeates our economic, political and societal life. Theology has always been a great theoretical discourse on hetero-normativity, prescribing sexual relations at home and in the public spheres of life. Without a theology of sexual stories, the last moment of the hermeneutical circle, that is, the moment of appropriation and action, will always have a partiality and a superficial approach to conflict resolution. For instance, during the past decade many BECs have been dissolved by the decision of Roman Catholic dioceses in Latin America. This has happened because the BECs have never been inscribed into canonical law: they were spontaneous, non-hierarchical movements of the church, outside the legal arrangements of ecclesial institutions. However, the hierarchical structures of the church which were finally decisive in the ending of many recognised BECs were only partially challenged. Gender and sexual issues remain conflictive and smoothed over in BECs and in Liberation Theology and where they could have been the issue which provided the challenge to the roots of hierarchical models. Sexual and gender issues are not addenda in the minutes of a meeting, but key epistemological and organisational elements which, if ignored, never allow us to think further and differently.

The time has come for a 'see–judge–act' analysis in theology as a material act of grounding Christianity in reality. Sex may be perceived as potentially chaotic, as the field of ambiguities and unruly life and theology has to struggle to put sex into tidy compartments, each one with a name, a colour, a function, and a positive or negative symbol at the door. If theology discovers that in reality there are more sexual behaviours than compartments, identities are essentialised. People are supposed to fit into boxes, even if just under the lid (or do sexual compartments have balconies, so one may be inside/outside at the same time?). Traditionally, the role of sexual stories in society has been precisely to give some sense of historical coherence to sexual lives, or a claim to a genealogy of 'natural' behaviour. The same can be said of the church and its centuries-long struggle to fit homosexuality in a theological box. This struggle will never end, because heterosexuality, like sex itself, is a very unstable category (Weeks 1995: 95). This is particularly evident in the role of sexual prayers as we have seen. Sexual stories perform some social ordering, register changes, tensions and have a political role to fulfil, apart from their narrative structures (Plummer 1995: 16, 22). The normalisation of sexual stories through prayer is a strategical device to demarcate sexual fences and political behaviour. These prayers convey social memories of sexual stories recycled and repeated in community, a work of crochet where people's own stories are linked with tentative stitches, in a movement of continuous searching for the unknown because not all our stories have had a voice in theology in the past.

Nationalistic X sex(es)

> *Entre una picha y la cubanía, la cubanía.*
> (Between a dick and Cuba, I choose Cuba)
> (Diego, a Cuban gay quoted in Quiroga 1997: 141)

We must now continue in our exploration of the hermeneutical circle of Liberation Theology stopping to reflect on the issue of nationality, which has been the counter-discourse of sexuality for many decades and affects the moment of praxis or action/reflection. This false dichotomy between being political and being sexual in Latin American is part of a long history of understanding life and social processes in the continent under the iron rules of *machismo*. Not surprisingly, Chiapas women in the struggle seldom mention any Christian belief, except general ones of love and justice. Moreover, the work of the Shuar community genderising centuries of sexual oppression in new categories of popular indigenous theology may even be offensive to them. 'Being political' means here that sense of everyday commitment that many Latin Americans have to the struggle for the liberation of their countries and continent from political and economic oppression. 'Being sexual', means to be able to find your identity and question the political identity of the 'oppression/liberation' dialectical pair with a suspicion of *machista* ideology. The point is that perhaps it is not so easy to choose between a dick and Cuba. At some level of the discourse, they may be the same. The Cuban Phallus, which beyond being a Cuban penis represents also the absent object of a desire, can be seen as a Cuban sigh, a lack, a nostalgia for the lost desire, or the desire that does not match *machista* ideology'. I know that under the present way of doing Liberation Theology somehow I cannot consider myself a true *patriota* (lover of my Argentinian nation) if I do not fully participate in the *machista* structure of the national myths of independence and the theological *imaginaire* of my people. The Virgin Mary in a vision to Don Manuel Belgrano (one of the National heroes of Argentina) told him to make a flag with the colours of her blue and white cloak. The songs which compare our flag with an eagle in serene flight, born from the Sun and a gift from God, were sung by children of my generation in primary school. These songs learnt in my childhood may still excite feelings of devotion and fidelity to my country, but they also remind me of the sexual persona which is attached to this notion of citizenship. They also increase my awareness of the dislocation of my desires in society. The configuration of sexual behaviour is the basis of political behaviour. Argentina is a way to be married, to dress in the streets, to determine love and security, it is a way to be decent. In the end, the love for our country is nothing else than a sexual story. The Bible is a collection of sexual stories, to the point that we might wonder if this was the real reason behind its exclusion from Latin American life during the last 500 years. The stories of liberation, or the ethos of political liberation, do not necessarily come across very clearly for the inexpert reader; they require some exegesis of liberation. The sexual stories of the Bible, to the contrary, always come clearly understood without exegesis. When the debate on the ordination of women in the Church of England reached its peak with a vote of approval, Gustavo Gutiérrez was interviewed by Spanish television and his opinion as a liberationist was sought. Gutiérrez's opinion, predictably, was along the lines that women in Latin America did not care about ordination, but about feeding their children. That is, between political and gender liberation, women in Latin America must choose political liberation. 'Between a dick, and Cuba, I choose Cuba.' The nastiness of Gutiérrez's comment lies in its force for the continuation of the false dichotomy we were considering. First of all, women are mothers according to idealist heterosexuality; this means exclusive motherhood, outside other pertinent interests in life. Second, their identity is reduced to children and meals, without considering what is the relationship between his assumptions and the political order which creates that situation of poverty. I have been a poor woman myself and I dreamed of warm clothes for my mother during winter, and nutritious meals for me and my family. But I also dreamt of having an education, a vocation in life to be a priest, and I dreamt of justice, love and lust in my life. Gutiérrez, according to this argument, should have spent his life cooking meals for the people who need them and not studying theology, pursuing a priestly and theological vocation and publishing books. Why would he, a Peruvian man, have any other interest in life except to cook meals for the poor? Many women in Latin America want to be *patriotas* (devoted to their nation's interests) and sexual personas too. Everybody, including Diego in Cuba, wants this. But even for Gutiérrez, the sexual stories, the sexual exegesis of the Bible comes first, and the political second or subordinate to the first.

Liberationists also have colonial dreams of an imperial nature: dreams of a hegemonic nature. Of course, we must not leave class analysis aside. The utopia of the Project of Liberation of the Kingdom takes cares of that. The God of the Poor has an option there, but gender/sexual boundaries are, apparently, closer to that God's heart. This heterosexual God, it is suggested, does not like to be French-kissed by women. Historically, God's closest relation is with (male) priests. Can they French-kiss him? Can 'the poor' French-kiss God? (A *Marica*-faggot-God?) Is that not indecent? What a sexual parody and comedy of contradictions! No wonder the male priesthood is classically confused with its own sexuality, and poor men feel their *macho* sexuality threatened by Christianity. Between a dick and Cuba, what would *you* choose? And between a dick and God? Why that false dichotomy, creeping in under the guise of theological purity? Our path, as we have said before, is that of obscenity. We should unveil and not cover up our search for divine truth, and for that purpose, we need to use popular resources, such as sexual stories from the grassroots. And all of these, in order to French-kiss God.

Oral sex: sexual *hi/storias* in oral theology

It is interesting to notice that in Spanish, the words 'story' and 'history' are written with the same word: *historia*. This means that as a Spanish speaker, my notion of the boundaries between interpreting a story and the meaning of history, is somehow blurred. Stories are historical events. History is made up of stories. A sexual story is always historically sexual, because sexual stories are not components of abstract worlds but they are rooted in political communities and obey concrete conditions of production, limited by race, class, age, degrees of accepted sexual normative discourse or resistance. Ken Plummer sees that the lives and events of people can only became sexual stories if people have a voice and can be heard (Plummer 1995: 22). These stories are related to their producers, and the conditions of life of a person, her class, sexuality, race or a combination of all these factors. The story of a poor heterosexual woman has more chance of being heard than a poor transvestite's. However, once the story is heard, it becomes part of an interactive social word, and negotiates its space of meaning and signification within a network of other unheard stories, and from that actions for transformation and challenge to the status quo may take place. For instance, when a person tells a story which seems unusual (because it has not been heard before), that person may be trying to find a language or an appropriate metaphor to express it. Someone else identifying herself with the story will then add another metaphor, another way of expressing it. Thus the story keeps being redefined, refined, because it is a story in search of self-expression. That experience in itself is what makes the telling of sexual stories a perpetual coming out, like the symbol of the Chinese cod quoted by Plummer, which stands erect gasping for fresh air, coming out for life (Plummer 1995: 22). According to Gayle Rubin's pattern of a sexual social pyramid, the sexual stories that we hear most are those belonging to the top, which are mainly heterosexual, marital and reproduction stories (Plummer 1995: 30). They are also the stories of elite men and women. For instance, in Argentina, these are the stories of traditional large families of the oligarchy, the ones who grow up in country estates but not the large families of the slums. They are heterosexual in their reproductive perspective, but not necessarily straight. Stories of rich homosexual men who were married and had extensive families also circulate. Names of wealthy, aristocratic gay men from Argentina who had only one wife and big families are well known. Anecdotes of their occasional trips to Egypt with a *beau* friend, and the names of what were euphemistically called 'nephews' (*sobrinos*) of rich men were well known. Curiously, there is no indecency in these stories. Their homosexuality is somehow spiritualised. It is the gayness of the poor married man, not of the rich, which fails to be heard. Poor gays are always indecent. The same can be said about women. Rich women's sexual liaisons with other women or men, including their illegitimate births, become part of an ontological discourse in which the protagonists are intelligent women searching for identity. Even sexual ambiguity becomes progressive. Poor women who sleep with many women or many men are part of the discourse on sexual promiscuity and church morals. The church may say '*necesitamos remediar esas relaciones*' (we need to make good [*remediar*] those relationships) but *remediar* means, literally, to give a remedy, a medicine for an ailment. In this, the church usually harks back to a medical discourse on abnormality, on the growth of people's unruly sexual life.

Rubin sees the prominence of the sexual stories at the top of the pyramid not only as coming from heterosexual but established couples, even if they are not heterosexual. Thus, gay and lesbian couples in long-standing relationships are located in her pyramid directly after the heterosexual hierarchies of married and unmarried people, but above the sea of what we can called the despised: this includes multitudes, from bar dykes, leather folk, S/Mers, transgendered, fetishists and rent boys to men into 'rough trade'. Marginality seems to be somehow the first condition of whether sexual stories are heard or not. At the top of Rubin's pyramid we can hear sexual stories told loudly and clearly, but somehow at the bottom the stories are shouted. The difference is that they are ignored. However, there are some contradictions here too. The ability of a story to be heard or not seems to depend not only on its position in the pyramid but also on the type of story. For instance, stories of incest and child abuse are more likely to be heard if they come from the bottom of the pyramid than from the top.

Sex and the children of the streets

In the upper and middle classes, stories of child abuse are not easily heard, but are silenced. These are not stories that can be shared with others. In Argentina, there are no stories of this kind which have become part of people's everyday knowledge. If they are known, only a limited number of people hear about them. Meanwhile, the stories of children of the street living under sexual abuse and direct exploitation are widely known and even shared. People usually say that the children of the streets are 'children of children'. It is a well-known fact that some Christian agencies prefer to help boys in the streets rather than girls, because girls are more complicated. They get pregnant, have babies, and require far more effective attention than boys in relation to sexual abuse. Take for instance the following story, as told by a 12-year-old girl of the street in Buenos Aires:

> [These people] come here when one is sleeping, and that is why I don't stay here anymore. One day, they took my sister and another friend, they gave them money (although very little), and they forced them to be with them in the ladies' bathroom. And if they resisted, they beat them. Then my sister told me that we mustn't sleep in that place anymore.
>
> (Montes de Oca 1995: 77)

The social setting of this story is that children are taken by force in daylight to perform sexual acts with men, amidst multitudes of people passing by who pretend not to see what is happening or not to hear the children's cry for help. A girl spoke of being forced to follow a man to a public toilet at lunchtime, and how not even the police intervened to her cries for help. These are not the kind of sexual stories of child abuse which require secrecy, because these children are marginal and devalued in relation to society. Are we facing a contradiction here? Are the stories of the marginal heard or not? The sexual stories of the marginalised people are known but devalued. Incest and child abuse (and stories of domestic violence) have been silenced amongst wealthy people, but amongst the poor there is another kind of silence: the silence of secrecy has given way to the silence of impotence. As a poor child, I knew about these stories from my friends. The children of the poor circulate around circles of promiscuity and loneliness and they hear and see many things: they know the names of the men to whose rooms they should never go because older girls or boys have told them not to do so; or the price some may ask you to pay for a gift of some sweets. Poor children also seem to care for their reputation at a very early age. For if a case of some form of child abuse is known in a community, s/he can be called a faggot or a prostitute (which happens frequently amongst the poor) and in practice this can be just an invitation to more abuse. The children of the poor are seldom treated with the same standards as other children. Their sexual stories receive no theological attention either, although theological sexual stories reinforce, for instance, virginity as institutionalised idealism, where the woman is responsible for its preservation. Once the little girl has been abused, she cannot be physically redeemed of that. In theology virginity is a category more closely connected with the control of sexuality rather than with respect.

The problem is usually the combination of desire and poverty. Stories of sexual abuse are not taken seriously enough, but the sexual taboo is extended to good sex too. Stories of sexual desire amongst the poor are a no-go area. Gutiérrez has said that poor Latin American women only care for food for their children, but I can tell him that we must care a lot about our orgasms too. If not, how is it that poor women end up having so many promiscuous relations in their lives? Is promiscuity an imposition or is it sometimes the flow of desire, a search for intimacy usually unfulfilled under the present conditions of sexual injustice? The taboo against poor women's sexual desires matches the taboo against the stories which other sexualities tell, including the (in)voluntary celibates in the struggle for liberation in the church. Consider the following sexual stories about a gay priest and adultery, two of the most common obsessions of the church, which deals with them without listening to their voices. The first is about poor people re-telling a sexual story of their priest, which contradicts the easy assumptions about culture, poverty, theology and sexuality. The second is about some transgressive theological meanings coming from adultery.

Retelling Father Mario's story

In September 1996, the media in Buenos Aires covered the news of the killing of a Roman Catholic priest called Father Mario. He was a young man who worked in a poor parish where a small Christian Community was flourishing. The first reaction to this crime was to relate it to the activities of the drug mafias in the poor areas. Father Mario was well known for organising the community to resist the drug trade. His funeral was impressive, although before his death he was only known to his community. All the people from the poor community were present, as well as the media and even a distinguished foreign priest travelled to Argentina to pay public homage to the exemplary nature of Father Mario's life. Father Mario was not just a priest; he belonged to a Charismatic group of Roman Catholic priests who believe in social justice and the charismatic gifts of the Spirit, such as healing, and who exercise a complex ministry of social justice and pastoral care. As the weeks went by, the story of Father Mario's death became more complicated. The public statement from the police that they could not yet say anything about the case had a hint of sexual secrecy. People started to wonder. In Argentina, when silence is imposed in particular ways on the media, for instance, with words which point to a self-righteous silence, people know that there is something sexual lurking somewhere. It was a sexual story. Father Mario had been killed in his car by a rent boy, after an argument. The police found that Father Mario had, behind a cupboard full of Bibles, what the media described as 'pornographic materials, books and videos', or, as understood by the people, a profusion of sexually exciting images of young men. The church silenced the story. A Monsignor spoke briefly on local TV to say how sad he was to know this story ('I feel as if I have lost a son!'), but no more was said. People were left to think that *todos los curas son maricones* ('all priests are faggots'; almost a popular proverb in Roman Catholic Argentina), but also that faggot equals bad. The problem was that Father Mario was not bad, only a per/verted priest: a priest with another, different interpretation of sexuality. However, the community spoke out at length against the view that Father Mario was bad. During the days when the TV cameras came to the poor neighbourhood where the parish was located, people spoke of their love for Father Mario and their desire to build a chapel to carry his name. Testimonies of his kindness and generosity, as well as his spirituality in the struggle, were abundant. But did they know or believe that he was killed by a rent boy? Yes, and they were sad for the crime, but some knew Father Mario was gay, and nobody thought much about it. It was not relevant. However, someone said that what was a pity was that Father Mario never spoke with anybody about his loneliness: otherwise they could have talked with him. They were sorry that they did not help this young man, driven by desperation and the denial of his sexuality to dangerous places and people who could not love him as he deserved. This was a community of the poor re-telling Father Mario's sexual story. For them, Father Mario was not gay, if by gay you mean that his life was defined only by the fact that sometimes he would sleep with men. He was gay, if by gay we mean a priest who fought for peace and social justice in his Christian Base Community and who was so full of love for his people that he also longed for abundant love in his own life, and for the love and company of another man. That is indecent theological thinking.

This sexual story shows us how the notion of community has changed even amongst the poor Christian communities. It illustrates the mainstream theory advocated by Liberation Theology which Anne Phillips in her article 'Universal Pretensions in Political Thought' defined as 'emphasis in justice or rationality that can give us any critical purchase on the communities in which we live' (Barret and Phillips 1992: 14). The community does not necessarily use universalising principles, not even sexual ones, with ease all the time. As Phillips remarks, the standards used are not the moralising universal ones, like the theological arguments we are so used to. On the contrary, communities decode the hidden values which are present and discern justice in the relationships already there. What may be happening is that liberationists re-address people's own elucidatory processes and impose their own. For instance, a typical liberationist statement on Father Mario's story would be one which denies the young priest's gay desires. Liberationists would accuse the priest of being so individualistic as to be driven by his desires. In this case, the cause of the poor should be the only driving force to be considered in one's life. 'See the poor people; consider their suffering; they do not have time to weep over some love problem as you do, because they have *real* problems.' This point was made to me some years ago by a minister of a militant church, and I have heard it repeated by theologians and ministers many times just when I had a lot of love problems to resolve in my own life. They always succeeded in making me feel guilty for suffering, as long as I was able to afford a meal per day. My life as a poor Christian woman was reduced to my meals; any extra, such as love, was superfluous. Therefore, for the one who has enough to eat and works with the poor, like Father Mario, it is the denial of sexuality which comes, this time, from the God of the poor. The statement is different as applied to the poor: they are essentialised in the discourse – 'they do not care for anything except food'. Sexual desire mobilises people's concept of citizenship and of justice. In political discourse, sex counts (Barret and Phillips 1992: 12) and in political theology, it is an essential source.

On adultery by divine command

> Dear Sir,
>
> In the life of King Charles the First, the company of stationers, into whose hands the printing of the Bible is committed by patent, made a very remarkable erratum or blunder in one of the editions: for instead of 'Thou shalt not commit adultery', they printed out several thousands of copies with 'Thou shalt commit adultery.' Archbishop Laud, to punish this negligence, laid a considerable fine upon that company in the star-chamber . . . [However] by the practice of the world, which prevails in this degenerate age, I am afraid that many young profligates of both sexes are possessed of this spurious edition of the Bible, and observe the commandment according to that faulty reading.
>
> (From a letter to *The Spectator*, Wednesday, August 11, 1714)

Are we not suspicious enough of marriage to ask ourselves why so many Christian people are adulterous? Adultery is not the characteristic of Christian people only, but it is still a common aspect of Christian life, and since Christian people reflect on God and their lives, therefore adultery is a characteristic theme of theology. Is that a divine commandment that theologians and people are reading in a faulty edition of their Bibles? A theologian cannot be very sure about the answer. In fact, adultery or some aspect of it may well be biblical and godly, although not inscribed in a commandment. There is a legal clause about property in the Bible, which includes reference to your neighbour's woman (Exodus 20:17). It is the neighbour's woman and not wife, since the concept of husband and wife as we know it is an anachronism when reading the Bible. Therefore, if the assumption implicit in the statement – that people are property – comes to be doubted, the commandment itself loses its performative function. If someone asks me to promise in God's name that I shall never steal my neighbour's camels, I may agree, but the commandment has lost its performative function in my context since I do not have neighbours who possess camels and I have never been in such company in my life. The order is unreal; the context does not match the injunction. In the same vein, if someone asks me to relate to other people like parcels of goods or private property, even if this is said in the language of 'respect', I shall always refuse, and any injunction based on that will not have any validity in my life. Of course, we have all noticed that the commandment speaks only of 'women' and not men. In biblical times the main source of income was ownership of land, and the family was just an economic unit, under the authority of a male head (Westbrook 1991: 11). Only the patriarch was entitled to have tents, and women, slaves, children and camels, in the order of his choice. Women may have kept personal items after entering into a patriarchal covenant or wedding but proprietary rights from the dowry became the possession of the male head of the family (Westbrook 1991: 152–3). Decisions concerning divorce, remarrying, the complications and punishment of adultery were complex legal issues concerning rights, lands and dowry property. Women were only recipients, although guilty ones, in adulterous relationships in accordance to Israel's proprietary laws.

> I was in the meeting when the bishop spoke with tears in his eyes and said: 'Today, there is not a minister in this church who is still married or if married, who is not known for having had a relationship with someone else.' The last drop of water in a glass already full (*la gota que colmó el vaso*) was the case of B. But she was not ashamed. She was happy, she had found a friend, a special one and it did not mean she did not love her husband, but she said that life is more than finding completeness in only one person. So, no divorce, just the rare joy of growing through the intimacy of someone else. The rest of the people did not say anything, they were scared. What a pity! We lost the opportunity to come clean on this, because they are excellent people and I know them so well. Good Christians, committed to the struggle and full of compassion towards the poor. They have transparent lives, but this adultery thing is because marriage is such a small box, and limits women so much.
>
> (An Argentinian minister)

I think I am a polygamist. C is my long standing partner, but this other man has suddenly become important to me. I thought I needed to separate from C and start a relation with F, but why bother? Both of them are different yet important in my life, so I spoke to them and we made an arrangement.

(A British female academic)

The first story was told to me by a minister friend in Argentina. The second, is from a British academic woman. These stories are non-traditional stories, which portray intimacy as a 'floating' category, in the words of Anthony Giddens, which needs to be negotiated, dialogued with others (Weeks 1995: 42). Traditional sexual stories of adultery always have a theological under-pinning and a storyline ending in disgrace. These are 'Anna Karenina' plots, built around a euthanasian pathos, that is, the death (symbolical, social or physical) of the adulterer, especially if that person is a woman. It is God's punishment. For the man, the tragedy usually centres around unhappiness for not being forgiven by his wife, the loss of domestic peace and in some extreme cases, by public scandal which could be redeemed by repentance, going back to the abandoned wife. So, X told me the following story:

When my children were small, I met this woman, also married, and we loved each other dearly. When my wife found out, it was so devastating. I separated from my friend, and I stayed with my wife but the conse-quences of that love devastated me for many years.

X is a man who has had innumerable affairs during his married life, many of them complicated and simultaneous. He felt guilty; he changed his ways, but yet as a Christian man he has never reflected theologically upon this. He became wiser in the art of departing from lovers and keeping his public image as a serious religious man, but this longing for relationships with different women seems to be detached in his mind. It has never become an issue for the theological reflection that everybody has in life, when considering life, suffering and God's discernment, although it is perhaps one of the most significant elements of his life. This may be unfortunate because his life has been driven by guilt instead of a genuine understanding which could have prevented the suffering of his family but also that of other women. What my Argentinian friend said in the case of B can be also applied to him: what a pity that he never searched for a theology out of the closet of decency, in order to be able to reflect in a dialogue with his desires about this. The stories of the Argentinian woman and this person (both Christians) challenges a heterosexual monotheistic system from the grass-roots of human relationships, the one God, one husband and one phallus system. They are not faulty people, but people for whom the spectrum of human relationships as it is presented is not satisfactory. As theology escapes from confronting reality except for condemnation, then reflection and understanding is always lacking. These stories of coming out as heterosexual women in relation to adultery are fraught with difficulties. Heterosexuals may find it harder to come out with their truth concerning the telling of their stories, because heterosexuality assumes a hegemonic state of presence which denies that heterosexuality can be anything other than the standard description found in the textbooks. Descriptions are presented as microcosms of interrelations, such as myths about the monogamic reproductive family. Jeffrey Weeks points out that intimacy is a sexual act and has come to be understood, as love, in a more fluid way (Weeks 1995: 39).

'Adultery' is in fact a specific legal and ecclesiatical term, that people do not commonly use when describing what they refer to as 'extramarital relationships' or 'affairs' (Lawson 1989: 7). In theological terms, it covers a more extensive field than that considered legally, because the ingrained belief in women as property for reproductive purposes has persisted in Christianity, even if in secular society such notions have long been challenged. In a way, the church's definitions of adultery are more 'proprietary', more concerned with the marking of lawful belongings rather than with relationships between people. 'Property' is a term which relates to 'properness', the proper, the decent valuation of a situation. It seems that adultery like decency in theology is marked by the ordering of properties (women, slaves). A poem about abortion from the Brazilian Methodist theologian Nancy Cardoso Pereira, may express women's longing for political and sexual transgression.

Kairos – I open my legs
a big mouth of small lips
and I make an abortion by my own decision.
I continue and go inside my legs, for
the agrarian reform of my own household.
(Cardoso Pereira 1994)

In theology, the agrarian reform for the reformation of women's property (and decent/proper) position in society is related to this theological category of impurity and ownership which is adultery. 'Adulterous' is a word from the Latin *adulterare*, probably from *alter*, hence 'to approach another, to commit adultery' (Collins English Dictionary). This is a sexual definition of the form which we might use to indicate if the jar of coffee has chicory apart from Colombian beans. Mixtures are necessary and welcome things in life, and people are not accused of being of an adulterous nature by the fact of being born with a proportion of female and male hormones in their body. However, to adulterate carries the negative connotation of secrecy. Even if one prefers coffee with chicory, it needs to be declared publicly. These are the rules of the ethics of advertising. The heterosexual marriage has been advertised as a relationship between a woman and a man for life. It is the unique case of a legal contract which discourages intimate friendships for life, while trying to see in the controlled setting of marriage a foundation for goodness in society. However, adultery often seems to be a desire to escape from the control and predictability of life, from the non-creative confinements of particular domestic and public ideologies (Lawson 1989: 5). Adultery is then a denunciation. It shows the arbitrariness of the setting of human relationships, which can be applied not only to one to one relationships but to the whole way in which society thinks. Adultery is therefore chaotic, not because it necessarily produces chaos but because it uncovers it in the supposed predictability of the ideal model of heterosexual marriage.

Adultery may not be a divine commandment but, in a real sense, intimacy with others has a divine nature, and is by far the more divine commandment. This longing for closeness with others need not be sexual but it is linked to sexuality. Adultery tells us something about our faulty constructions of human relations beyond institutional marriage. For instance, it establishes power and forms of control and identity in society. Sociological research done on this theme tends to show that women have far more sense of control of their relationships in liaisons than in actual marriages. Theirs is the power to start relationships, to finish them, to choose the number of partners and to remain in a way detached from a partner (Lawson 1989: 31). The Shuar community quoted earlier pinned down adultery alongside sinful structures of political power, but this can also be interpreted as a symptom of gender/sexual trouble in the community; adultery sometimes functions as a disciplining or purging of gender/sexual transgressions in society. Popular theology has not been able to go beyond the accustomed 'crime and punishment' theological genre of adultery. Such stories exist and circulate in order to exemplarise a bad end outside the ruling proprietary order, and to be educational pieces for the rescuing of the stratification of society and the defence against any long-due 'agrarian reform'. In a way, theology has succeeded in creating a loving un-learning process, and a dehumanisation of relationships. In Christianity, it is probably the myth of Genesis which has been fundamental for a narrative of the punishment of transgressions, in which the symbolics of sexuality may be included. However, stories of adultery sometimes have a subversive power. They act as denunciation narratives of the structures of sexual sin, and the politics of friendship in heterosexual systems which have been so influential in Christian dogma. Take, for instance, the Trinity as a divine structure of marriage: Father, Son and Holy Spirit are supposed to have an exclusive, faithful, eternal and pure (unmixed with other Gods, for instance) relationship. The essentialism that we perceive in Trinitarian models comes from these marriage assumptions which exclude dissension, plurality and longing for intimacy outside the circle. Peruvian writer Mario Vargas Llosa once said to me that fictions do not portray reality but what people dreamt as the ideal reality. People need lies; not imposed ones, but collective lies which may be the utopias of the future. The pattern of relationships that adultery breaks is an imposed lie, and the Trinitarian model does not reflect reality but dreams of hegemonic ideologies. The suffering and pain of adulterous relationships exist, as they exist in marriage too. It is the secrecy of adultery which destabilises power and puts people in vulnerable situations. In fact, secrecy is the main element of adultery; without secrecy, adultery is not adultery (Lawson 1989: 30).

Recently, people have begun establishing different patterns of relationships outside proprietary concerns. In Argentina, during the past decade, the concept of *amigovio* has become socially acceptable. *Amigovio* is a word composed of two other words: *amigo/a* (friend) and *novio/a* (boy/girlfriend). *Amigovismo* is a transitional category of relationship which usually involves sex, but also a sense of friendship which trespasses beyond the heterosexual patterns of friendship in Argentina. It has been defined as a genuine, sincere relationship, or as someone said to me once 'a space to be human', beyond many sexual conventions in friendship. Women in this sort of relationship involve themselves with men beyond the stereotypical condemnation of women having sex outside committed relationships, such as marriage or engagement. *Amigovios* do not necessarily marry each other, but remain in close, intimate friendship in a different pattern from that of lovers or ex-lovers. The relationships are not necessarily kept secret and do not carry a social stigma. Perhaps *amigovios* show a new pattern of sexual friendships and relationships lived in the moment, in the movement of life and not in the fixity of systems. Perhaps, following our previous example, a Trinity based on *amigovios* instead of medieval conceptions of family would be richer and more credible than the actual property, boundary concerned laws based on objectification of people and their control.

Systematic theology from the margins of sexuality

During the past few years we have become accustomed to one very important pattern of sexual stories, the 'coming out'. Plummer describes the narratives of coming out as organised around a plot loosely constructed in the following way. A person perceives a difference in herself, perhaps in her childhood. Then, later on in life there is a moment of crisis, described as 'not fitting' in society in general, or in a place of study or family life. That crisis is sometimes explained as a desire to commit suicide, for instance. After that, something happens: a friend, a book, a sudden understanding and the person 'comes out'. These are didactic stories which are shared in community, and become enriched with messages of triumph over discrimination and loneliness, a kind of rebirth experience. A friend of mine told me the following story.

> I was working in reception at the Theological Seminary when R. came in. He said to me: 'Good morning, How are you? And, by the way, did I tell you that I am gay?' Although I knew it, I almost fell off my chair at that moment, but then, Bishop F came to reception, and seeing R, came to greet him. He said, 'Hello R, Are you getting ready for your ordination ceremony?' And R said, 'Good morning Bishop. I'm doing

fine, thanks. By the way Bishop, did I tell you that I am gay?' And the Bishop almost fell on his backside.

R was a close friend of mine. He remembered that morning in Buenos Aires as a morning of triumph in his life, the morning of coming out.

> Yes, I still remember it. I was simply fed up with the church psychologist and exhausted from so much misery in my life. I said to myself: I only have one problem, I'm gay, but I don't think it is a problem anymore. My problem is that I do not feel loved by anybody. I need friends and lovers and a family who will say welcome to the real me, and not the one they wanted me to be, the false R. It was glorious, even if a voice inside me kept telling me: wait a minute, you may regret this. But I said to myself, that if I went to human rights demonstrations during the dictatorship because I cared for others, then, I could face my own coming out too, because I cared for me. I did it in the name of God.

Coming out cost R many things, including his job, part of his family and the church's refusal to ordain him, yet the feeling of coming out was for him even more important than the suffering he needed to endure. The happy ending came with R's pioneering work in the founding of the Metropolitan Community Church in Argentina. His courageous story told and retold by others was part of that network of meaningful tools for self-understanding which are community experiences. In Latin America the traditional role of *testimonios* (testimonials) in worship is that they are a form of coming out stories but from the experience of denial. People 'come out' in testimonials in order to deny themselves, that is to say that now they are not anymore what they are supposed to be. *Testimonios* usually mark the ultimate acceptance of established norms and sexual regulations. The sexual stories of coming out, to the contrary, give a testimonial with an affirmation of what normativity has denied. The first creates an order of conformity, the second, a network of rebellious people, the sort of rebellion which nurtures theology with a deeper questioning of life.

Stories of coming out are stories of courage; they open doors for a courageous standing in life. In my own Quaker tradition, this is what is called 'To speak truth to power'. Christian communities re-telling stories like that can find new sources and more strength for the struggle of liberation than in many liturgies. In fact, re-telling stories is a liturgical act in itself, of gathering, silence, dialogue and an exchange of the peace of God amongst each other. Somehow, they are more authentic than church liturgies, and more effective too. However, there are still many other stories which as Rubin says, remain at the bottom of the sexual pyramid without a voice. Yet, without them, we cannot have a theology.

In his seminal book *The Intimate Connection*, Nelson has differentiated between the theologies of sexuality and the Sexual Theologies (Nelson 1992:

128). The first speak about issues of sex and may address sexual stories, following a methodological movement from an idealist conception. Therefore, they establish first an understanding of God and the Bible which comes from their political heterosexual options. Then sexuality needs to fit that pattern, as in the Christian ethical approach to adultery. This is a commandment approach which finds fault with a well-known aspect of human behaviour and festers with guilt and destruction, instead of listening to the longings in human relationships and facing their complexity. As a result, sexuality and God get reduced in the process and the theological vocabulary gets increased with words such as 'control', 'reprimand', 'repress'. The reference is not a god of justice, but a god of social ordering who never existed anyway. Faithfulness to a marriage contract has been construed as faithfulness to God, but we have learnt that in the case of the sexual position of women in the Scriptures, for instance, to be unfaithful to a misogynist god is a duty which carries the risk of women committing ontological suicide. Transgressions have always been with us. Sexual theologies are the opposite of idealistic processes. They are materialist theologies which have their starting points in people's actions, or sexual acts without polarising the social from the symbolic. It is from human sexuality that theology starts to search and understand the sacred, and not vice versa. Indecent theologies are sexual theologies without pages cut from the books of our sexual experiences.

Pornography and sadomasochism have been the object of theological reflection basically through Mary Daly's pioneering books *Gyn/Ecology* and *Pure Lust*. In *Gyn/Ecology* Daly reflects on pornography and sado-rituals such as female excisions and infibulations from the perspective of women's objectification under patriarchy. She also refers to Paul Tillich's pornographic compulsion, as told by his wife Hannah, fixated around images of bondage and Christian crosses (Daly 1978: 94). As Daly points out, in Christianity, 'female suffering is joy'. However, in *Pure Lust* Daly establishes a difference in the definition of lust, depending on whether we are considering it from a patriarchal perspective or from a feminist redefined one. Patriarchally speaking, lust is 'phallic lust, violent and self indulgent, level(ling) all life, dismembering spirit/matter . . . Its refined cultural products, from the sadistic pornography of the kind characterised by the Marquis de Sade to the sadomasochistic theology of Karl Barth . . . (represent) unmitigated malevolence' (Daly 1984: 2). Daly has constructed a theology of denunciation of patriarchal sexual stories at the bottom of the sexual pyramid. However, if she can re-appropriate the meaning of lust for women and redefine it as 'Pure passion: unadulterated, absolute, simple sheer striving for the abundance of be-ing' (Daly 1984:3), then we could also re-appropriate stories of women with fetishist passions for high-heeled boots and bondage games. Liberation Theology has not dealt with these issues because the fear of homosexuality in Latin America surpasses any other fear, and it is an active fear which silences and suppress sexualities. Feminist

Liberation Theology still remains working with stories at the top of the pyramid (even if amongst the poor) preoccupied by stories of heterosexual reproductive sex and a gender role, neither a sexual role nor reflection on it.

However, we need to consider seriously the fact that it is oral sex we are dealing with (the retelling of sexual stories in the gathering of communities), which can build the Project of Liberation of the Kingdom better than the heterosexual reproductive stories we are used to. Sexual stories at the bottom of the pyramid are crucial for the building of the Project of Liberation of the Kingdom for two main reasons. First of all, because in their complexity and diversity they challenge the monolithic assumption of the Project of the Kingdom as a *Heteropia*, instead of a Utopia. We define heteropias as the location of 'coexisting different orders of space, the materiality of different forms of social relations and modes of belonging' (Probyn 1996: 10). Probyn, as a sociologist, has developed Foucault's thought on heteropias as places of 'disturbance, the shattering of tangled common names . . . and the syntax which causes words and things to hold together' (Foucault, quoted in Probyn 1996: 8). Following Foucault she sees heteropias as relations of proximity amongst the diverse, and as a process of surfacing where lines of political, social and historical forces interact. A Project of the Kingdom built upon a heteropian model is multiple and changing. It may present a kind of quicksand surface where theology may walk with uneasiness, but that is the crucial element of the Project of Liberation of the Kingdom: a certain uneasiness and a community made with the juxtaposition of elements which do not belong, who are outsiders to any hegemonic definitions.

The second reason why we need to retell these oral sexual stories is because God is desire. It was the late Uruguayan theologian Juan Luis Segundo who said 'God is society' (Segundo 1973: 39). That point was further developed in relation to Trinitarian models of God, presenting God-self to humanity not as a God-individual but as a community or a society. Let us consider how Deleuze and Guattari have defined desire, as a process of becoming which does not dichotomise between the symbolic and the social order, or the soul and the material. Desire is a social process.

> Knowing how to love does not mean remaining a man or a woman; it means extracting from one sex . . . the flow, the *n* sexes . . . that constitute the girl of *that* sexuality . . . When the man of war disguises himself as a woman and flees, disguised as a girl, hides as a girl, it is not shameful . . . To hide, to camouflage oneself, is a warrior function.
>
> (Deleuze and Guattari 1988: 277)

Society is made by the flow of desire which provokes one thousand coming outs in each individual life as part of warrior-like survival strategies. Heterosexuality is a sexual system permanently on the mend with the help of legal social contracts which give it hegemonic powers, but splits are unavoidable. They are produced constantly because humanity's life is driven by social desires. This requires transversalities manifested through gender challenges and sex dubiousness as a hermeneutical category of suspicion. God is desire in history and in the events of everyday life in society. Sexual stories unveil and facilitate the coming out of God and the heterotopic (instead of Utopic) Project of Liberation of the Kingdom.

Black leather: doing theology in corsetlaced boots

> Religion could be . . . conceived as a revelation of the *absolute essence* in *representational* form or figure, halfway between art and philosophy: a revelation that has, however, yet to attain the form most adequate to the Truth, its conceptual form.
>
> (Trías 1998: 97)

> Fetish with style: *Marquis,* fetish fantasy magazine, renowned for its informative and entertaining articles from the bizarre world of Fetishism. Each new issue published in glorious full colour, updates the reader with all the latest information on real life happenings on the scene world-wide, and contains a wealth of offerings from talented artists and photographers...
>
> (Advert, *Skin Two*, Autumn 1998; p. 27)

> Once a Catholic, always a perv, some say . . . Nothing else comes closer to the habit of a nun than a full rubber catsuit.
>
> (Collings 1998b)

Religion as the representation of an absolute essence is a Hegelian idea which has been disputed by the liberationist Marxist approach, through an understanding that the absolute essence is nothing more than a political ideology homologising itself with a God-like discourse of sacred authority. Revelation is also a contested concept amongst liberationists, because revelation is not considered anymore as the almost mediumistic art of pulling down a Platonic idea of an abstract absolute idea of God. In any case, revelation reveals (unveils, undresses) God in our historical circumstances, and assumes a materialist twist in our understanding. That is the point of doing theology from people's experiences and from their sexual stories, because they reveal the falsity of the border limits between the material and divine dimension of our lives. Yet, the belief in absolute essences and Platonic, idealist revelations still pervades the most radical of theologies and their representation persists in the liberation movement. Liberation Theology in its discourse on ideology and theology went through the same process of idealist temptation which challenges traditional North Atlantic theologies. This is shown in the reluctance of liberationists to face a way of doing theology which could challenge doctrinal and traditional standpoints of the Christian Church.

However, theology has its own deconstructive forces, its own instabilities and imprecisions which always create tensions and open new ways of understanding. This has made of theology something still worth the effort, a path of permanent revelation and rediscovery of the engagement between the sensual and the divine in our lives. Theological representation of absolutes has been part of Liberation Theology because there have been problems accepting the farce of a simplistic confrontation between oppressive and liberative aspects of our lives. In the end, Liberation Theology and structures of oppression both share a common epistemological field. Achilles Mbembe, in an article concerned with what is frequently the futility of many elaborated colonial strategies of resistance, made the following point: only in the 'conviviality' and 'familiarity' of the common epistemological field of colonisers and colonial subject can the possibility of dismantling them occur (Mbembe, quoted in Probyn 1996: 29). Colonial ways of thinking, organising society and theologising have ramifications, and grow inside our colonial souls in a play of opposition and camouflage, in tension and in acceptance. Camouflage has been the name of that theology, adapting and continuing ways of reflecting and acting with minimal change.

Sexual stories of fetishism are in proximity to Christian theology; there is a familiarity and conviviality between them, but also a criss-crossing and dissent which unveils and produces a revelation of theological camouflage. The neighbourhood fences between fetishism and Christianity do not separate them but point towards a common flow between them. The border is arbitrary and a product of colonial procedures into theological methods, that is, of the play between identity and the *Otherness* which needs to be created to establish the limits of that theological identity. What is fetishism? The Collins English Dictionary describes fetishism as 'a condition in which the handling of an inanimate object or a specific part of the body other than the sexual organs is a source of sexual satisfaction.' The characteristic aspect of this definition lies precisely in this element of bordering. Fetishism is described as full of borders, frontiers, and this is given by the word 'condition' (a medical term), and a particular definition of what constitutes sexual organs: a kind of robotic epistemology concerning the difference between animate and inanimate objects, or between animated sexual organs and inanimate ones. This is what forms the line of dualistic opposition which is obviously on display here, the relation between animate/inanimate. However, fetishism is hard to define and fix, because it seems to carry a certain undecidability or indecision in itself, for instance in that which constitutes the 'organs of pleasure'. A fetish is defined as an inanimate object believed to be alive, like an idol of magic worship. For instance, consider the following paragraph taken from an Umbanda handbook from Brazil dedicated to the worship of the goddess *Pomba Gira*.

Fetishes are elements which carry with them a vibration related to a certain (spiritual) entity. In them are allocated temporarily the energy of the entity. In the case of the *Pomba Gira* these elements are . . . seven coins, a tambourine, a golden ring. . .

(Arcadio 1996: 9)

This definition, which comes from the Umbanda worship as practised today in Brazil and Argentina, shows that the fetish is understood as both inanimate and animate at the same time. This is very queer, because there is no either/or for the fetish, but on the contrary it is everything and nothing at the same time. Animated and dead, and dead and alive *temporarily*, are the characteristics of life in our universe. However, there is another dimension to fetishes. Etymologically, fetish is a word which comes from the Latin word *facticius*, which means artificial, something made as a work of art, and not a natural product. Fetishism is then the realm of the mythological field of fictitious or unproved characters, the animated inanimate, the living dead. Christianity as mythology is also the realm of stories and religious systems elaborated around the living dead, and talking inanimate beings. For instance, resurrection is a case of dead yet alive, although it is not the 'dead yet alive' of the Zombies because in the Christian narrative Jesus does not remain physically around his town, but departs from the physical world at a certain point in time. The presence of the Holy Spirit saved Jesus from becoming a Zombie. Christianity is not a natural product either, but artificial in that it is a religious collective construction, and we may say that in a way it is an artificiality which participates in the artificiality of any creative process. Creativity shows by its mere existence that humanity is not natural and static, but in a continuous process of production of material and symbolic realms. But fetishism is also something else, because it makes sexuality explicit in this process. Fetishism can also be described as part of the process of the movement of desires in search of their own objectification or placement (Deleuze and Guattari 1988: 10). This is part of a process which we can call an approximation to a location of identity, or of finding that identity through non-traditional associations with improbable neighbours, by a way of splits and fictitious sexual creations. If we associate the body of a child called Jesus with the body of the God of Israel, as in the doctrine of the Trinity for instance, what we are doing is placing God, fixing God, and if you want fetishising it. Take the story of the virginal conception. There are no sexual organs in this narrative of sexual reproduction of a human being, but rather an objectification of sexual organs in the spirit which descended upon Mary. And even then we do not know what it descended upon. (Her vagina? Her womb? Her "heart"?) Between that and getting yourself a leather suit or high-heeled corsetlaced boots and making of them the guardians of your desires, there is conceptually not much difference. The fetishist epistemology is the same.

Fetishism is also a political option. Marx saw fetishisation processes in Capitalism in a similar frame to that which we have already discussed. It is the objectification of social desire through the alienated product of the workers. The transgression of boundaries in fetishism is done by blurring materiality, and therefore rendering indistinct the perceived division between sensuality and spirituality. In Marxist-inspired Theologies of Liberation, this leads us to a condemnation of the idolatrous process of replacing the animate with the inanimate, or God with an ideology. However, this assumes an original hegemonic definition of what should be considered animate. God is assumed to be the animate part which is threatened but we are not asking what God has displaced in the struggle of establishing who is alive and who is dead, or where sexual organs are located. In the end, it is a struggle of authority. Marx saw fetishism as the element at the base of Christianity, as an ideology, or as the location of the evil in Christianity. Derrida calls our attention to how the figures of evil in Marx 'discredit and credit' the credibility of Christian faith (Derrida 1998: 14). Fetishism unveils Christianity in its political hegemonic ambitions, but in doing so it re-projects the ideal of a Christian faith. The accreditation and disaccreditation procedures are processes of legal authority, of validation and invalidation of gods and fetishes. What was a god today, is a fetish tomorrow. It seems that fetishism may have things to teach us about the validation and invalidation of theological processes.

Stories of sexual fetishism carry many theological elements to reflect upon. This can be done in three different ways. First, it proceeds in parallel with Christianity, without challenging the binary logic of theology. This has been the usual procedure of justifying things with the Bible in hand, courageously finding new forms of justice and solidarity through biblical teaching but within the limits of, for instance, heterosexual concepts of justice. The second way may be done by reverting that logic, by privileging the subaltern concept of opposition. For instance, it is no longer possible to justify exegetically the claim that Israel was guided by God in the pillage of Canaan. Theologians like myself who come from continents which have suffered colonial invasions and genocide have, during the past decade, privileged a reading of the story from the Canaanite experience, that is, with the memory of the nations and cultures massacred by other nations which claimed that God had given them the power to do so. This has been the path of Liberation Theology. The third way is the indecent one. It is the path of reflecting the theologically *different*. The parallel line of reflection assumes that sexual misreadings and interpretative per/versions are evil, and that heterosexual idealism in theology is good. This is parallel thinking: everything and everybody needs to align with heterosexual theology; gays need to repent or be celibate, and women should be treated equally in the church whilst considering their particular 'gifts' as mothers and carers in the community. It usually ends in farce, with a tendency towards naïveté. It ignores the historical links between spirituality and sexual options, or between bondage and Christianity, or fetishism and the doctrine of salvation.

A story of fetishism and salvation

My great-aunt, an ordinary churchgoer, had on the wall of her dining room a picture of the Sacred Heart, Christ opening his body to reveal a bleeding, vermilion organ of compassion. On her drawing room mantelpiece the Virgin

Mary was permanently in tears. In the tiny country church my family attended, the stations of the cross serialised each cruel stage of Christ's passion . . .

Like all Catholics, I was brought up on images of gory suffering . . . Later on, I caught up. That's what adult life is: like Christ, to be betrayed, subjected to humiliation in all kinds of ways, to be tortured by unrequited love or frustrated ambitions, and worst of all, mortal.

Perhaps that's why people say, once a Catholic, always a Catholic. Having once been exposed to the imagery, only the most stolid of us could find it forgettable.

. . . But lapsed Catholics who become masochists – and I have it from a reliable source that they are legion – are cheating their way to heaven. We are too modern, too sceptical to attend Mass. But we haven't lost the taste for the combination of sensual excess and aesthetic sublimation that Catholics enjoy.

(Phillips 1998: 65)

What is the meaning of Christian salvation? Salvation, deliverance and preservation are three similar concepts. They imply to escape from 'harm' (sexual sin, in Christianity), and to preserve us as 'natural,' to keep us without (artificial) changes. In heterosexual Systematic Theology, there has always been a heavy emphasis on salvation from sexual transgressions, including the act of robbery such as taking a woman who belongs to someone else. Salvation shares with fetishism in being a category of the natural and at the same time of the artificial. Salvation is a creation/natural theology to save us from the natural/artificial state of sin. The story from Phillips somehow shares this theological indecision: religion is suffering, life is suffering, and salvation from suffering is found in suffering. Christ is the human supplement of God the Father: as supplement, Jesus adds pain as a theological category and a spiritual must. God the Father was not completed until the Jesus project started, thus the supplement is not an addendum; it is part of God the Father theology.

Salvation then becomes the theological place of what Derrida has called 'the safe and sound, the unscathed <indemne>, the immune (sacer, sanctus, heilig, holy . . .)' (Derrida 1998: 2) but simultaneously, as Phillips says, it is that place of sensual excess, which carries with it pleasures of insecurity, or the excitation of the unsafeness of the unknown (Phillips 1998). This is the trace of fetishism in salvation, another obscene trace of bondage, rehearsed by submission and control but unfortunately, not always optional, as in fetishist practices. From my own experience of living in Argentina, I am somehow familiar with what Phillips describes in her story. My grandmother's bedroom was a dark room illuminated with candles to the Virgin Mary, whose heart was pierced by seven swords, and to the crucified images of Christ, always bleeding and in pain. Reading stories from the life of saints, I as a child rehearsed some forms of their bodily punishment. I secretly avoided putting sugar in my tea, deprived myself of my toys and would not use a sweater even if it was bitterly cold. As I grew up, I saw suffering and spirituality bonded at other levels, in the general context of the oppression of my people. The narrative of the punishment of the bodies of the saints was a divine pedagogy to understand reality. I saw people's hearts pierced by swords of hunger, political repression and economic injustice. Sado/masochistic practices in the terrorism of the state in alliance with the church became torture and infinite forms of human pain inflicted on the people. I myself in my early youth ended up in hospital with acute malnutrition brought about by the conditions of poverty in which I was living at that time. At that moment I accepted it with resignation to the sadistic economic policies of my country which had the spiritual blessing and support of the institutional church. This was the spirituality of political sadism.

In the traditional Christianity of the 1970s in Argentina, salvation became a difficult category to understand outside the S/M scene. Stories of torture and the sexual pleasure that this produced for the torturers have been made known in past years.[4] This was the time when liberationists reorganised the discourse of salvation as liberation, in concrete political terms, but in order to do that they needed to discredit salvation as the location of the safe. In a reverse theological movement, salvation presented the traces of insecurity, of riskiness materialised in the option for the liberation struggle. That implied a transgression of the religious political order of a magnitude that North Atlantic theology and new generations even in my country would find difficult to comprehend. That alone turned the Christian discourse in Argentina and in other Latin American countries upside down. No wonder Liberation Theology was called a source of destabilisation of society. It discredited safety, the realm of the unscathed but credited hurt, and voluntary hurt, as in the case of the people who joined the struggle for liberation. Women and people of non-heterosexual options needed to submit their identities and struggles for the sake of the struggle for political liberation, a struggle which did not have them on its agenda. That hurt too, and a lot. Fetishism in all its complexity moved there with categories of suffering and submission, of the discarded and those considered irrelevant, the inanimate and the animate in simultaneous relations of transgression.

However, stories of sexual fetishism present us with a mimicry of salvation by a representation of the safe unsafety of heterosexual hierarchies. God the master and the Christian as the submissive slave subject, the top/bottom relationship of S/M people, is a master sketch of Christianity done in a moment. Again, salvation cannot be sketched so easily, because it has a dimension in itself which may subvert the fatefulness of heterosexual submission to certain orders of the sexual and political realms which are so closely related to each other. Desire for a whip in a fetish scenario is not the same as experiencing the whip of God the Father. The Father's whip, that whole chapter of sex and punishment of Systematic Sexual Theology, works close to political ideologies of economic submission. Salvation, in this context, as a call, can mobilise people to step out from the safety of the organised order and destabilise theo/social conceptions.

> It is not surprising that many people with a fervent Christian background end up at least sniffing around the leather and S/M scene. After all, many Christian sects urge their followers to be like Christ, and they all learn about his passion and suffering. Ever wonder how a crown of thorns may feel, or had fantasies about crucifixion? . . . I am acquainted with five members of the Christian clergy – three of them Catholic priests – who are very much into the leather and S/M scene. From what I have been able to observe, these men suffer no apparent spiritual conflict, and are altogether fine guys who are bright, interesting (and) have a good sense of humour . . .
>
> (Baldwin 1993: 35)

This statement seems to find some echoes with the words of Collings.

> Offering oneself up to a higher truth is the purest thing that one can do. Whenever I enter into a sub-dom relationship, it is an attempt to emulate the offering up of the self to God. Over and over as a Catholic schoolgirl, I heard the words of Mary quoted and recited: "I am the handmaid of the Lord". It instilled in us the command to go out and be submissive . . .
>   . . . The act of masochistic submission is symbolic of the greater, religious submission . . . we are asked to put our faith completely in the higher force . . . As in Catholicism so in SM, in that without consent, the act of submission is meaningless. The experience of emotional/physical pain is nothing unless given into gracefully.
>
> (Collings 1998b: 64)

Without consent, the act of submission is indeed meaningless, and so it is with salvation. A consensual salvation is always risqué, unsafe, unsettled but meaningful because it recognises the body as the space of salvation. Eroticism and hunger are sites of pain and liberation.

Theological misfortunes: from bottoms to tops

The two previous sexual stories present us with a binary methodology, making parallels and oppositions between Christianity and fetishism and S/M practices. Binary methodologies work by privileging the part of the binary opposition which is considered truthful. For instance, between God the Father and the Pomba Gira María Mulambo (a goddess from Umbanda Worship), God the Father is God and María Mulambo is a fetish, a little Brazilian statue of a naked red woman with long black hair. The reason for that is that Christian theology recognises reason (logos) and hegemonic authority from the construction of God the Father and any binary opposition with him loses out by becoming subject to him, and devalued. However, we can subvert orders of logic, which are the orders of *logos* and of the *logos spermatikos* of theology (Battersby 1989: 8). The logic of theology follows models of spermatic flow, of ideas of male reproduction which defy modern science but are established firmly in the sexual symbolics of theology. The sperm is the metaphoric vehicle of reason and logic. The following paragraph from Colin Wilson's *The Outsider* illustrates this last point.

> In sexual excitement, it is as if the spirit itself becomes erect, and becomes capable of penetrating the meaning of life. Normal consciousness is limp and flaccid; its attitude towards reality is defensive.
>
> (Wilson, cited in Battersby 1989: 140)

The question is, how can we cool down this erection of the *logos spermatikos* in theology? One way is by giving privilege to the subordinated part of binary compositions, what 'leather' people would call the prevalence of 'bottoms' (submissive partners) over 'tops' (dominant partners). The other is by trying to find the different (not belonging to the binary pair in conceptual opposition). Let us see first how the subversion of logical order, its displacement or misfortune in a theology of fetishism may allow the traces of the obscene to became more obvious.

Building the Un-Just Messiah

Christianity is the religion of the Messiah. I have said elsewhere that the understanding of the conceptual production of Messianism is crucial for any theological reflection relevant for our present times (Althaus-Reid 1995). That production of Messianism has two main characteristics. First, it is a collective process, which comes from a community which developed the expectancy of a project of Messianship, and second, this community's theological construction produces the Messiah himself. In the case of Jesus, and although historically there were many men claiming to be the Messiah of Israel at that time, only Jesus was accepted. That means that between that community and Jesus there was a commonality made by mutual understanding of Messianic codes and expectations, and corrections were also necessarily made during the process. Jesus learnt the expectation of his community, and therefore he learnt to be Messiah. This is a dialogical model of understanding Jesus as Messiah, in dialogue with the community and outside the hierarchical model or top down approach of authoritarianism. That dialogic Messianism has been built around two main issues. One is justice as 'a desire for justice' (social, sexual), that Derrida sees as Messianically independent of Christianity, Jesus or the Bible (Derrida 1998: 18), and the other is the mediatory role of Messianism. This mediation is based on an asymmetry, a non-coincidence between the divine and human beings; therefore the mediation of Christ is of a reconciliatory nature. The two pairs of oppositions in which Jesus as Messiah stands are then:

Messiah → Justice/injustice; Fairness/unfairness, the Unjust (outside the accepted standard)
Messiah → Mediator with humanity/Divine persona himself

The Messiah as the just man is the righteous (the one who keeps the law or has the law on his side), the fair (unbiased), the proper one, but it is also what in Spanish we would call *El Justo*, which means 'the correct', 'the precise' and 'the exact measure' as if weighing merchandise, or describing something which is very tight (like clothes which do not fit), restrictive, and even scarce. *Tengo lo justo para vivir* : I have enough to live on (money for food and bills), no more, no less. This *justeza* constitutes the trace of the Just Messiah: a restrictiveness, a space that is tight and cannot be exceeded, the area of the predefinitions of Messianship that cannot be discussed. However, Jesus did not have an easy time as Messiah. He did not occupy the *espacio justo* (space of justice, but also restrictive, scarce space) all the time. He exceeded his space, and became an *Unjust* Messiah, larger than life, sometimes outside the defined boundaries of justice, and definitively not in accordance with accepted standards of what is to be human and/or divine. Sometimes Jesus exceeded the box of expectations, the constructions of justice, although we must stress the *sometimes* because Jesus does not present a coherent record of consciousness of justice especially in relation to women. However, there are enough examples of Jesus' refusal of tight theological and social spaces, enough to make of him an Un-Just Messiah, occupied in un-just relationships, that is, unrestricted, open, larger relationships than the one prevalent in Jesus' historical times. In this lies the permanent conflict between the intuition of a larger Christ and a larger justice, and the tight fitted Just Christ of social and sexual restrictions of centuries of hetero-sexual ideology in Christianity. There is a curious story about Alexander Cruden, the eighteenth-century author of *Cruden's Concordance to the Holy Scriptures*. He was so convinced that people in Great Britain were exceeding his understanding of the Just way of living (for instance, English people not respecting the Sabbath) that he asked King George and his Council to give him the official title of 'Alexander, The Corrector'. It may sound as if this is really a storyline for the *Rocky Horror Show*, but no, it happens that Cruden believed people needed a living Table of the Law, a Civil Corrector in their lives, pointing out to them the Just ways (Cruden:1909, ii-iii). 'The Just' as a theological category was apparently taken by Cruden in his full dimension, and this makes a striking contrast with what we have called the path of the 'Un-Just' Messiah. Excessiveness and Un-justice, Justice and Restriction are also important pairs of oppositions in the fetishist binary system. Fetishism, as in Alexander the Corrector's ideal job, restricts movements, even the possibility of a sexual relation in itself, while exceeding the realms of sexuality. Fetishism articulates restriction and excess through clothes and objects. Fetishist adverts like sexual stories have received little attention in Sexual Theologies, yet they present this articulation with graphic clarity. For instance, restriction is the realm of chastity belts as the following advert conveys.

> The chastity belt is a classic S/M fantasy. It signifies total sexual control, absolute power, complete ownership, in a way that no other erotic bondage device can. Many different chastity belts are available to cater to this fantasy, ranging from the purely decorative to the fully functional. At the decorative end are products such as Rude Metals' spiky leather belt. It is easy to wear and for an outlay of around £89–90, would certainly look fierce, teamed up with other fetish garments . . .
>
> *Made to Measure Clothes. Drag Queen 'XXX' Dressers*
>
> Period costumes, Maids' Uniforms, School Girls' Uniforms, Corsets, Basques, Frilly Petticoats, Hip Pads, Make-up, Lingerie, Stockings, Boots, Wigs, Breast Forms, Leather and PVC Fantasy Clothes . . .
>
> Dominion: For adventure and escapism try this *tight fitting* new women's leather collection which combines the softest, sexiest leather with daring design . . . Also for the more daring – bondage equipment to really get attached to.
>
> (*Skin Two* 1998)

Are the stories behind these adverts stories of justice as restriction? The scarce space of justice is presented in the sexual restriction of chastity belts and forms of punishment (for instance, spanking). There is an excess of just/ice in fetishism. Sexual organs are excessive and therefore do not need to be biologically located. Sexual contact is not necessarily the point; restriction as a condition for excess, may be. This is somehow a familiar scene in theology with the Christian discourses on sexuality and virgin mothers, except for the fact that Christian theology de-eroticises even sexual organs, while fetishism eroticises the whole body, even the hairs of the head which appear powerfully erotic covered with leather wigs. Yet the photographs behind those adverts do not portray restriction but excess, the excess of restriction, the excess of justice (*lo justo*) and the un-justice of excess. All this un-justice is played around hierarchical theological systems: nuns with whips and ladies with crosses on their corsets which are designed to bring the waist in by up to four inches, parodies of theological authority, of domination and subjugation, in an unstable system where those orders are established temporarily and reversed for pleasure. Fetishism and S/M are seen by some people as fulfilling the role of religious groups. However, we are aware of some forms of religious reversal of the kind we are unravelling in fetishism. Julia Collings expresses it as follows.

> Religion is often considered the arch-enemy of Sadomasochism. It is a war fought with equal venom on both sides. The pious think we are depraved and immoral; we view them as hypocritical negaters of personal freedom. But it is a battle where the two camps have more in common than they either would care to admit . . . It's easy for an SMer to look at the strange world of religious fanatics and think, "Ha! They're just perverts like me". It's a bit harder to realise that *you* might actually be like *them* – that the naughty world of perversion hidden in your closet could be just another variation of the centuries-old routine of pain and worship
>
> (Collings 1998a: 50)

Is fetishism an obscene trace of Christianity then? In fetishism, pain and worship seem to produce a subversion of Christianity, in relationship to the Scriptures and from there to Messianism which is represented through the visual and tactile elements of fetishism: clothes and photographs are the text of fetishism, and their authoritative (W)ord. These seem to be closer to the in-built authority of the Virgin Mary in Latin America. Not by her Word, but by her clothes and images we believe in her. However, in Christian theology, the written Word of God has never been the only source of ultimate authority. The written Word has been subordinated to Orality. In the process of writing the Scriptures, people's experience, manifested in oral accounts, has been a hermeneutical key in the search for a final text, which ultimately is difficult to produce (Croatto 1973: 29–31). At institutional levels, for instance, this process tends to disappear if sermons and church documents are produced as epistles (letters) to be read (heard) excluding any dialogue with them. The Vatican encyclicals are an example of this. They are letters sent by the Pope to the 'circle of bishops' around the world to be read to the people who must hear what they say. Therefore, this suggests that if God is the Word (or Verb), the final authority in discernment is also speech, and not *ecriture*. In fetishism, sexual stories as told, for instance, in magazines are only partially effective in transmitting people's actual experiences. The pictorial element of photographs and drawings are the arena of dialogue and linking experiences, and therefore become the real significative texts. From the pages of classified adverts in *Skin Two*, issue 27, we choose at random the following texts.

Fetish Designers

'We would like to hear from experienced freelance designers of rubber, leather and PVC fetish-wear, who can produce professional patterns and samples . . .'

'Photo processing dark room studios for your private development . . .'

'Wolfang Eichler – Erotic Photographs. A de-luxe *Marquis* Edition book featuring 128 plates from one of the most prominent photographers of erotica. Eichler women are sexy, beautiful and always "in control"'

'Fetish Witch. A portrait of one of Germany's most exciting dominatrix, 128 pages of photos featuring this long-legged fetish tigress. It is no wonder men worship her feet . . .'

'Fetish Images. Every year, *Marquis* holds a reader's competition to discover new and exciting photographers, illustrators and authors . . .'

(*Skin Two* 1998)

Many pages are dedicated to professional illustrators and graphic artists, commenting on the artistic characteristics of their work. Photographs, catalogues and illustrations are the locus of a different theological order. Instead of the Christian order of Word-Word (speech of God – the written text of the Bible) and Speech-Word (the orality of church documents presented as letters and sermons), fetishism presents us with the following: photographs-photographs, or from the visual to the visual. However, this is the point of disorder. As Barthes said, photography is always a disorder, because it is 'unclassifiable' (Barthes 1993: 4). Barthes attributes this disorder of photographs partly to the fact that photographs carry in themselves their own referent (in contrast to the referent of the written word, which can be untraceable), and partly to what he describes by using sexual metaphors with fetishist undertones: according to Barthes, photographs are 'affected by *amorous* or *funereal immobility . . . glued* together *limb by limb*, like the *condemned man* and *the corpse in certain tortures* or even like those pairs of fish . . . which navigate in convoy, as though *united in eternal coitus* (Barthes 1993: 6; italics mine). What disturbs us in photographs is the presence of 'pricks, wounds or marks' in the images that Barthes calls *punctum*. *Punctum* is 'sting, speck, cut, little hole . . . that accident which pricks me but also bruises . . . is poignant to (oneself)' (Barthes 1993: 27). This describes what fetishist texts are: photographs *par excellence*, in that amorousness of funereal immobilities, whipping scenes, and the eternal coitus of the non-sexual organs. They are also *punctums* in themselves: everything in them de-adjusts and takes away the coherence of heterosexual representations such as the photographs in pornographic magazines where women (mostly) and men fulfil and repeat the heterosexual logic of gender orders. Fetishism makes it difficult to discern gender and sexualities, and only the temporal momentum of the top/bottom relation gives it some sense of stability. This may be why, contrary to fetishist material, pornographic magazines rely on words as much as photographs. The trangressive element of fetishist photographs lies in the fact that they are not texts, and somehow they escape or confound the logic of binarism. The religious elements of fetishism, as if coming from sexual stories, confound the theological writing–speech order, because they give authority to *punctum* disorders: a woman (probably) dressed as a nun with the attire and appropriate religious symbols, yet with purple eyelashes and a whip, and leather buttons and a coifed head. Religious fetishism represents a disordered Christianity, but so does Jesus. Which is the *punctum* in Jesus' 'photograph', the discordance which, as in fetishist adverts, makes people relate in wonder to what is unclear, unsettling or transgressive? Jesus is an unsatisfied Messiah, a Messiah in pain. He is a man, sometimes hungry and thirsty, sometimes asking 'Who do you think I am?' as if in a sort of identity quest for himself, a God surrounded by angels and voices from the God of the Universe, a Christ with the red eyes of a tortured body. The Virgin Mary crying permanently on the dressing table in the bedroom. Christ resurrected: a living dead, but not yet a Zombie. A transgressor, a passive recipient of Roman colonial law and order. A disorder, his own text.

On mediation: does Messianism submit to sexual desires?

Following from that disorder in the Christian text of fetishism, Messianism also becomes incomparable with the theology of God the Father. This happens because Jesus Messiah works in a reversal relationship with God. Following a fetishist binary system of tops and bottoms, God is top (master, Lord) while Jesus is bottom (slave, the suffering Servant). In Jesus' relationship with the world, he somehow continues to be bottom while the world (Greek *sarx*, the flesh) is constructed as the top. Jesus suffered in subordination to the world, and as the Apostles Creed says 'he suffered under (the political regime of) Pontius Pilate'. It does not say, 'he rebelled against the political regime of Pontius Pilate', but 'suffered'. If, following Deleuze and Guattari, sexual desire is also social desire, we may say that Jesus Messiah lived and suffered under that social and sexual flow of desire. He submitted himself to the flow of sexual desire, he did not want to master it. 'My Kingdom does not belong to this World' (John 18:36). This is an interesting point because in traditional heterosexual theology Jesus cannot be thought of submitting himself to social desires, while in reality they mean 'sexual desires'. Social desires are sub-versive (they come from below, or from the grassroots) and rely on per/verted interpretations (exegetical options, changes in the hermeneutical road originally taken). For instance, Jesus was presented as submissive in relation to issues of Roman colonisation and indifferent towards Jewish political independence. So the struggle to present Jesus as not submitted to social desires is true but only in relation to sexuality, and with a very tight (*justo*) restrictive biological understanding of sexuality. But if Jesus stood amidst the real conflicts of his time, it is evident that he stood amidst forces of political and social desires and the sexual ones which conform to human reality. Sex does not belong to any chapter in Idealism, except in heterosexual (fictional) literature. He may have submitted to sexual desires in the sense that he passively accepted the temporal construction of sex of his time without any insight of historical consciousness different from his contemporaries. It may be, for instance, that on issues of sexuality, there was not much difference between Nero and Jesus and they both considered that patriarchy had divine support, women were born to be subjugated and so on. Or, it could be said that Jesus' sexuality exceeded the biological locations (although not necessarily excluding them) and that Messianship is a sexual project, and that an Indecent Theology can undress the goodness of the erotics of liberation in the Project of Liberation of the Kingdom. This could be the point in Goss's Queer Theology, which struggles against the reification of oppressive social practices in Christianity, and sees liberation as tentative and always in process or as we have already said 'always exceeding'(Goss 1993: 141).

However, orders of submission in Jesus have been relocated in Christianity to restore an otherwise threatened theological order. Therefore, the submissive Lamb of God becomes sometimes Lord and vice versa, in a complete reversal which has created not a few theological contradictions in Christianity, not only in relationship to doctrinal aspects but to the structural organisation of churches. Humility and submissiveness were demanded of the social groups considered weak and vulnerable to punishment, including economic sanctions in the curtailing of job possibilities. This has been, and still is being done with the theological representation of Jesus Messiah, 'Jesus-bottom.' At the same time, the church organises itself in tight classist, sexist and racial compartments of tops which master, rule and punish. We are at the point of considering that these church structures get sadistic pleasure from this, otherwise this system of imposed divine punishment administered by the church would not be maintained with the fierceness that is still prevalent. The flesh rules the church, not 'God', in a way that Christ Messiah is not only represented by suffering women, for instance, but the church itself gets pleasure from submitting itself to heterosexual desires of law and order. Sadomasochistic complexities move here. The sexual story undertone of church teaching on sexism, and the evident pleasure in it are shown, for instance, in the following piece entitled 'At Last the Truth Hits Home'written about the theme of inclusive worship in the Roman Catholic Church, as appeared in The Catholic World Report issue of November 1997:

At the June meeting of the US bishops Donald Trautman of Erie, Pennsylvania, singled out Matthew 5:23–4 as an instance where the Vatican rejection of inclusive language had a negative impact on translation. This was the version originally submitted to Rome by the American bishops: Therefore, if you bring your gift to the altar, and there recall that your brother *or sister* has anything against you, leave your gift there at the altar, go first and be reconciled with your brother *or sister* [my italics] . . .

The article is a virulent attack on any form of inclusive language as an open door to immorality, even on the grounds of translation, which diminishes disadvantaged people. The words used to oppose such a simple inclusion as the words 'or sister' in the text speak for themselves:

> Is this natural English? . . . Logical coherence and disciplined adherence to principle (of Greek translations) have never been a major concern of feminists or other groups that use the weapon of political correctness to achieve their goals. Will 'inclusive language' translations sound natural to an ordinary young reader?
>
> (*The Catholic World Report*, November 1997: 46–7)

Shockingly, the picture supporting this last statement in the article is one of a young boy of around six or seven years old, seated with an open book on his lap, bearing on its front cover the word "Blessings". And sitting in the same ample chair with him there is a life-size dolly, an imitation of a little girl made in plastic with a bonnet and girl's clothes as his companion! It is clear that this is a fetishist image of a boy relating to the Bible and to a plastic (inflatable?) girl, in a setting of the sexual submissiveness of women to men. The illustration of the article against sexual disorder in inclusive translations of the Bible has been illustrated with a plastic girl which acts as a *punctum*, or point of inner destabilisation in the photograph. The dolly works here as supporting a logic and a discipline which seems to belong to the chain of compulsory S/M locations in the church. Fetishist desires: women need to be excluded, crossed out, even from the simple additions of the word 'sisters' in a reading, and reconstructed as plastic women. The Scripture and Christianity are desexualised. The plastic dollies are sexualised.

Fetishist Theology is a theology of photographs, but Christianity instead fixes its pictures of submission and control without the consensuality of S/M. S/M'ers, according to some sexual stories, get pleasure in reversing and reorganising the lines of top/bottom relationships or Master/Slave. Some people are 'switches', and like to swap the roles of dominant and submissive in their relationships. Another point in Jesus Messiah as mediator is his submission to God is his submission to the flesh. The flesh (world and desires) is what decided his fate and suffering, his persecution and trial and final death. That was a point made in Liberation Theology: Jesus died for coherence's sake. Although liberationists see that coherence in Jesus' refusal to accept the ways of the world, there is in reality more coherence in his submission than in any active refusal to obey the ways of the world. He did not join any postcolonial, liberationist guerrilla army of his time, for instance. He submitted himself to the flow of desire which we have called sexual, that is social. Therefore we get little concrete from the Gospels about the Project of Liberation of the Kingdom, only general values and intention. The late Juan Luis Segundo wrote during the 1970s that Jesus committed ideological mistakes; he knew where to go, but he did not organise clear strategies for that (Segundo 1982: 158). For Segundo, Jesus' failure was in the difficulty he had effectively combining his faith, in the terms of goals or values, and his ideology, considered as a methodology or strategy for achieving those goals, such as the Project of the Kingdom. Jesus' politics were based on passivity, or submission to the political order of his time. However Jesus as mediator between humanity and God does not fit a living parable of submission, at least not all the time. Jesus sometimes seems to behave more like a fetishist photograph than a text, and as such is *punctum*, disturbance, scandal although not a planned action. Reading Jesus' life is a voyeurism, an experience similar to that of Baudelaire watching through a window:

> Across the heaving waves of roof-tops I can see a woman who looks middle-aged: her face is already wrinkled and furrowed; she is poor; . . . With her face and dress and movements, with almost no clues at all I have reconstituted that woman's history, or rather her legend . . .
>
> Then I go to bed, feeling proud of having lived and suffered in others, not myself.
>
> Perhaps you will ask me 'Are you sure that legend is the true one?' But does it matter what the reality outside myself is, so long as it can help me to live, to feel that I am, and what I am?
>
> (Baudelaire 1989: 155)

This confronts us with the point that Jesus cannot be organised easily in any theological logic. There are mediation and forms of Messianism in the fetishist photographs, a mediation of voyeurism into his life from conception and what may have been his hidden Messianic fantasies of pleasure (a Theocracy?), perhaps in a way similar to the photographs of crucified girls which fell from Tillich's books when his wife opened them. Jesus as a fetish photograph works like the window for voyeurs, and as the pinning down of particular events of suffering and pain without that sense of transcendence and ownership built by theology. Jesus' events happened only once in history. His life is a series of photographs which do not belong to anybody, and yet, to everybody. Jesus Messiah is a window where our lives project their sexual/social pain and hopes. Jesus' stories are stories from our own experiences, our own stories. Sexual stories of fetishism give us food for thought for a Jesus Messiah in whom we may find the particulars of our life concretised and not transcendentalised, divinely sensualised, socially sexualised, and always for our time and the precise present moment. However, Jesus represents a disordered Christianity because he does not coincide with himself in his divine personality, and as in the fetishist photographs, one looks at him in order 'to make another [divine, in this case] body' for ourselves (Barthes 1993: 10). As we learn to indecent this process, multiple bodies of Jesus Messiah appear, and the richness of his contradictions help us to continue a journey outside the realm of heterosexual theology. Mediation is a way to express theologically that the relation between God the Father and Son is about being in the middle of a road with two ends, one of departure and the other of arrival: the human one, and the divine. It is also a transferring of an understanding about society and sexuality. In the end, it seems that it is not a good model. Mediation presupposes conflict and a privilege of power. Stories from the bottom of Rubin's sexual pyramid open the way for new forms of model, not mediatory but multiple, plurivocal, including the economic readings of theology we are going to consider in the next chapter. Economy, like fetishism, is about restriction and excess, and a heterosexual understanding of human relationships. It is about theological struggles between flexibility and inflexibility and the human need for adultery, that is, the need for creativity, for intimate longings to be acknowledged and the questioning of the taken for granted. Above all, economic systems are about paradigms of coming out from this crossroads of theology, sexual hegemonies and economics, looking for the way out for political, economic and sexual justice in our societies. To take. seriously. history as a space of faith is, in the words of J. Severino Croatto, a struggle for people to 'say their own word' (Croatto 1973: 14), and we may add, to recognise the freedom needed to do an Indecent Theology of people's indecent, unruly lives of suffering.

5 *Grandes medidas económicas*
Big economic measures: conceptualising global erection processes

'Qué pasó, dónde se fué mi palabra que dejé?'
What happened? Where has my word gone, the one I just left?
(Juana, a woman from Chiapas in Pérez 1995)

Chiapas reminds us in a brutal way that a thought or political project does not have value if it is not concerned with *cotidianidad* [everyday life, and the everyday quality of our history] and with the suffering of people. Inequality suffered by women, yes, but also by indigenous people, peasants, the marginalised, prostitutes, homosexuals, young people this persists in our country without any apparent congruence with the development we have reached in many areas . . .
(Marta Lamas (1994), Mexican feminist and
Director of the Journal *Debate Feminista*)

When we first had the idea to start a trade union for prostitutes it was twelve years ago, and at that time we were in jail and the country did not have democracy and *éramos locas* (we were mad, indecent women). And yet, we are here.
(Susana Rivero (1996), co-founder of AMEPU,
the Association of Public Prostitutes of Uruguay)

Colonial souls and the erotic desires of economy

Whatever happened to our words of passion and justice, the ones 'we just left', in our women's socio-theological discourses? Behind me, there are shelves full of books and research written by women on issues of gender and sexual oppression, politics and religion. Whatever happened to those words? Why is it that every so often we feel that we need to return to old arguments, repeat them and reframe them, because 'they are not part of the discussion anymore' as if they had departed? The words of Juana, full of indignation because women's demands for modifications in the law concerning midwives in Mexico were not met. This reminds us of other voices, for instance, the voices of Chiapa's women after having seen that their testimony against the soldiers who raped them, written in some document as a simple protest from indigenous women whose river had been polluted with the soldiers' condoms. We are witnessing here the dialectics of silence and representation in our societies. It is not that poor women's words are not heard, but that, as in Juana's case, they are relocated, forced to enter a new grammar (and therefore we cannot recognise them any more), or are simply gone. Yet sometimes poor women's words, although misconstrued and reshaped, may reappear forcefully intact from their retreat, as in Uruguay, amongst the few sufficiently indecent and courageous women who founded AMEPU to legally represent prostitutes. This was a dream of justice which began between two prostitutes one night in a prison cell, and in a country driven by a dictatorial regime. The dreams of indecent women, dreams of deviants can make words of protest and cries of injustice reappear in society in actions of transformation. They become a sort of resurrection, or the incarnation of women's voices in justice.

This chapter is an attempt to reflect on the interrelation between the dominant theological and political discourses from the perspective of a Sexual Theology, centred on the intimate connections between the sexual and socio-political hegemonic constructions to be found at the base of capitalism, the market economy and in the present globalisation movement allied to a neo-liberal ideology. The perspective is that of a Collocation Community,[1] a perspective of dialogue. Economic desires walk hand in hand with erotic desires and theological needs. An economic model is a relationship model based on erotic considerations concerning the economy of bodies in society, their intimacy and distance and the patterns of accepted and unaccepted needs in the market and the making of the politics of satisfaction. The economy of bodies considers the basics of what we need, while intimacy and distance are to be seen in the way society is organised and how the mechanisms of production for meeting those needs are regulated. Of course, this implies the identification of who is the subject of the economic process, and who thereby determines the distribution of goods to those identified subjects. The economic subject is an erotic subject, and economic theories deal with unique identities where sexual and racial components interrelate with class and gender constructions, producing complex results in terms of oppression. This happens because economic desires are a contentious field, not easily defined due to the fact that needs and desires are negotiated amongst different peoples and cultures in different ways, and the whole erotic/economic model relies on definitions and exclusions. The theological models are, in this sense, not far from the economic ones. Traditionally, we may consider that theology deals with a market of souls and the definition of their needs: sacraments, prayers, ritual ordinances and an allegiance to beliefs which regulate people's lives, in order to effectively distribute the spiritual goods of redemption or forgiveness or even eternal life amongst them, the spiritual clientele. The mechanisms of distribution are organised structurally in highly erotic elaborated church rituals, with their phraseology and conceptualisations of exclusion and inclusion, while sexual ecclesiologies determine the efficacy of faith according to the ideal created identities of officials such as priests and theologians. For instance, when some churches debate the ordination of women or gays, what they are effectively saying at the bottom line of any argument is that women or gays may or may not be effective in the delivering of spiritual goods in the socio-judicial organisation of the distribution of divine goods in society. Of course, it also implies a question of fixing identities, or defining who is who in the market of souls, for instance, who is supposed to enjoy the goods and how; dependency relations, and elements which have made of the 'shepherding' of the church a somewhat common problem of clientage.

Developmentalist thought as part of an applied theological reflection on issues of poverty and wealth distribution has sometimes ignored the close links between these two markets, the theological and the social. This may have happened at times through the sheer authoritative weight of the theological meta-narratives which tend to obscure a self-questioning process, and at other times through a theological instinct of self-preservation. It is not only that Christianity can challenge the economic order (as well as support it), but it is fair to say that challenging economic orders also means challenging the order of the divine constructs of Christianity. Unfortunately, much of the current field of development and theology has fallen into a kind of 'application' model. It has been easy in church circles to say that the freedom of the market contravenes the idea of freedom in the Gospels, or that equality for the neo-liberal models is not the equality of the Project of the Kingdom. However, concepts such as freedom and equality in Christianity have been positively contested throughout history by the advance in consciousness coming from secular society. Women voted for presidents and became presidents of nations before becoming bishops. In some Latin American countries, women can become presidents but not go to church on Sunday and read the Scriptures if they happen to be menstruating that day.

Developmental/theological thoughts may benefit from challenging their traditional notions of, for instance, 'freedom' which can be not only more oppressive than those of the market, but also at the root of the oppressive conceptions of any economic model which is also a sexed and gendered model. The problem is that in development and theology it is easy to follow implicit hegemonic theological orders, no matter how well disguised they may be in terms of participation and 'empowerment.' The discourse of equality as (supposedly) based on the Gospel is an example of this. In the end, Christianity seems to be all for equality between men and women, but to have been sadly misinterpreted for twenty centuries. Christianity is prevented from coming of age, and is not allowed to reflect on its prejudices and mistakes. There is always an epistemological ceiling, called faith, or patriarchal faith, which is not removed. This I call the ceiling of decency.

Decency keeps fixing the needs of this market of souls and bodies both in the Third World and in the First World alike. Some positive elements such as decentralisation and the rights of individuals are demonised in the name of a Christian theology which likes to keep central controls, to homogenise and obliterate the rights of people in the name of general, constructions imposed on life. Laclau and Mouffe have pointed out that popular movements and many political organisations which are interrupting our social constructions, such as the Zapatistas, are 'surplus' value from the social order (Smith 1998: 2). The importance in terms of resistance and creative development of such surplus threatens the identity construction of the erotic subject of theology. For instance, the romantic assumptions of developmental theological thought are based on popular identity constructions which are the product of theological discourses and in contradiction with the identities created by the surplus of people's resistance to precisely such constructions. However, Liberation Theologies are more ready to support that surplus and disengage with colonial identity constructions of the developing countries. The fact that we still make a distinction between a liberationist and a developmentalist discourse proves that there is a gap in conception between one and the other, basically in the understanding of decentralisation both in politics and in theology.

Decentralisation is part of a catalogue of indecent social gestures. As such, we must welcome it. Throughout this book I have been using the term 'indecent', in a positive, subversive sense, referring to a counter-discourse for the unmasking and unclothing of the sexual assumptions built into Liberation Theology during the past decades but also today when confronting issues of globalisation and the new neo-liberal world order. Indecency as a social gesture is extremely political and erotic, and relates to the construction of the identity of the subject through the subversion of economic, religious and sexual identities. Developmental thought, like traditional Sexual Theology, constructs identities through coherence, that is, with the 'what we have in common' mentality. It needs to assume and stress commonality amongst the community, and commonality in relation to what is common understanding in a Western sense about a developing country. Meanwhile, postcolonial thinking has introduced us to the complexities of national identities and the strength which may lie in the different, not the common struggle of the people. The constant mislocation of 'fragility' and 'strength' in poor communities from well-intentioned developmental agencies is an example of faulty thinking. It comes as the result of misunderstanding the local structures of knowledge of survival of different people. Poor women's strength may be found in the masking of their female identities with the excess which characterises the story of Ruth and Naomi: two friends trying to survive together using a strategy of high femininity in order to get a man/provider (Wilson 1995: 159), just as a modern middle-class woman might get cosmetic surgery in order to apply for a job. However, oppression is perhaps what we cannot have in common, because oppression is built in overlapping levels of multiple and contradictory elements which, according to context, produce variably dense, saturated effects. Ruth, the Moabite woman, had a different layered organisation of oppression from that of Naomi, yet at one point she succeeds (at least as a piece of narrative, not of history) by summing up differences. If identity as a summing up of commonalities is not effective because it is not realistic enough, only identity construction by subversion may confront us, since it is the multiplicity and not the singularity of oppression which we need to challenge. This refers specifically to what Chantal Mouffe addresses when she talks about the 'contingent and precarious' identity of a multiple, contradictory oppressed subject (Mouffe 1992: 372). Therefore, any theology concerned with issues of wealth and poverty needs to consider more the incoherence of oppression and its multiple dimensions rather than its commonalities. At this point, we need to remember the erotic constitutive element of our identities, in the politics of food and of pleasure. The problem with Ruth and Naomi's story lies with the assumption that an excess of femininity is the only erotic strategy. Thus Ruth is not a Moabite judge who challenges the judicial system to her advantage; the result of the triumph by excess of femininity is not always a happy one. Bread is exchanged for bitter intimacy. That excess of femininity relies on an excess of hetero-masculinity too; in this context, erotic excess is decent. Otherwise (as in surplus), it may be indecent.

It may well be that indecency and decency were historically created in the colonial world to ensure the regulation of the surplus of social order. This would be true also for the co-ordination of the coherence and good functioning of the religious–political market which has been sustained mainly by women indoctrinated into that complex state called 'decency'. What the colonial masters made illegal for native men and for their society in terms of economic organisation, jurisprudence, religious and educational structures, for women and for those of other sexual orientations was termed *indecent*. Indecency also has obvious socio-economic, political, legal and religious implications but of an overtly erotic nature which organises and controls the public and private spheres of the lives of women and transvestites – that is, anybody outside the imposed sexual regulations. It is interesting to notice that in Latin America the adjective decent, when applied to a man, refers to economic honesty and proper social exchange as in the expression *¡Qué hombre decente!* (What a decent man!). But it is not applied in the area of men's sexual exchange, where different codes of sexual regulations function for men and for women, and for men and women outside the boundaries of heterosexuality. *¡Qué mujer decente!* (What a decent woman!) applies only to either her sexual inexperience or marital fidelity to a legal sexual contract. In economic terms, women need to subvert political systems whose definitions of decency contravene their pleasure, because women's pleasure is not linked to centralisation, state property or assignments based on reproductive planning. In this, obviously, we have implicitly described the elements of a centralised economic model as ontologically negative. One cannot submit to sexual decency master codes without tacitly submitting to political master codes too. Decent Christian women, unfortunately, make decent citizens too. However, it is from indecent Christians and subversive citizens that action for transformation occurs in history. Indecency may be the last chance for a surplus of Christianity to transform political structures.

Theology uses a sense of hetero-normativity, where political and religious autonomy *and* sexual autonomy are linked concepts in mutual contradiction. Economic theories in which women are reduced to units of consumption due to the invisibility of their domestic work (including the affective, erotic work which nurtures the workforce) are theories not of autonomy but of dependency. In that division between the private and the public we also find the core of traditional Sexual Theology too. Women are the traditional consumers, not producers of theology. Other sexual identities such as bisexuality or lesbianism fall into the same economic relation of dependency, in the sense that people's lives are regulated in the market or in theology in dependence on hegemonic definitions of which goods people need, how to distribute them and for whom this model is effective in terms of satisfaction and happiness. Transvestites prostituting themselves on the *Panamericana* Highway in Buenos Aires are not confined to the same definitions as women prostitutes, yet they have their own gender/sexual constraints. For instance, their identities are construed in terms of the realms of the private and not the public life of citizens, and the job market also differs for them. That distinction between the public and the private is exclusionary and produces a sense of societal coherence through disjunction. Binary thought has construed the private/public relationship as one of dependence/independence and transvestites have needed to align themselves into feminine or masculine categories as part of their identities of survival in poverty and restricted market economies. The gender spaces and multiple sites or locations of society are sexed and gendered; you go either with the men, or with the women. My understanding is that a sexual critique of political thought and of the theological structure which supports heterosexuality as an ideological primal system will help us to throw some light onto the present crisis of the global neo-liberal process and Christian theology alike, but it is not the only critique which is required. As we have said before, oppression is multiple, and although patriarchal thought is foundational, it is only at the intersection of the unpacked multiple layers of suffering that we find its core.

Let us take, for example, the fact that recently, much has been written about the crisis of Liberation Theology and the impasse in the sociology of development. Basically, it is claimed that ideas and reflections have ceased to produce innovative visions and strategies for action. Where is this crisis located? In the failure to keep selling books in the theological market, in the crisis of the Christian subject of development or in the changes in the political international field? The crisis can probably be seen as touching all these areas, but amongst the various reasons given for the perceived crisis, is mentioned the fall of trusted paradigms such as developmentalism and

Marxism and the difficulties in understanding the full implications of the new globalisation process. However, the crisis of the theological subject of development is not receiving the necessary attention. NGOs which helped to strengthen the people's struggle against violations of human rights, and the Basic Ecclesial Community movement, for instance, are now giving way to popular movements which are far beyond ecclesiastical expectations. These movements are not only the response of the struggle presented by Latin Americans to the current crisis but also a highly positive consequence of the socio/theological decentralisation of praxis, and as such a positive consequence of postmodernism and globalisation. Decentralisation is a feature of the market economy, and amongst Latin American Christians – its spirit has come to defy the protectionist ethos of church ecclesiology, and church-theological dependency. Socio/theologically speaking, we are moving in complex circles here. Our reflections, caught between a faith which in the church seems to be still in struggle with modernism and a difficulty in coming to grips with postmodernism, are not as efficacious as they should be for the transformation of our society. Basically, so much time has been spent denouncing what is perceived to threaten Christianity, i.e. its plurality and difference, that there is a tendency to forget the difficulties created in the lives of Latin American people by totalitarian Christianity. Difference and the presence of the *Others* amongst us do not always need to mean exclusion, nor does plurality need to be homologised with incoherence. From Developmental Theology to Liberation Theology, there is a core of assumptions which has never been the object of ontological suspicion, a kind of master-concept which gives a false sense of coherence to any praxis. These are concepts related to the universalisation of the needs of a soul market, regulated through the codification of sexuality, but also race and culture (and we may include economics in cultural patterns too). However, we should refer here to what Maria Mies calls the capitalist–patriarchy concept (Mies 1986). Mies disagrees with Marx on the grounds that it is not capitalism which alienates the man–woman relation in society but that, on the contrary, capitalism is born from and depends on patriarchy. Capitalism, according to Mies, is a development of patriarchy, although one can see it not as in a linear, unique and uniform style of production but in a more complex articulation between patriarchy and race, culture, sexual identities and religion. All forms of capitalism are patriarchal derivatives, from the Democratic forms based on democracy as a support system, to the functioning of the market and a cultural political platform based on Creation Theology (Misfud 1997: 24), to Savage Capitalism, constituting economy as an end in itself. In this context, globalisation as an extreme form of neo-liberalism may just be the latest development of this articulation, especially in relation to the totalitarian enforcement of neo-liberal economic policies. Following Mies, the main characteristics of capitalism could be considered to be a binary economic epistemology, or a process of capital accumulation based on hierarchical exploitation (based on the man–woman heterosexual relation) and dominion produced through warfare and force. As with every economic model, we seldom know or need to know the theoretical framework of capitalism (or its motivation) but by its fruits we know them very well. People do not need to know how to define capitalism or patriarchy, or be theologically literate, but they know what these conceptual frames produce in their lives by experience. The conceptual economic model is mediated in our everyday lives by the reality of its implementation, that is, the motivations or 'spirit' of the model (legitimisation processes); the judicial institutions created in relation to this and the technical mechanisms which guarantee the implementation of the economic model (Mifsud 1997: 11–12). Therefore, we realise that in analysing an economic model theology has very often been partial. By this we mean that instead of understanding the wholeness of the model, theologians sometimes just take one aspect, looking for instance for the 'spirit' of the model on its own. This could be one of the reasons why patriarchalism and capitalism have never been taken seriously enough amongst liberationists. They would concentrate on the spirit of capitalism following homosocial constructions, but then contemplate how the implementation of such a 'spirit' is negative in relation to women. Following Mies, I consider that patriarchal criticism seems to be pertinent to all these constitutive elements, and unless they are fully considered in their multiple interaction (together with other co-ordinates such as race and religion, for instance), we lose sight of reality. In particular, we lose sight of an important chain of what Laclau and Mouffe call struggle's equivalences (Mouffe 1992: 372). Men and women are sexually posited in different moments and spaces of oppression in the three constitutive elements of an economic model, and their struggles need to be linked while differences are respected.

In colonial processes, patriarchalism has reinforced chains of oppression when the male colonial subjects felt that their maleness was diminished by the colonial masters. Christianity has been present in the stages of institutionalisation and the organisation of procedures of economic distribution through the distribution of several myths, such as myths of divinely-ordained racial superiority, men's superiority and mastery over women and nature, and economic superiority. As part of the colonial Christian mythopoetics, the male colonisers genderised their subjects as women, depriving them of the male status of their own patriarchal societies and therefore produced in them a reinforcement of heterosexual stereotypes regarding women in their societies in forms which were sometimes unknown before colonisation processes. Women have been forced to react to that with different strategies of rebelliousness, including the 'masking' of themselves into the excessive feminine stereotypes socially organised in order to survive. What I recognise sometimes as a syndrome of split personality amongst women in my country may be related to this. Women master the art of assuming different gendered expectations amongst different groups in society: Capitalist, job orientated expectations, churches' expectations and cultural expectations related to the marriage or love market. However, the colonial masters also produced a theological artefact, such as the concept of the native, or in Latin America, of '*el Indio*'.This concept was not developed scientifically but theologically. It is a false frame of reference which conveys a false historical meaning, and it produces the verbal illusion of an explanation born of a metaphysical, ethical and logical conquest (Mendiola 1994: 459). The concept of *el Indio* also implies a continuity that according to Dupeyron (Dupeyron 1992) ignores the break produced by the *Conquista*. Developmentalists who engage in the cultural paradigm without acknowledging this tend to use the continuity of the conceptualisation of natives and native forms of organisation which in fact, according to Mendiola, may just be a disorder, or 'a belic device' masking an imperialist rationalisation of other people's lives (Mendiola 1994: 458).

Heterosexuality is the ideology of patriarchalism, and also its true God, and Christianity reinforced this alliance of heterosexually constructed gods in continents such as Latin America. As Mendiola says, the concept of 'woman' is like the concept '*indio*': they are equivalent illusions (Mendiola 1994: 460). Heterosexuality became divinised, and that which cannot be discussed, or re-theorised, because it has God-like qualities: like capital in Marx's criticism, it has become an abstract concept, a given, a meta-narrative which claims to be natural and not created. In the Third World, a reallocation of different meta-narratives has constructed our souls. For Latin Americans, the birth of modernism (although modernism has had more than one emergence in history) was the praxis of violence of the *Conquista* of América, when the Christian meta-narrative of centre and periphery was constituted (Dussel 1995: 11). Our souls are in reality *colonial souls*, born of that religious violence based on exclusion, and exclusion seems to have its origin in sexual violence or the primary conceptualisation of the world according to sexual differences. In Latin America, Christian people are the descendants of mothers raped by Christians, in their bodies and in their religious beliefs, cultures, philosophical and economic systems. Christian theology performed here as an overvalued penis, in a globalisation mode of international intervention and destruction of the local state, but without any of the benefits of decentralised thinking. This is our biggest contradiction: to recognise that we have a faith born of an entanglement of patriarchal traditional cultures in alliance with oppressive gendered Christian and political ideologies. Those elements are still present.

However, in the new market of souls that the colonies were, not only were the goods of salvation dispensed but their needs were *created* too. The people of the Original Nations did not need 'redemption' or 'eternal salvation'. They had their own provision and distribution of goods for the soul, according to their beliefs, but superfluous Christian beliefs created superfluous needs too. Those needs and their political framework were and still are, a form of sexual discourse which fulfils functions of 'differentiation in Sameness' (Evans 1996: 3–4). Now all Latin Americans were supposed to have a commonwealth of Christian needs and desires to be fulfilled, apart from political struggles. National identities became entangled with a mixture of Christian patriarchalism and their own heterosexual cultural ideologies, and even after a period of postcolonial critical thinking on theories of development, the cultural subsuming of sexual injustices under the guise of traditions continues underlining the whole praxis of development (Kiely 1995: 156). It is obvious that the developmental crisis cannot be sorted if we remain in the terrain of the heterosexual ideology which sustains capitalism and Christianity, although we must recognise also that there is a patriarchal substratum in the 'gift economy' system, as used for instance in Paraguay, or in any other form of economy and/or religious exchange. In that sense, deconstruction is a very welcome cultural project too. Deconstruction is not destruction, nor is indecency or improper behaviour destructive. On the contrary, we need to leave decency and advocate a deviant, per/verted Sexual Theology for social change. Deviancy is a category which can act as a reminder that an economic model, such as theology, is basically a social relationship model, conceptually linked to social science theory and classifications of anatomy and erotic conduct, definitions of nature and needs and desires, while implementing laws and regulations to ensure its efficacy in society. Therefore, the criticism of one implies the other too. Let us consider, for instance, the main point of dismissal of Savage Capitalism, as it has been made by liberationists and developmentalists alike. It is basically summed up in one phrase: Savage Capitalism has made a Grand Narrative of economy, or a God-like narrative of life. Why a Grand Narrative? Because it has the following characteristics:

1   It implies a natural order, a pre-discourse or metaphysics of presence in Derrida's term.
2   In that sense, capitalism is almost a cultural ontology, with a theory of being and a metaphysics of the world uniquely constituted.

However, the liberationist critique is inadequate if it remains only in the sphere of accusing Savage Capitalism of having taken the place of God (such as in the traditional idolatry argument from Hinkelammert or Dussel); if, by doing that, we are just replacing one omniscient theo/social authority with another. One meta-narrative is replaced by another, and the whole debate gets reduced to their particular hegemonic struggles. Meanwhile, we are not reflecting on the fact that capitalism is an embodied, incarnated theory which creates a cultural reality based on having a certain being and a certain body. As such, capitalism has answers for drives, and desires which characterise the nature of a person. These are based on binary oppositions, dualistic thought and discourses of subordination. It is interesting to notice that it is not only that capitalism is based on inequalities in the labour force, especially gender inequalities. It is more than that, because it resembles the heterosexual assumption of the naturalness of a model of thought based on two sexes and their specific constructed relationship based on an invested erotic model.

To replace hegemonic divine concepts by deviant (unnatural) styles of thinking, helping people to develop their own identities outside the closure and boundaries of theo/social systems, could provide more scope for alternative patterns of thought and actions than providing the locus for a mere struggle between patriarchal meta-narratives. The concept of the 'Structures of Human Sacrifices' (Hinkelammert: 1991: 20) is effective in relation to the external debt, but it must be applied first of all in relation to sexual sacrifices. Hinkelammert has said that modernisation was brought about by a structure of human sacrifices, literally, the death of the poor who paid with their lives for the new economic and political conditions (Hinkelammert 1991: 43), but Mary Daly had made this point before, in her powerful denunciation of the assassination of women throughout history, sacrificed to die the many deaths of patriarchal society (Daly 1978). Christianity has been an immense sacrificial altar for women, and, moreover, its life seems to have been nurtured by that sacrificial death of the *Other* throughout history.

The problem is that heterosexuality stratifies and compartmentalises our vision of the present, constructs our past according to its own categories of important selected historical events, and therefore, controls our community projections of the future. When we read and listen to stories about developmental initiatives, we usually find that these are stories of tension not only between men and women in their gendered and sexual roles in a certain moment in society but something more important than that shown in the struggle of women to overcome the geographical limits of our heterosexual frame of thought. Stories of developmental initiatives are somehow sexual stories too, or erotic dilemmas where the allegiance needs to be either to patriarchalism or to economic liberation; or faith or social consciousness. We are not far from the words of Diego, the Cuban gay who needed to say *'Entre una picha y la cubanía, la cubanía'* (between a dick and Cuba, I choose Cuba). This happens because the politics of traditionalism reinforces heterosexual idealism like its own version of the book of Genesis. Any deep challenge to the story of the mythical origins of societal harmony is seen as part of the problem and not of the solution. Therefore, the Chile of Pinochet reinforced women's domestic role through *Centros de Madres* (Mothers' Centres) and Nigeria in 1983 forbade women to use trousers and tried to *discipline* the country in traditional heterosexual discourses (Waylen 1996: 99). The term 'discipline' is crucial here, because heterosexuality is a discipline of bodies, including political ones, although not by mutual consent as in S/M practices. However, developmental projects, as we are going to see later, do not differ radically from this enforced disciplinarian effort, because they are also based on gendered visions and assumptions about economy and politics. Theologies of Development may also be at risk of becoming inheritors of the title of 'Alexander the Corrector'.

I will be referring here to the concept of 'heterosexualism' instead of patriarchalism for the sake of conceptual efficacy. Heterosexualism is a less contested and more pervasive assumption than patriarchalism (a historical term), and it is more straightforward when addressing the core of meta-discourses. I use the term following Adrienne Rich's classical definition of heterosexuality as a compulsory political institution with different but interconnected manifestations (Rich 1980). Using this concept has the advantage of challenging us at the level of current theological praxis including action and reflection on justice and development. Heterosexuality is responsible for the capitalist metaphors based on male body experience reflected in concepts of growth, penetration, determinism, etc. But metaphors are texts in miniature, where the new meaning produced by the metaphoric twist is nurtured by the assumed commonplace of the metaphor itself (Ricoeur 1978). It is not a coincidence that the paradigm that there are two genders founded in two biological sexes began to predominate in Europe in the eighteenth century, when the economic trend showed a tendency towards domesticity and the objectification of wealth. The housewife and decent mother was a concept born at that time, when family was a concept with class connotations. It is useful to remember here that capitalism was born from the family institution. Still, all these discourses on family, decency and capitalism support each other. For instance, the Mothers of *Plaza de Mayo* in Argentina were called *las locas* of *Plaza de Mayo* by the media. *Locas* means 'mad' but in the gendered discourse of Argentina, the term mad when applied to a woman implies two different connotations: mental madness or prostitution. The political challenge of the Mothers was delegitimised on the sexual grounds of the rules of decency apart from a discourse of rationality. To challenge the military regime which used the 'Chicago boys' economic rules in my country required some indecent contestation, coming from mad women and at other times from lesbian and gay communities.

Indecency, theology and development

Our basic assumption is that all political theories are sexual theories with theological frames of support. Moreover, all the corpus of Systematic Theology including Liberation Theologies are, as we have seen, Sexual Theologies since they are based on a simple set of ontological and material assumptions about sexuality and women's humanity. The sexual construct is at the base of theology and economics at the level of what is desirable and the strategies for achieving that including counting the costs. The relation with God has been constructed as sexually unequal, as a centre-periphery relation, subdivided in a multiplicity of sub-peripheries. Historically there has not been an equal relationship theology between God and humanity, and centre-peripheries models disguise the plural fields of oppression in the same country or regions of that country. In spite of the superficial message of equality in theological discourse, different sets of needs, duties and spiritu-

ality have been devised for different people. Typically, the theology women
and non-heterosexuals have been receiving for centuries is different from the
one heterosexual men have been receiving. The divisions of class and race,
not to mention sexualities, complicate this fragmented spiritual teaching to
the limits. Those theologies have been using one pattern of sexuality and a
rigid genderisation code while addressing themselves to people who have
substantial differences in their experience of life. Yet, we pretend that there is
a basic normative unitary theological discourse that we may follow with
some minor differences 'in interpretation'. Interpretation becomes here a
mere device to unify, to hegemonise discourses which are in need of
subversion and per/version and diversification in issues and in methodology.
However, theology has problems with plurality, and so does capitalism. In
reality, we are not living in a capitalist world, as least not in The Capitalist
World. We live in a world where several economic theories coexist. Parts of
the northern areas of Argentina have a quasi-feudal structure. The
Fazendados (Land owners) in Brazil may still have slave workers, but we also
have, for instance, the feudal economy of love which makes women decent,
that is, marriage structures and the family based on ownership and
immobility. Local economies in Third World countries are seldom studied
seriously or counted except to be subsumed in capitalism. There is no
novelty in saying that the structure of capitalism in terms of hegemonic
thought reminds us of North Atlantic theology, but what is the basis of this
common thought? I claim that it is heterosexualism, not as a sort of
transparent foundation but as a strong force in the developing of essentialised identities in our political society, while mixed with different and
conflicting ideological projects.

Theology follows political thought, and political thought follows heterosexual principles

It is well known how the discourse of development as a theme and as an
interpretative theological category was superseded by Latin American
Liberation Theology at the beginning of the decade of the 1960s. Basically
the Theology of Development, as it was called, came from the same concerns
as those of the liberationists. Both were based on theories of the centre–
periphery relationship of power. Developmental Theologies saw the centre as
a model and a promoter of models for development while Liberation
Theology saw it as the problem. The first was a project from modernism; the
second questioned the modernity myth of production of goods and their
distribution. In this last point, distribution, we find the problem of the
construction of the identity of the subject, and especially the colonial
subject, because s/he is the subject who produces and needs the goods. In
Liberation Theology, liberation from the centre with all its cultural and even
religious implications was the goal and the strategy for development, because
the positioning of the Latin American subject changed. At the core of

Developmental Theology was a belief in the modernisation discourse and evolutionary theories of progress. It is important to notice that Marxism was used in its orthodox form by developmentalists, since imperialism was perceived as a process in the stages of the division of the labour force, which would contribute to a new phase of capitalism. Once again, we are confronting androcentric body theories of progress, unity, accumulation and reproduction, i.e. a difference which excludes, for instance, contradictory women's body categories such as menstruation, birth, abortion and meno-pause where the body changes, fluctuates and continues or ceases, in order to start life without reproduction. Other bodies (or the bodies of the *Other*) are irregular, cyclic or even multiple, inclusive bodies such as those of trans-sexuals. One wonders how indecent would it be for us to listen to sexual stories to reflect theologically on them at the crossroads of theology, sex and economics? But following an Indecent Theology of denunciation of sameness, while acknowledging identity formation as necessary, is a process of coming out from closets as human beings, questioning sexual assump-tions. This could help us to find space for the alternative in economics, which comes from embracing diversity in identity beyond dualism.

Liberation Theology, born from the contradictions and divisions of orthodox Marxist praxis in Latin America and the hardship of the dictatorships of the 1970s, stressed socialism and revolution. Production was the object of liberationist theological analysis and not the circulation of goods and commodities as in developmentalism. Today, Latin American analysts have been moving towards a post-Marxist approach, de-emphasis-ing the role of the working classes in the struggle and centring their discourse on pluralism. Amongst other things, in practice this means that socialism could be achieved effectively by stimulating secular and even religious alliances amongst popular movements in resistance to oppression and inequality. This bird's-eye view of the changes to Marxist analysis in Latin America could also be applied to the evolution of the Developmental/ Liberation Theology discourse in the continent. In fact, from orthodox Marxism to post-Marxism we find a reflection which has been mirrored theologically in the liberationist movement. With the exception of the Argentinian theologian Enrique Dussel, who claims that we need to revise original Marxist thought beyond the 1930s commentaries on Marx, liber-ation theologians are now either engaged in the debate on development from a Culture and Gospel discourse, or confronting the evil of globalisation, for instance, from traditional categories such as idolatry (Hinkelammert), a philosophy, almost an ontology, from the poor (Scannone), or the eco-theology of Leonardo Boff. It is no longer class analysis on its own which is being stressed in political Latin American theology, but, and especially from women, a de-hegemonisation and the need for intercultural and secular or inter-religious alliances to build a democratic, populist opposition to the present systems of oppression. One may ask why Latin American women theologians have developed practically nothing on the lines of systematic political reflections. Latin American women's theology, as we have seen in previous chapters, the theology with 'women's eyes', has remained in the domestic more than in the public side of the economic gaze. In general, we can say that from Dussel's Marxist negative theology of unmasking the idols of capitalism to the early work of Porfirio Miranda's theology which sees Marx as an example of Christian critical theology, by way of Hinkelamert's critique on the globalisation process (from idolatry) and the pluralist, post-Marxist discourses of Latin American feminist theologians, there is something that remains in this debate, and this is the essential *decency* of our political and theological discourses. There are essentialist sexual assumptions about womanhood and manhood which are seldom addressed and which come from *Machista* ideology. Roles may be discussed; sexuality, never. The exceptions can be seen in considering the debate about equality in some forms of Liberation Theology and in the more evolved thought on 'equality in difference' of postcolonial approaches. However, equality presupposes a heterosexual model which even dares to claim that heterosexuality is a homogenous category with a constructed subject with whom women must be equal, which is not far from the old developmentalist theories which encouraged countries from the periphery to aim for the progress of the centre. In other words, this is a model of welfare as equality with the hegemonic powers which have constructed themselves, precisely, by a logic of hierarchies and inequality. This is faulty thinking. As de Beauvoir observed, 'one is not born a woman', and may I add, one is only legitimised as a woman by theology, culture and political thought. The discourse on gender and development, if it is incorporated into discourses of essentialism and equality, only reinforces the lack of options and decisions that women may take at micro or macro economic–theological levels. This happens because, historically speaking, women do not make social pacts but are the objects of socio-economic pacts and their possibilities of political struggle depend on concessions made to them. Equality is part of the discourse of essential decency (Archenti 1994: 26). It fixes limits or boundaries and defines strategies of action too. Women who want to irrupt into current political and theological thought need to question the decency, that is, the sexual constructions underlying the sacred legitimisation of conditions of production and reproduction in their societies. Indecent Theology is a call for a deviant Sexual Theology, which would challenge the normalcy of women's oppression in its ultimate consequences. By this we mean that from that dialectic of decency/indecency in our lives we must think politics and theology at the same time. The starting question may be: what do the constructions of sexuality and gender tell us about God, human rights and development? What do sexual stories tell us about hegemonic thought and subversion, the confinement of imagination and alternative models of thought? Binary thought can only be challenged in theology and capitalism alike by people whose bodies are living parables of transgression. From patterns of love and friendship between lesbians, gays, bisexuals and transsexuals, from stories of adultery and fetishism, we may be able to learn something about difference. Recently, theological essays on theology and development have started to talk about the 're-awakening' of Third World countries, especially in relation to globalisation. For instance, essays on the 're-awakening of Africa' or the 'coming back to life' of Latin America. This 'Sleeping Beauty' talk seems to assume that in our traditional cultures (or what has been left of them) there was a higher consciousness and understanding sadly asleep which is now awakening again. In an article entitled precisely 'Africa is Re-Awakening', Sam Kobia of the 'Unit of Justice, Peace and Creation' of the World Council of Churches writes the following in relation to this:

> While the church should be concerned about, and indeed support, the building of democratic systems, even more fundamental to her social calling is the articulation and promotion of democracy as a vision. That would be in keeping with the prophetic messages of the Old Testament prophets, and with Christ's Gospel. At the centre of such a vision are three basic elements – equality, liberty and justice. These are part of the jubilee motif as announced by Jesus at the beginning of his ministry.
>
> (Kobia 1998: 7)

While not disagreeing in principle with this rhetoric of prophetism and justice, one may ask what justice, what equality and what liberty are at the core of the theological reflection on globalisation processes? Are these the Enlightenment ideals? African cultural concepts? Or some general universalisation which requires us never to be explicit about their tenets? Which equality is our idea of equality? Does it include diversity and even opposition? In the same vein, one can also ask if Jesus, living two thousand years ago in Palestine under Roman occupation and Patriarchal Judaism, would have had a concept of, say, 'equality' as we now have at the beginning of the twenty-first century. Are 'Kingdoms' egalitarian projects? This lightness in our theological reflections betrays our inability to think of original concepts which can be rooted in real human experiences beyond the approved texts of the church and with strategic values for change. The reality is that our cultures (including our colonial Christian inheritance) cannot deny that heterosexual constructions of divine and political order existed before colonisation processes, and that in them lie many of the problems of our present crisis. Reading texts from some of the indigenous women in Chiapas who may be Christian, we discover many cultural and indigenous religious traditions of dehumanisation, which seem to belong to the same heterosexual matrix where international trade agreements and church declarations are made. For instance, in a dialogue between the *Comandante* Ramona and the *Comandante* Javier of the *Ejército Zapatista de Liberación Nacional*, issues of the traditional sexual contracts in the indigenous communities become more explicit. It is interesting to notice that in his interview, we are told that *Comandante* Javier became emotional when telling how they had inherited old traditions from their great-grandfathers which, as he says, 'are very sad ones because in indigenous communities the life of women is miserable'.

> Women usually get up between 2 and 3a.m. to prepare some food, and as soon as the sun is coming up, they leave the house with their man (to go to work in the field). The man goes on his horse and the woman runs after the horse with her child on her back. When they arrive, they do the same work: they harvest or collect coffee, but when they go home, the woman does another job because she needs to cook. Many of us men do not have a consciousness of this, and we just give orders, but for the woman, well! (¡de veras!) The children are crying and she needs to look after them, and grind the maize for tortillas and also clean her house, and very late at night she goes out to wash clothes because she couldn't do it during the day.
>
> (Pérez and Castellanos 1994)

Yet the Zapatistas understood that the political and economic changes they required would entail a radical revision of gender roles and sexual assumptions in their cultures. Some Zapatista guerrilla women known as *insurgentes* refuse to marry in a society where women's reproductive role is their traditionally meaningful mission in life, and although they do not deprive themselves of sexual relations they use contraceptive systems which allow them to join the struggle for liberation at the level they require. The *insurgentes* constitute 30 per cent of the Zapatista women's population. Choosing this lifestyle is a very daring action which challenges gender roles in their society at a deep level, and transgresses cultural identities without resorting to Jesus' thought twenty centuries ago, or at least, to the easy Jesus construction of unreflective, decent theology. As far as I am aware the only other case of Latin American women who seldom marry are the *Mai do Santos* or priestesses of the Brazilian Umbanda religion, as they would like to remain legally free (although neither celibate nor childless) in order to have a relationship with God not mediated or obscured by their legal subjection to a man, which happens in marital contracts especially amongst poor women. Christian theology cannot match these new developments in socio-political and sexual understanding unless it can confront the limitations of heteronomy as a hegemonic system of organisation and thought. For instance, as we have already noted, in the New Testament Jesus stopped the bleeding of the woman who touched him but did not challenge the menstruation taboos of his time. Repeating Jesus' praxis without challenging the sometimes sad decency of Jesus' own acts works as the sleep of reason which produces monsters. These monsters are the ones which end up reinforcing oppression. Indecenting Jesus and the tradition of his time is not always possible, but in many cases such work could give a more positive ground for finding heterotopic visions in community.

A case study on the sexuality of economics: the case of the shrinking penis

Continuing with a Sexual Theology of stories, we will refer now to a case which happened in Ghana in 1997. This is a sexual story from everyday life. Curiously, it was brought to my attention not by the *Tamale Culture and Development Seminar* of May 1997 (Tamale 1997) but by an article in an Argentinian magazine on the same subject. Both the Argentinian article and that from the Tamale Institute of Ghana present similar analyses, except for the fact that the African work engages in a dialogue with the described witchcraft mentality, while in Argentina this was not the case. This is a sexual story in which we can engage ourselves and start a theological and sexual–economic dialogue.

Briefly, the substance of this story seems to have originated in Southern Ghana, and to have been later extended to Tamale in February 1997. The Argentine article I refer to describes the case briefly and ends with the question of whether such cases could also start to occur in Argentina, and even mentions some cases which have been reported to the media and could have been similar in nature. The shrinking penis phenomenon refers to the experience of a man who, having been greeted by another in the street, by shaking hands, found afterwards that his genitalia had shrunk. The solution to this, as seen from the victim's perspective, was either to offer money to a third man who would appear on the scene offering to remedy the problem, or to kill (or beat) the suspected perpetrator of the shrinkage. Police were called on many occasions although it usually proved that the complaint was false. For instance, when the alleged victim went to a public toilet with a policeman, the latter usually verified that, in his opinion, the penis of the victim looked of normal size. However, instead of this being taken as a proof that the accusations were false, the result was sometimes the opposite. It was taken by the crowd to mean that if the accused man was caught and beaten the witchcraft could be reversed. Therefore, if the police had arrived after the perpetrator of the shrinkage was punished by the crowd, that action was viewed as restorative of the penis's order. The impact of a witchcraft mentality in the community was very damaging, especially in terms of creating a culture of suspicion and mistrust. It also caused religious problems related to traditional Muslim greetings amongst Dagomba men in the streets, since men became wary of touching other men in case their virile organ disappeared. Also, it produced considerable disruption of the developmental work organised on a community basis, as with for instance NGOs or other local developmental projects. Homosolidarity was lost. This was a case of penis disorder with physical, economic and theological implications. Correlated with this case which brought empirical corroboration of the belief in damaging witchcraft, were also the cases of Ghanaians resisting the polio immunisation campaign for fear of vaccines carrying the AIDS virus, or the outbreak of meningitis in upper Ghana which resulted in the killing of many old women accused of witchcraft. Therefore, while men were shrinking other men's penises, foreign vaccines were allegedly also trying to shrink the size of the healthy population of women and men, and old women went shrinking villages of children, young women and men by afflicting them with meningitis. This happened amongst people who were struggling with the shrinkage effects of poverty in their midst; decrease in salaries and constricted economies: people who needed to 'tighten their belts' and saw their lives becoming shrunken, narrower in hopes and possibilities day by day. If shrinkage comes from witchcraft, then economic theories may be another form of the 'Book of Shadows'. It is true that the witchcraft mentality is seen by many as an obstacle to development work in various countries, and a number of different measures are taken by developmental workers, such as living in the so called witches' villas (compounds where women accused of witchcraft are condemned to live on their own), or dialoguing with priests from traditional religions, but the sexual and economic project of witchcraft persecutions is not always addressed.

The analysis of this case by the Tamale Institute of Cross Cultural Studies was related to the Gospel and Culture style of reflection. It shows ambiguity in condemning the witchcraft mentality as false consciousness, whilst accepting it as part of the community's world-view. It outlines the weak points of the witchcraft mentality, such as the inability of people to take responsibility for their own actions, thus blaming the witches, along with suspicious attitudes towards the community instead of solidarity and fatalism. It was stressed that self-reliance programmes for development need to overcome this through education, gradual changes involving patience and renegotiations and involving traditional models when trying to resolve conflicts. For instance, this may involve dialogue with Diviners and Shrine Custodians and interventions from NGOs, also through dialogue with Diviners. This is the Gospel, Culture and Development ideal of a dialogue to respect traditions and mediate only in times of crisis, for instance, in cases when development projects are at risk. Therefore, the shrinking penis phenomenon was seen at the level of community solidarity and work as homosolidarity, as if homosolidarity were the basis of community life. It is interesting here to note that the case of the shrinking penis tests reactions to the symbolic alterations that a diminished penis can inflict on community life, while women's clitoridectony in Ghana (a reduction in size of women's sexual organ and pleasure) is not seen as affecting community life, neither as an act of witchcraft nor as a punishable act. This is culture, theology and tradition. The ingrained witchcraft mentality in our current theological reflections is reflected in men's fear of seeing a diminishing penis or phallocratic discourse in areas of body control and economics. In the area of body control, if a man shrinks the penis of another, this could suggest that there is a man and not a woman who threatens virility and a reproductive understanding of sexuality, thus reinforcing taboos on homosexuality. Meanwhile, development projects are trying to address and challenge the diminishing of women's bodies in poor countries, for instance through hunger, violence and genital mutilation. Also, if women cannot be workers except in the unpaid area of motherhood (as sexual procreators and child carers), there is a diminishing body of women who can do whatever they want. In the area of economy and theology, the phallus of heterosexual hierarchies and assumptions is validated by subjugation and discrimination in the workforce and by male authoritative discourses of the sacred (the divine construction of the phallus of God). Development, however, is more than the idea of self-sustained community programmes for immediate relief and future progress. Development is about consciousness raising, and the community's critical awareness of traditions and mentalities.

In the case of the Tamale community, questionnaires and dialogue with the local people showed overwhelming support for the belief in witchcraft, even if partial. That is to say, although many cases such as the shrinking penis phenomenon could be thought to be the product of collective imagination, the participants in these reflections claimed that there was some truth in what was said to have happened. We need to confront ourselves with the truth of the Dagomba proverb: 'there is no smoke without fire', or perhaps we could make a new proverb from this experience such as 'there is no penis which seems to be small which is not small'. However, witchcraft mentality and the fear of losing penises is not just a Ghanaian phenomenon. It is also at the core of the Argentinian external debt. The problem is that we reflect on witchcraft mentality with the colonial naïveté which constructs the *Other*. The *Other* is constructed as pagan and primitive, and that reinforces our belief in hegemonic capitalistic thinking as non-primitive and civilised, but in reality, this binary pair of oppositions does not exist. Heterosexual economic thinking, and not popular thought, is the primitiveness we need to denounce.

Reflecting on the external debt and the shrinking penis phenomenon in Argentina

Studies of the history of the external debt in Argentina show the theological linkage between witchcraft mentality and the current process of impoverishment and disempowerment of the poor (Vitale 1986: 181–200). According to statistics from 1997, every person in Argentina, including newborn children, is in debt to the tune of $2600 each. In five years we cannot say how much the debt for living will be. We are living with the legitimisation of slavery. The debt changes human bodies and the shape of whole communities, and produces shrinkages too. Children go to school with alopecia; cholera and illnesses such as TB can be registered even in the midst of the wealthy capital city of Buenos Aires. Hunger changes bodies too, through swollen stomachs, mouths without teeth and malnourishment affecting brain function. It also changes the body language of the people through uncertainty and fear. Why do the poor tend to look smaller? Is it due to the way they hunch their tired backs? Why do poor women look down? Capitalism always risks sexual boundaries, in the sense that the market does not respect gender positions at certain levels although it is not true to say that the market is gender blind. Still, in Latin America there are collisions between patriarchal expectations and gender ones. The latter seem to be built on theoretical assumptions: 'Our grandmothers stayed at home and cleaned and cooked, and cared for children.' Some may have done, but other grandmothers worked hard, didn't have a husband, hated children or were not even heterosexual women. My great aunt was a lesbian and did not care to cook, nor did she like to stay at home and even when she was seventy-five years old she systematically went out for meals with her partner. Capitalism shrinks bodies and memories in a thousand different ways, and so does heterosexualism. If the streets at night have no women walking for fear of rape, there is a shrinkage of humanity at night. If people do not get jobs or lose those they have because of a different sexual orientation, there is a shrinkage in the labour force.

In Argentina, the external debt policy was born from patterns of shrinkage through fear of the size of the masculine power and hegemonic thought of the army, that heterosexual patriarchal institution *par excellence*. The external debt was contracted by a dictatorship working with the assumption of a male alliance between the State and divine symbolics. 'First the Pope, second the Nation and third the family' was the dictum of hierarchy imposed by the army, always looking for the consensus of *Machista* traditions. The faculties which had amongst their students high numbers of women, such as psychology, sociology and philosophy were closed down. In the concentration camps, women prisoners heard phrases such as *'Si es psicóloga, es puta'* (If she is a psychologist, she is a whore). Decency needed to ensure political and religious order in the country, because the economic crisis was a shrinking penis phenomenon. Male psychologists or philosophers were portrayed by the media as mad, and sociologists and lawyers as Communists (mad and evil), but women philosophers, sociologists, lawyers and especially psychologists were called whores, indecent women; they were amongst the most cruelly persecuted and most often kidnapped by state terrorism. These women were objects of fear because of their questioning of the Christian/patriarchal structures of thought taken as normative in Argentinian society. The Mothers of *Plaza de Mayo* are another example of defiance towards the political and religious values of society. The army needed to impose tough, harsh measures in all spheres of life including the economic, while guarding the decency and morality of these indecent, questioning activists. There were plans, supported by the church, to create a ghetto in Patagonia where lesbians and gays could live apart from society. These plans were made explicit and explained by a Roman Catholic bishop on TV in Buenos Aires.

James Nelson, in his classic work on Sexual Theology, has questioned the theological practice of overvaluing the phallus. He says 'in a man's world, small, soft and down pales beside big, hard and up' (Nelson 1992: 95). From an issue-based methodology, we may be able to see how God as a masculine constructed divinity supports the same discourse, and although Jesus has been considered as different in relation to the Father-God's rhetoric in some Feminist and Liberation Theology, due to the fact that he is theologically narrated as sexually neutral, that neutrality renders him powerless to counterbalance this sexual discourse. Witchcraft is a gendered social and religious activity and a female gendered concept. While for the military dictatorship in Argentina the discourse on order and decency in society was supported by order and decency in the church, from a distorted male spiritual conception, the political dissenters were seen as sexual deviants, that is homosexuals, lesbians or whores who by their political actions were a menace to the size and power of the military ideology. In a way, any heterosexual categorisation of the non-heterosexual is in a double tension of being resisted and needed at the same time. The non-heterosexual reaffirms the heterosexual ideal, while at the same time marginalising it. The same happens with the virility concept of the military regimes, which is always contested in highly patriarchal societies such as the Latin American one because the limits of homosociability are unclear and, by this position of unclarity, threaten ideal heterosexuality.

On torture and debts

The military Junta had a sexual project. It sexualised the so-called Communist menace using categories of *Machismo*. Graziano analyses this point from the perspective of the process of objectification of the enemy developed by military powers. The enemy was feminised or located outside the existent definition of virility. When human rights campaigners outside the country questioned at international level the systematic abduction and killing of citizens, the military Junta printed stickers with the legend: *Los argentinos somos derechos y humanos* (Argentinian people are straight and human). The word *derecho* in Spanish means both right and straight. *Derecho* also means a heterosexual man. The military Junta fetishised the patriarchal phallus and linked it symbolically to objects such as the *picana eléctrica*, that electric device of torture which had a privileged position amongst other forms of torture. The *picana*, a stick or club, was a tool invested with *Machista* power and used for the purpose of sexual rape (Graziano 1992: 158). Symbolically they represented a form of exchange with male sexual organs, a fetish.

Those men considered to be the enemy were not real men; they were considered feminised or gay. But women fell into another category, that of 'witches'. Witches (*brujas*) is another popular name for sexually deviant women in my society. The solutions were perceived as similar to the African case, that is, death to the accused, because they also represented a threat to virility. Even ecological interests were portrayed as the interest of feminised men and deviant women, in contrast with the interests of real macho men and real wives and mothers. The shrinking penis of an African man is somehow no different to the threat of shrinking hierarchical, *Machista* ideology which needs to be preserved intact, that is, hard and high, against the ill will of less than human rebels. This is the point: the enemy were dehumanised by a process of rendering them as powerless as women in a traditional society such as Latin America. The external debt was then contracted by an army in alliance with men using this ideology and at war against what we can call the penis disorder syndrome. The external debt was contracted under the National Security Doctrine which created a warlike internal conflict by establishing the theory of 'the enemy within'. This is witchcraft ideology; the enemy could be any man who shakes my hand, even if he is my brother. The enemy within has been described by the military Junta as a condition, or illness, which overtook people and created a menace without name, in a far deeper ontology than that which divided humanity into Communists and straight people. For instance, in a curious discourse during the peak of the dictatorial regime, a general of the Junta spoke about the disappearance of people in the following terms:

> The enemy do not have a flag or a uniform; moreover, the enemy do not even have a face. [Therefore] the enemy's fellow citizens and friends get confused [and think that the enemy] is a person like themselves [*lo confunden con lo propio*] and then, what happens is that they do not understand his absence [by abduction]. And only the enemy, if you were able to open his head, only he himself in the depth of his mind knows that he is the enemy.
>
> (Discourse from General Viola, 29 May 1979, quoted in Abós 1985: 31–2)

That enmity was not simply the enmity of a Communist Party. It was a vague and obscure inner subversion of thinking which acquires demonic character- istics. Therefore the policies imposed by the dictatorship were constructed from the values of subordination and forced labour, carried out under the auspices of theological thought, and deeply ingrained in sexual under- standings of life and society. 'Subordination and Courage' (*Subordinación y Valor*) was the motto. We never had such a highly heterosexual moral discourse as when people were disappearing in their thousands during the political persecutions in my country.

Ernesto Laclau, in a discussion about deconstruction, pragmatism and hegemony, considers that by and large, the goal of any political reflection in history has been the 'elimination of politics' (Laclau 1996: 65). By that, Laclau refers to the almost systematic process of elimination or regulation of any element of indeterminacy or ambiguity as found in any social structure. This is done for the sake of coherence. Theology has been through similar processes. As part of any relevant political strategy, the institution of the social can only succeed by what Laclau calls 'hegemonic victory over conflicting wills' (Laclau

1996: 66). Yet what Laclau calls for is the recognition of an element of 'structured undecidability', or dislocation, present in every social institution and for a reconsideration of the closure produced by hegemonic regulations in society. At the same time, these considerations open a door for us to understand how hegemonic decisions are made and to what extent they are limited by a dialectic undecidability/decision. At the core of this process lies the fact that political processes are transient although hegemonic, and that social pacts are rooted in contradictions and disagreements too. From there, liberation processes can start; for instance, in recognising the transience of sexuality and its instability. There are no 'real men and real women' as the military Junta liked to think, nor can political transgression be organised except outside the closure of Christian traditional Sexual Theology. Christianity has curtailed 'the possibility of profanation' (Bataille 1994: 127) and this is a political possibility too. Even in our fragmented postmodern world order, there is a core of coherence which cannot be profaned, perhaps due to the fact that coherence is rooted in a hegemonic decision for a heterosexual and exclusive world-view. One cannot challenge one without challenging the other. However, if we assume the characteristics of instability and contingency in the political discourse are taken seriously (Laclau 1996: 59), then there could not be a more democratic project than the deconstruction of sexuality in the social formation. Take, for instance, the discourse of the military Junta. It was firmly based on a decision about sexual mores. Pamphlets were distributed in schools teaching girls and boys how to dress properly, with pictures of girls with skirts and boys with short hair. There was even instruction on how to stand up properly: boys looking straight ahead and girls with their eyes slightly downcast. In contrast, the enemies were portrayed as young girls in trousers looking boldly into men's eyes (a masculine stereotype for less feminine and decent girls), while boys were portrayed as feminised with long hair and untidy informal clothes. It would be naive to conceive of these gender strategies as irrelevant in relation to the economic and political tactics which were deployed. We do not live in split realities but, on the contrary, people's identities are formed and reinforced, or split and shattered through the concurrence of a wealth of symbolic manifestations which provide a final closure and stability to *Other* discourses. Although there was resistance to the Juntas, it was never enough, perhaps due to the fact that the heterosexual symbolics were approved of and welcomed by many people who were brought up in a deep *Machista* culture and found it difficult to disengage a political discourse on the nation and a religious discourse on Christianity from gender and sexual roles in society. The contravening of these roles by any theology or political system qualify them as indecent.

Economic erections, global erections

Is globalisation a big *macho* thing? Would that be a negative statement? The answer may well depend on your sexual position, and on your submission to the inerrancy or otherwise of sexuality statements. Erections can hurt or disseminate pleasure and knowledge amongst people of different sexualities. Clitoridectomy is a surgical measure against women's erections. Global neo-liberalism has produced a decentralisation of the role of the State, whose function consists of being receptive to strategies developed at international economic levels. A battle of erections. At the same time, an open and competitive market acts as a co-ordinator of the economic actions of society, but also more than that, their relationships and praxis. Finally, market competition seems to be related to justice in the regulation of the efficiency of the process.

The market assumes a presence which is thought to be unique and pervasive, and is described by liberationists as 'idolatrous' (Hinkelammert 1991: 24). Yet, there is a breakthrough of social and political transgressions for transformation which might not have happened under the traditional paternalistic state, for instance the 'Movement of the People without Land', or the hundreds of popular organisations around issues of care for youth and children, or human rights. States may be fathers, but not necessarily good ones; the gender metaphor of State–Father is, as in the case of the God-Father, oppressive and small; they tend to shrink people instead of letting them grow. Globalisation processes have also been compared with casinos. Globalisation refers to a tremendous increase in international capital flow, with turnovers of up to US$1,500 billion on the foreign exchange markets circulating every day around the world. Paradoxically, only a small percentage of that money (about 2–3%) is used for production, national services and direct foreign investment. The global markets are characterised by speculative money or casino finance.[2] This casino finance system creates its own laws of survival and growth by policies of de-regulation and overruling of national laws and agreements. The elite of financiers are basically men trained in North Atlantic institutions. As a result of these policies, the economic instability of countries and the most vulnerable people has increased dramatically. Poverty gave way to a newer, more greatly feared form of social exclusion. People became disposable outside mechanisms of productivity. The casino economy does not have any forms of local control, as countries negotiate their interests under hegemonic rulers. Yet sexual economies are casino economies too, and few have ever blinked an eye to their exclusionary effects in society. For instance, cultural traditions, when confronted with Christianity, double gamble on women's lives in what are supposed to be their 'Father-Faiths' and 'Father-Cultures'. In a story told by the Kenyan theologian Grace Wamue about the suffering of a Kenyan woman, we find metaphors for neo-liberal globalisation, or casino processes too. Witchcraft, domestic abuse and a form of casino economy mentality which is sustained by the division between the domestic and the public realm of law and spirituality as it happens in globalisation processes, seem to interlink. The story told by Wamue is as follows:

My mother was married in 1950 in Church but unfortunately was bereaved in early 1954. . . . she was left . . . with two children and expecting a third one. To my mother, life became one long dark struggle against many odds. This was also the period of the struggle for Kenya's independence. She was left under the dominance of her father-in-law, who turned her into a slave. He forced her and her children to work for him; depriving them of any material support. She was turned into a beast of burden serving the big extended family of her husband's kith and kin.

She received constant beatings from her father-in-law, as well as abuse from his sons and their wives . . . all in-laws would gang against her; accusing her of all sorts of evils, mainly witchcraft and prostitution. Having had a Christian marriage, my mother could not enter into a leviratic union with any of the brothers-in-law. The Church highly condemned this. Unfortunately, the Church regarded and viewed her as a social misfit and a sinner . . . she was denied sacrament like holy communion and the children born after her husband's death were denied baptism.

(Wamue and Getui 1996: 43–4)

The widowhood case presented by Wamue is to be read at the intersection of several heterosexual/economic systems. The most important one is the issue of investment. Society invests in a woman, but the State cannot protect her efficiently, nor can Christian (foreign) intervention. She becomes exploited in the economic market and in the soul market too, because although the church seems to reject her, she remains a Christian person thus supporting the establishment at some level. The basic elements of the story may be considered as follows:

1   The widow is a redundant worker. She will not procreate her husband anymore and ceases to have a useful life.
2   The patriarchal rules which legislated for her life continue after her redundancy as procreator. She now needs to work hard. She is indebted for life (a slave) and so are her children. Her debt is quasi-ontological; she is a debtor and the enemy. Her whole sphere of rights is reduced to the domestic realm where women's rights are tenuous and overruled by legislation and custom.
3   Caught between Levirate traditions (to marry one of her husband's brothers) and the Christian overruling of this tradition, she inclines towards Christianity, although with such a family, who could blame her? However, Christianity shows no gratitude. Having lost domestic status, she loses church status too. She becomes *indecent*, and has more children after her husband's death.

As Wamue says, the community traditions which existed to protect widows such as Levirate custom, even if still oppressive, showed a certain flexibility in patriarchal thought which Christianity destroyed. Now she has become a redundant Christian too. Her slave work and her children's contribution must have produced an overflow of goods into that family, even a surplus of savings, but these were not to be used for her benefit. Beside this, she has become socially excluded, an outcast, reduced to invisibility and hardship in the midst of the wealth she is creating. Her sexual difference and probably her need for pleasure has led her to exclusion. Because this form of violence was sanctioned by society and even by the church (if only with the indifference shown towards her), the economic violence perpetrated and the oppression of this woman are a case of global violence. The woman is violated by a religious hegemony which invades the community's legislation on widowhood, and more than that, because gender categorisation, as in globalisation processes, deregulates and overrules women's lives, leaving little if any space for autonomy to live. However, it would be naive to accuse modernisation processes and the apogee of individualism (or secularism, which is not necessarily the case in Third World countries) as the culprit of these problems in community. One may ask Wamue, for instance, how it happens that a community orientated people, as she described her people, can show at times such a degree of indifference and lack of solidarity towards members of the society. Perhaps the answer is to be given in terms of communities built on homosolidarity values in struggle for supremacies of power. Take, for instance, our description of globalisation processes; they rely on a great deal of solidarity. No elite group could impose such processes with such force onto other countries if there were not many people supporting them. A widow would not be enslaved if other women were standing together against it. If the breakthrough of decentralisation could become a praxis in people's everyday life, then it would be revolutionary. The question here concerns heterose(x)olidarity. This form of homosolidarity profits from a multitude of alliances between social and religious myths, but globalisation also relies on alliances of myths such as free competition and equality.

Indecent Theology challenges the organic assumptions in our theological and economic structures built around the belief in these myths and their functions of obedience. Some of these functions may be visible or represent-able while others are domestic and invisible, but they provide meaning to our lives. For instance, in macroeconomic analysis, 'efficiency' can be defined as a shifting of cost from the public to the domestic sphere. An example of this is the 'care in the community' policy in Britain which makes hospitals more cost efficient by sending patients to be cared for by their relatives or friends. Meanwhile, the household work of women increases. 'Adjustment with a Human Face' is the name given to such initiatives, which assume, amongst other things, that women's work at home is part of leisure time and that households are units of common interest and duties. The binary opposition discourse permeates economic theory, which includes categories of mastery, submission of differences, organic developmental theories and conceptualisation of growth. The future becomes a better, revised version of the present. Equality discourses shake hands with the 'God the Father and Mother' discourse, while some people may ask why we need a God-Father or a God-Mother at all. Moreover, if there are concerns about sexual roles and their theological production, we should avoid metaphors of biological repro-ductive discourses. The problem starts when the parental divine metaphor entangled with the imaginary of a feudal structure of the family supposedly becomes a metaphor to contest capitalism, which is absurd. God-Father and the Trinity male society need to shrink their penises' (dis)proportion too. No wonder, many are now talking about the impasse in developmental thinking and/or in Christian theology alike. Globalisation, which has been criticised for using heavy sexual metaphors such as 'the penetrative ideology' or 'the new form of colonial rape', has not been challenged at its core, which is the universal claim of a model of erection and mastery. Indeed, globalisation, as some feminist economists have claimed, may be a rape process, a violation of people's rights; but the point is that that we should not assume rape as part of normal human experience, or consider even the inevitability of rape. If globalisation is only a case of overvalued erectitude and forcefully exercised mastery, a criminal act of power, it will be difficult to take an ethical stand apart from condemning it. However, globalisation also has some elements linking it to postmodernism which need to be considered too, such as decentralisation and changes in people's praxis.

How do we contest globalisation? If globalisation in the neo-liberal form is rape, should we be arguing with the rapists' ideology to see if it can be changed? This is the discourse of 'respect authority and negotiate as diplomatically as you can', which is advocated too many times at so many levels, from women advised to dialogue with husbands who mistreat them to factory workers prevented from going to their Trade Unions but, instead, having to negotiate with their superiors. Why not use women's historical experience of rape and fear as an empirical model from which strategies for change in current epistemology could come? Rape victims know that adjusting or adapting to gender-role expectations may not be conducive to surviving the criminal attempt, and that going outside the limits of gender expectations has more possibilities of success. From the leaflets of women's groups one reads of how not being polite with a stranger at night may save your life. They also remark on the difficulties that women experience in not being polite, shouting, and insulting in a deep, unfeminine voice, or crossing the street several times, if being followed. I have heard women asking 'How many times should one cross the street if one feels followed?' Women who have been attacked have sometimes related that they thought it was improper (indecent) or offensive towards the person who was following them (and they were unsure even if they were followed or if it was just a coincidence) to cross the street more than once. However, if the inner logic of patriarchal heterosexuality gets confused when a woman does not show the expected fear and submission which is part of the reward of rape, or the politeness and ethics of women's subordinate education, perhaps this could be applied to other levels of civic society. To contradict and to present new sexual models is then a prophetic task: the Mothers of *Plaza de Mayo* or the Widows in Guatemala have done that to some important degree. I was told that an important leader from the Metropolitan Community Church was surprised that, when visiting Buenos Aires years ago he was welcomed and a reception was organised for him by a community of poor transvestites. These were members of a Christian Community from a slum, who gathered to read the Bible and discuss politics every week as members of the MCC. They dressed with high heels and women's clothes, and their sexual identity gave them different perceptions and experiences of life which produced different challenges at political and religious levels. The leader's initial shock changed into some admiration for the work the church was doing, but the contradiction of sexual, political and religious models was highly and beautifully subversive. There is no transgression in theology as powerful as real transgressions of the patterns of stereotyped believers, and also beliefs.

In the same sense, we need to reflect on the lessons from the 'Reclaim the Night' campaigns to reconsider strategies for confronting structural adjustment policies. Or, is it not the case that women have been structurally adjusted for centuries? There are lessons on how people stop questioning things and acting in solidarity for their rights which come from women's traditionally divided loyalties between loving men and loving themselves. Moreover, the work done by women working in projects related to domestic violence could enable us to identify key mechanisms in the area of domestic violence and the strategies to end it, which could be applied to current strategic thought in opposition to the policies of Savage Capitalism. After all, domestic violence is public violence and encompasses ideas and strategical thinking from women's historical experiences which are part of the epistemology of the *Other*. Structural adjustment policies are a case of domestic violence economically institutionalised. Heterosexuality, as the main framework of economic ideas, needs to be rethought from lesbigay and even transsexual perspectives, based on different social experiences in dealing with hegemonies. This is issue-based theology, based on sexual stories of people at the margins of the heterosexual system who produce economic thought. It is time to consider whether we have been sleeping with the enemy for such a long time that we are blind to its presence. The plural discourse for subversion of hegemonic thought in economy will in the end subvert theological thought too. But such subversion needs to became an organised sexual transgression in order to be able to begin with that starting point of Liberation Theology which says that more important than having the right answers is the ability to ask the right questions. 'Decency' is what fits, in symmetrically formed binary thought. It is time to break the capitalist-heterosexual symmetry which produces clones. Clones will not ask the right questions, nor defy the constructed sameness of the discourses of theology, culture and development.

An Indecent Theology using deviancy as a methodological source, would have a better chance of challenging the accepted which is at the root of the powers which control and dehumanise people's lives. Indecent proposals in economics could decolonise our spiritual souls, which are also economic souls.

Sexually dubious, economically deviant: theology *contra natura*

> Sexuality is one of the concrete forms of the face-to-face relationship which is part of the game of 'human-sex-to-human-sex' (coitus) where the sexualization of the *Other* does not depend only on the genital biological level . . . but on the encounter of two exteriorities, two people who cannot leave aside the mystery and the freedom of the *Other*. If the *Other* is constituted as a mere object sexualised by an erotic intention of the subject, this act becomes *homosexual* and as such an *alienation* of the *Other* who is now (constituted into) a mere mediation of autoeroticism.
>
> (Dussel 1977: 72; italics mine)

> We know what Hegel has said: self consciousness has a wrong side but it does not know it. To which Francois Mauriac responded that he remembered as a child he believed that important people did not have bottoms. The irruption of praxis takes philosophy by its rear . . . To have an exterior space and to have a rear is the same. But to have a 'behind' is to have an unexpected exterior. And this happens to philosophy.
>
> (Althusser, in Navarro 1988: 56–7)

The rear of philosophy that Althusser refers to here is the idealist enterprise of dominating the world by subjecting every social practice to their own 'law of truth' (Navarro 1988: 58). That project which Althusser calls violent, because it entails an appropriation leading towards a hegemony of power/ knowledge in society, faces an irruption when confronted by a materialist approach. That irruption, or recognition of the invested interests of pre-tended universal and neutral philosophy, reminds us that even philosophical systems have a rear. Theology has a rear too, and the threat posed by questioning its sexual constructs has been seen as sodomy; an unnatural act/reflection or praxis *contra natura* which is against the utopia of the project of social justice and political liberation as heterosexualised. Enrique Dussel, for instance, considered homosexuality and lesbianism to be the enemies of the liberation project, and as such, part of what he claims to be the autoerotic individualist project of a hegemonic Totality (Dussel 1977: 117). And perhaps, after all, he is right, and this is a justified comment to make if we consider that only by irrupting into self-righteous hegemonic systems and confronting our enmity with oppressive sexual constructions will we be able to move forward. Dussel's concept of Totality, as so often in

Liberation Theology, is univocal: the oppressed–oppressor categories are subsumed into heterosexualism; good heterosexualism (reproductive) and bad ones (sodomy, for instance). Sodomy is an interesting concept which is indebted to nineteenth-century understandings of science and nature, under the influence of evolutionism (Van der Meer 1993: 187). It originated together with the concept that nature's evolution required to follow a certain order or it would degenerate and perish. For instance, arguments relating the supposed heterosexuality of animals (which has now been proved false) were used to naturalise sexuality. Natural and procreative were exchangeable terms for the sexual act and sodomy, mutual masturbation or other pleasures outside the limits of vaginal penetration were the basis of theological casuists, the judges' court of Christianity. But what was sinful in sodomy was not considered or at least it was far more than the sexual act relating penetrative sex between a man and another man, and was seen as a threat to the social order. Sodomy, by its mere structure of the man/man relating pattern, presented to society a fracture into the hierarchical men/women ethos; this was considered to be damaging for the life of society, the constitution of states and the relationship of humanity with God. According to Theo van der Meer, eighteenth-century political discourses from the Netherlands explicitly mention sodomy as a case for class insubordination as it threatens and weakens the borders between the rulers and ruled, the masters and subjects, the male as active and the female as the passive recipient of sex (van der Meer 1993: 186). The sodomite was thought to feminise his partner, making man become subject to man, instead of keeping the order of women being subjected to men. They were betrayers of sexual hierarchies, and incidentally, in eighteenth-century Netherlands they were penalised with the form of death reserved for cowards and for women, that is, garrotting (Van der Meer 1993: 197). The threat of homosexuality and lesbianism to Liberation Theology is of the nature of sodomy because it confuses hierarchies and removes the struggle for liberation from manly concerns and manly virtues which are represented, in the case of Dussel, as liberative and authentic, as opposed to the inauthentic and oppressive practices of European thought. The autoerotic threat is linked to the capitalist threat. In order to understand Dussel's theory of the sodomite war against Latin America, we propose to carry out here a parallel reading between Dussel's Philosophy of Liberation and a sexual story from Nicaragua.

On Queers, revolutionaries and theologians

In an article written during the time of the Sandinista revolution, Roger Lancaster analysed the story of everyday life in Nicaragua, and the relationship between a blouse and a boy called Guto (Lancaster 1997). The story of Guto is the story of coming out as a transvestite in Nicaragua during the revolution. This is the story of 'The Blouse'.

It was early evening at the end of a typically sweltering day in Managua. Aida, my *comadre*, had returned home from work with an exquisite rarity in Nicaragua's devastated economy, a new blouse, a distinctively feminine blouse, soft to the touch, with good thread-work and careful attention to detail (. . .) When Aida arrived home, she beckoned everyone come see her new garment. Her teenage brother, Guto, arose from where he had been lounging shirtless . . . With a broad yet pointed gesture, Guto wrapped himself in the white, frilly blouse, and began a coquettish routine that would last for fifteen or twenty minutes. . . . The seventeen year-old added a purse and a necklace to his ensemble. Brothers, sisters, even his mother, egged on this performance shouting festive remarks: *¡Qué fina, bonita muñequita!* (What a delicate, pretty doll!).

Guto added to his performance with make up and a skirt while Aida made the following remark to Lancaster: 'See Roger . . . Look, Guto's a *cochón* (Queer)'.

(Lancaster 1997: 9–10)

This story, whose simplicity is deceptive, is in itself a chapter of Latin American erotic economy. A *cochón* (*marica*, Queer; the word *marica* comes from a derivative of the name *María*) comes out spontaneously and playfully in the presence of his family who play the game with him in his imitation of a Drag Queen. Guto represents a Drag Queen because he is forming and informing his own identity. The question here is that the space of the public/private disappears in this story. The devastating economic situation of Nicaragua is present in that blouse, fruit of arduous exchanges with its owner from whom Aida is able to finally obtain it. The blouse, originally from the USA and symbolic of wealth amongst poverty and imperial economic abundance, in contrast with the restricted economy of the Contra war, becomes entangled with a symbol of femininity. The flowing movement between the private and the public spheres of life, which are not separated from each other in substantial ways, relates to a process of simultaneous formation of political representation and sexual identity.

Who is the subject of our political theology? What is the condition of representation in a political theology such as Dussel's Philosophy of Liberation? In Dussel's perspective, the erotic representation of the Latin American subject[3] depends on the heavy binary pair of oppositions and the genderisation of oppression. The *Conquistador*, the Coloniser or the Imperial systems, subjugated and exercised power over the Latin American continent in a metaphor full of overtones of heterosexual rape and sexual abuse.

In the process of the *Conquista* of America, the European not only dominated the indigenous men, but raped the indigenous women. Cortés had a sexual relationship with Malinche, an indigenous woman and the mother of the *mestizo*. The *ego cogito* has founded ontologically the "I Conquest" and the *ego* phallic, two dimensions of the domination of men over men [sic] but now it is [seen in] one nation over another, one social class over another. Sexuality is something like the reproduction of the political, economic and cultural domination.

(Dussel 1985: 100)

The European (the Spanish *Conquistador*, for instance) is then the one who brings about an erotic process of economic dependence in Latin America based on heterosexual violence, which draws women and alienated men into phallic, economic forms of domination which he supposes did not exist before in the continent (Dussel 1985: 101). These false assumptions, contradicted by history and by the indigenous people's particular ways of sexual oppression still preserved in Latin America, allow him then to say that men need to recover 'their lost sensibility' (sic) in a new way of relating with women which retains heterosexual principles but is liberated from erotic domination. Here we find another form of 'The Sleeping Beauty' theology, or the awakening of a Latin American non-oppressive sexual understanding and gender distribution of roles which never existed historically in the first place but which construct the Latin American persona to be represented.

Representation is an issue of transparency. According to Laclau, representation requires that condition of transparency. What is represented is some form of crystal clear transmission of an existing original (Laclau 1996: 48–9). In political terms, the struggle of representativity follows this hope. Liberation Theology re-presents the voice of the voiceless, the excluded from political participation, because class, sexuality and racial issues are still knives cutting across definitions of citizenship in Latin America. But as Laclau suggests, the act of representing adds to or supplements what is represented. It constitutes the identity of the represented. The issues of democratic representation in Latin America today are still debated towards a pretended sexual indifference, but the liberationist oppressor/oppressed dialectic is based on the sexual men/women division of labour and humanity. Dussel's fear of heterosexual deconstructionism shows the cul-de-sac of Liberation Theology, but at the same time, his model of exclusion acts as a paradigm to show us with clarity what it is that is excluded. Exclusions are living proofs of a reality which cannot be homologised and required for safety reasons to be compartmentalised into regional frontiers and ghettos of life and thought.

Guto's story, as analysed by Lancaster, tests this ground, because it works as a test for the person who is the witness of such an event (Lancaster 1997: 14). '*Un test para el testigo*'; these two words which are dissimilar in their epistemological origin, sound similar in Spanish: *test* and *testigo* (witness). A test is a trial and a method of discernment, a kind of laboratory practice, and a witness is the person or evidence presented about a fact. That fact, in the case of Guto, is a fact of sexual ambivalence and political disorder, in the laboratory test of the playful act of Guto's transvestism. Did we ever think that Sandinistas were *cochones* (Queers)? The Queerness of defying the established Somoza dictatorship and his foreign political supporters, which surpassed in numbers and in power the initial handful of ill-equipped rebels, is difficult to overlook. The Sandinista revolution was a Queer act because it defied the status quo, the normality of oppression, and by a strange means: a mixture of Marx, Latin American socialism and Christianity. Why then did we assume that such an abnormal movement was to be produced by 'normal' (decent) people? If we need to talk here about popular rebellion, we need to understand rebellion as integral rebellion. When people come out as people and take to the streets, some, like Guto, can do it with his fishnet tights on too. Dussel has not seen rebellion as integral. In Dussel's political ontology, which has been so influential in Liberation Theology, the sin of homosexuality and lesbianism (which he considers even worse than homosexuality) is, as in the eighteenthth-century Netherlands, the sin of hierarchical transgression. Martha Zapata, a Mexican feminist, in her own critique, has pointed out how for Dussel, sexuality outside the reproductive limits of the (ideal) heterosexual relationship and gender roles is a chaotic threat (Zapata 1997: 69–97). For Dussel, sexuality is a service (*servicial*; Dussel 1977: 73), performed within a scheme of biological determinants: the politically liberated Latin American heterosexual men and women do not oppress each other but complement each other in the factory and the home where children are raised. The love for social justice is based on that relationship which overthrows individualistic and egoistic capitalist ethos. Homosexuality is, according to Dussel, the category of 'sameness'; together with masturbation, it shows, in his opinion, that the other is destroyed and a person can only love its biological equal. Lesbianism is an extreme case; women sin by rejecting maternity and their ontological *apertura* (opening), which he relates to the Genesis account of creation (openness in the sense of the opening of the vagina as a metaphor for the opening to the world). In the same vein, sodomy is anti-Christian because it symbolises the desire of Adam to be 'a totality in himself', an arrogant individualist desire which excludes the *Other* or the Alterity of our relationships (Dussel 1977: note 374).

However, Guto's story defies Dussel's idealistic sexual theology. Transvestism is a carnal practice of what Lancaster calls 'the space in-between' (Lancaster 1997: 14). Neither here nor there, transvestism is a case of cross journeying between race, class and sexuality. This in-betweeness reminds us of Althusser's perspective on Marxism: not a total system but an Aleatory Marxism, opposed to what he calls 'Registered [trade mark] Marxism' (Navarro 1988: 33). This Aleatory Marxism proposed by Althusser is a materialism of encounters, of things that are added and may change the existing ones or contribute to them, but always in a space of contingency, of provisionality. Not only texts, but a 'simple gesture' is, according to Althusser, a contribution to this non-teleological Marxism: gestures such as Guto's coming out story, for instance, which adds new meaning to Marx's concept of 'sensuous practice' (Lancaster 1997: 25). Sensuous practice for Marx is that condition of human life which requires a relationship with the sensuous material world, as he criticised the objectification of that world, for instance, in the alienation of the worker's relationship to production (Easton and Guddat 1967: 290). Transvestism is a gratuitous sensuous practice; risky, ambivalent, impractical as a game. That impracticability makes of it a popular sexual story to be rejected by liberationists such as Dussel, who have rejected the impracticability of the poor as sinful or a remnant of colonial practices, but have never learnt anything from that. Lancaster compares transvestism with popular carnivals in Latin America, as part of the 'revolt of the Queers' festival (Lancaster 1997: 21). I have been the witness of several carnivals in my own country, Argentina, which is also Dussel's country. I have seen the transvestite Jesuses, surrounded by their Drag Queen versions of the Veronica and the Magdalena (this last one, the object of veneration in many transgender communities of the poor). Jesuses with false eyelashes surrounding big, sad gay eyes and Magdalenes with wigs, penises and breasts, marching at night in the illuminated city and provoking the admiration from the public by the finery of their clothes and presentation. Why do the poor, on the only annual occasion where anyone can publicly represent herself as she pleases, present shows with transvestite Jesuses? Why this sexual and gender confusion in a popular festival where songs assume politically critical tones and entire poor communities live and work just for that annual celebration? Because political identities are sexual identities. Gender and sexual confusion are chaotic in intention: it is not, however, the chaos of the flesh, but the chaos of sexual premises in our trusted ideologies which we should be scared of.

As the situation in Latin America deteriorates economically under the Savage Capitalism which does not recognise restraint in its virile sexual assumptions and hierarchical urges, and globalisation processes govern the world as if it were a domestic scene where the weak (as in a symbolic of women) are to be told and must obey, sexuality in the Third World is still considered a peripheral issue. For developmentalists, it is an issue of balance and gender equality in the context of what is generally perceived as women's role in societies anyway; for neo-liberals, a discourse which glosses over the contradiction of patriarchalism and capitalism, and the sex/class/race realism which obliterates market opportunities. For North Atlantic theologians still disengaged from theological reflections from the Third World it is not even an issue to address. For liberationists, the panorama is as for developmentalism, a sexual equilibrium of a yin/yang mystique. In Feminist Theologies, and especially in Queer Theology, the yin/yang mystique has been supplanted by indecent thinking as constitutive of the integral theologians we want to be. Integral theologians are theologians who come out in their pursuit of honesty and engagement with the real and, like Guto, grab a blouse and a lipstick and per/vert the normative socio/theological script, unveil obscenity and are able to see, from sexual stories at the bottom of Rubin's sexual pyramid, tales of God and criticism of political systems. Indecent Sexual Theologies do not need to have a teleology, or a system, yet they may be effective as long as they represent the resurrection of the excessive in our contexts, and a passion for organising the lusty transgressions of theological and political thought. The excessiveness of our hungry lives: our hunger for food, hunger for the touch of other bodies, for love and for God; a multitude of hungers never satisfied which grow and expand and put us into risky situations and challenge, like a carnival of the poor, the textbooks of the normalisers of life. The hypocritical adulterers who preach marriage morals on Sunday while in their own lives they know that monogamous relationships cannot always be satisfactory. The theologians of heterosexuality, who lust in secret silence for the sight of some of their own biological sex. The unhappiness of the just, who have not seen that only in the longing for a world of economic and sexual justice together, and not subordinated to one another, can the encounter with the divine take place. But this is an encounter to be found at the crossroads of desire, when one dares to leave the ideological order of the heterosexual pervasive normative. This is an encounter with indecency, and with the indecency of God and Christianity. The way of Per/versions, and the path of Un-Just Messiahs, of twisted hermeneutical options in the road of thinking theology, politics and gender from our sexual experiences and identities. Thinking theology without using underwear.

Notes

Introduction: The fragrance of Women's Liberation Theology

1 By *out-of-the-closet-heterosexuality* we refer to the understanding that hetero-sexuality as a sexual option cannot be defined by compulsory heterosexual definitions. In the same way that gay, lesbian and bisexual identities need to be liberated from heterosexual patterns of understanding, so does the reality of heterosexual experience which is also in the closet. This point is further developed in Chapter 4.

1 Indecent proposals for women who would like to do theology without using underwear

1 An example of this is the worship of the 'Bandit Saints' in Argentina. Bandits who were supposed to be good in their communities have acquired saintly status, and their persecution by police is mythologised as a struggle of the bandits against evil laws in society. Consider also Santa Librada, who is a crucified woman Christ in Argentina, and also protector of minor thieves.
2 For rituals of symbolic political legitimisation of order, their justification and motivations for subordination, see Fedel 1991: 70.
3 Althusser said that during the 1960s he was a kind of philosophical warrior, 'cutting' reality with the (knife) of class only. Later he understood other sorts of cuttings were necessary (Navarro 1988).
4 See, for instance, Sobrino and Ellacuría 1993b. Of sixteen chapters, the only chapter written by Latin American women theologians is that by Ivonne Gebara and Maria C. Bingemer entitled, 'Mary'. In *Vida, clamor y Esperanza. Aportes desde Latinoamérica* (Autores Varios 1992), of forty-two articles, only three are written by women theologians: Maria C. Bingemer on the church of the poor, which curiously does not mention women in the reflection, Ivonne Gebara writing on Mary, and Ana Maria Tepedino and Maragrida Brandao writing an article on women as modern Mary Magdalenes, or theology with a woman's 'heart'. In *Presente y Future de la Teología de la Liberacion* by J. J. Tamayo (1994) of 213 pages only 8 are dedicated to Feminist Theology.
5 In 1948, during the debate on the modification of law 13010, allowing women to vote, the then deputy Eduardo Colon spoke in the Parliament in Buenos Aires in support of women's voting, full of confidence about the exquisite sensibility of the Argentinian woman who would not turn – as he claimed the Anglo-Saxon women did – to fight for equal rights with men even if they voted (Navarro 1981: 222).

6 This argument follows Daphne Hampson's seminal point on Jesus Christ's resurrection as having broken the historical causal nexus with nature; resurrection cannot happen in human history (Hampson 1990: 10).

2 The indecent Virgin

1 The painting *Portrait of the Artist as the Virgin of Guadalupe* by Yolanda López has been reproduced for the 'Calendario de la Raza 1999' (USA: Pomegranate, 1998).

2 The seers of the apparitions of the Virgin Mary frequently go through processes of fasting and silence. See, for instance, the modern case of the woman who claims to have been seeing the Virgin of San Nicolás in Argentina. The report from her priest, Father Pérez, to the bishop reads '. . . She is learning to be silent in her house and among the few people she normally speaks with . . . [her dialogue with] the Lord makes her quieter, at the cost of any desire to communicate what she is experiencing' (Laurentin 1995: 37). Also, she claims that the Virgin asked her to fast. "After fasting . . . I eat little. Each time I need less [food]' (Laurentin 1995: 42).

3 The faithfulness to the cause of liberation in Latin America is such a strong theological commitment that it is common for theologians to sign personal letters with words such as 'For God's project of justice and liberation of Latin America" or "Let us keep faithful to our God of liberation. . .'

4 Although outdated, and not a textbook to recommend to readers of Feminist Theology, it is worth noticing that Leonardo Boff published 'The Maternal Face of God' in 1985. The book is another Mariological reflection with emphasis on a liberal complementarity and equality between 'the two sexes' while introducing Marxist analysis, and apparently unaware of his own contradictions. Curiously, the book does not mention any work from Latin American women theologians, which were already well known.

5 See, for instance, Leonardo Boff's 'Good News to the Poor' (L. Boff 1992), where he attempts to elaborate a whole 'hermeneutical circle' from the Virgin of Guadalupe story. Enrique Dussel mentions the Virgin of Guadalupe in several of his articles and in his book 'La Invención de las Américas' (Dussel 1995).

6 One of the messages of the Virgin of San Nicolás expresses this in clear words: 'I give you biblical citations with my messages so that the world may see that they are authentic' (Laurentin 1995: 91).

7 See for instance, Luis Rivera Pagán's comments on the feminist zeal of the *Guadalupana* in Rivera Pagán 1995.

8 During the repression of the 1970s in Argentina, dogs were set to bite and dismember the male genitalia of political prisoners. This becomes meaningful in the context of the discourses of 'subversive communists' as non-virile, or effeminate persons. Therefore, it seems that the *Aperramiento* model identified the homosexual and determined his ritual killing too in Latin America. Castration was a widespread practice (Graziano 1992: 155).

9 For this point concerning hegemonic definitions of the poor, contrasted with the diversity of the communities such as BECs, see Vázquez 1998, especially part IV.

10 For the use of the term *Basileia* see Schüssler Fiorenza 1993: 10. The *Mujerista* theologian Ada Isasi Diaz has used the term 'Kindom' which unfortunately only makes sense in English. The fact is that to say Kingdom, *Reino* or Kindom carries with it the contextualisation of the concept according to either grounded political experiences and expectations or to idealistic theological conceptualisations. However, Kingdom is a site of contest both in contextual theologies and feminist (not always contextualised) theologies too.

11 The so-called Indian Virgins in Latin America made of dark wood therefore have dark faces. In many instances, the Roman Catholic Church has covered them with silver or gold to give an illusion of whiteness (Puchuri de Martini 1984: 14, 22).

3 Talking obscenities to theology: theology as a sexual act

1 Butler defines the heterosexual matrix as '(the) grid of cultural intelligibility through which bodies, genders and desires are naturalised' (Butler 1990: 151).
2 *Sous rature* is Derrida's term for his concept of 'under erasure'. It means that a word may be inadequate or inaccurate to express a concept, yet it needs to remain legible. Derrida usually strikes through words that are 'sous rature'. See Sarup 1988: 35.
3 See, for instance, Daphne Hampson's argument on the difficulties of presenting a female Christ (Hampson 1990). Her main point is that although it may be easy to have a black Christ, to have a female one is more complicated since maleness (in the sense of heterosexual constructions) seems to be quintessential to the conceptualisation of Christ. Although Hampson does not have any sexual theory and indulges in dualistic analysis such as 'low Christologies' and 'high Christologies', her equation of Christ and heterosexual man in Systematic Theology is correct.
4 This is a popular exegesis which was suggested to me in dialogue with some friends of the Metropolitan Community Church in Argentina. It owes a lot to the Liberation Theology style of starting from experience and then approaching the text for further illumination on the subject. As a result of sharing some sexual stories, someone made the comment that perhaps Lazarus did not want to compromise Jesus in public, but Jesus could not stand that. Lustful and passionate, this is about good love between two men and the difficulties of damaging the public image of one of them.

4 The theology of sexual stories

1 '*Laberinto de Pasiones*: About the Struggle and Hopes of Christian Women on Reaching Some Promised Land', a conference paper presented to the Forum of European Ecumenical Women, El Escorial, Spain, June 1998. Printed for internal distribution.
2 'Admiracao' in Portuguese. This is the term Paulo Freire used to describe Paul Ricoeur's concept of hermeneutical distanciation, originally from Husserl (Ricoeur 1991: 75); (Freire 1970: 90).
3 *Taitien* means 'daddy' in Quechua.
4 See, for instance, the Informe Nunca Mas (CONADEP 1994). For a detailed study of the link between torture, sexuality and military repression in Argentina see Graziano 1992.

5 *Grandes medidas económicas*

1 Collocation Community is a concept which comes from Italian feminist thought (Collocazione Symbolica). It refers to the community of women who engage in dialogue outside the boundaries of time and space and allows us to relate to the experience and struggle of women in other times, past , present or even future – in the future of a dreamed utopia – and from different geographical contexts.
2 Statistics from 'A Letter of Concern and Hope' signed by twenty-eight European based theologians, 30 June 1998.

3 In Spanish, 'Subject' is *Sujeto,* a masculine noun, and is used in such terms as *'Sujeto Histórico'* (Historical subject). The feminine noun, *'Sujeta'* has other connotations heavily relying on concepts of subordination and physical or moral constraint, which are lost in the masculine version.

Bibliography

Abelove, H., Barale, M.A. and Halperin, D.M. (1993) *The Lesbian and Gay Studies Reader,* New York: Routledge.

Abós, A. (1985) *El Poder Carnívoro,* Buenos Aires: Legasa.

Althaus-Reid, M.M. (1993) 'Walking with women serpents', *Ministerial Formation,* 62: 31–41.

—— (1994) 'When God is a rich white woman who does not walk. The Hermeneutical Circle of Mariology in Latin America', *Theology and Sexuality,* 1 (September): 55–72.

—— (1995) 'Do not stop the flood of my blood. A critical Christology of hope amongst Latin American women', *Studies in World Christianity,* 1, (2): 143–59.

—— (1996) 'Doing the Theology of the Memory' in M. Best and P. Hussey (eds) *Life Out of Death. The Feminine Spirit in El Salvador,* London: CIIR.

—— (1997) 'Sexual strategies in Practical Theology: Indecent Theology and the plotting of desire with some degree of success', *Theology and Sexuality,* 7 (September): 45–52.

—— (1998) 'Reconciliation in the struggle. Theological reflections from the rebellious women from Latin America' in B. Butler (ed.) *Open Hands. Reconciliation, Justice & Peace around the World,* Suffolk: Kevin Mayhew.

—— (1999) 'On using skirts without using underwear. Indecent Theology contesting the Liberation Theology of the Pueblo. Poor women contesting Christ', *Feminist Theology,* 20 (January): 39–51.

Althusser, L. (1971) 'Ideology and ideological state apparatuses' in B. Brewster (trans.) *Lenin and Philosophy and other Essays,* London: New Left Books.

—— (1984) *Essays on Ideology,* London: Verso.

Altizer, T.J.J. and Myers, M. (1982) (eds) *De-Construction and Theology,* New York: Crossroad.

Arcadio (1996), *Trabajos de Medianoche con Exú y Pomba Gira,* Haedo: Bermejo.

Archenti, N. (1994) 'Las Mujeres, la Política y el Poder. De la Lógica del Príncipe a la Lógica de la Acción Colectiva', in D.H. Maffia and C. Kuschnir (eds) *Capacitación Política para Mujeres. Género y Cambio Social en la Argentina Actual,* Buenos Aires: Femimaria.

Audi, R. (1995) (ed.) *The Cambridge Dictionary of Philosophy,* Cambridge: Cambridge University Press.

Autores Varios (1992) *Vida, Clamor y Esperanza. Aportes desde Latinoamérica,* Buenos Aires: Paulinas.

Bahbha, H.K. (1994) *The Location of Culture,* London: Routledge.

Bajo, García P. (1980) *Maria Reina y Madre de los Argentinos. Breve Reseña de Historia Mariana Argentina*, Buenos Aires: Gram.

Baldwin, G. (1993) *Ties that Bind. The S/M/Leather/Fetish Erotic Style*, San Francisco: Daedalus.

Barrett, M. and Phillips, A. (1992) *Destabililising Theory. Contemporary Feminist Debates*, Standford, California: Standford University Press.

Barthes, R. (1993) *Camera Lucida. Reflections on Photography*, trans. R. Howard, London: Vintage.

Battaille, G. (1994) *Eroticism*, trans. M. Dalwood, London: Marion Boyars.

Battersby, C. (1989) *Gender and Genius. Towards a Feminist Aesthetics*, London: The Women's Press.

Baudelaire (1989) in F. Scarfe (ed., introd. and trans.) *Baudelaire Vol. II The Poems in Prose and La Fanfarlo*, London: Anvil Press Poetry.

Baudrillard, J. (1990) *Seduction*, New York: St Martin's Press.

Beckford, R. (1998) *Jesus is Dread. Black Theology and Black Culture in Britain*, London: Darton, Longman and Todd.

Benhabib, S., Butler, J., Cornell, D. and Fraser, N. (1990) *Feminist Contentions. A Philosophical Exchange*, London: Routledge.

Bernal Diaz (1963) *The Conquest of New Spain*, trans. and introd. J.M. Cohen, Harmondsworth, Middlesex: Penguin Books.

Blaustein, E. And Zubieta, M. (1999) (eds) *Deciamos Ayer. La Prensa Argentina bajo el Proceso*, Buenos Aires: Ediciones Colihue.

Bocchetti, A. (1993) 'La Indecente Diferencia', *Debate Feminista*, 3, 16: 219–34.

Boff, C. (1987) *Theology and Praxis. Epistemological Foundations*, New York: Orbis.

Boff, L. (1986) *Y La Iglesia se Hizo Pueblo. Ecclesiogénesis: La Iglesia que Nace de la Fé del Pueblo*, Santander: Sal Terrae.

—— (1985) *El Rostro Materno de Dios. Ensayo Interdisciplinar sobre lo Femenino y sus Formas Religiosas*, Buenos Aires: Paulinas.

—— (1992) *Good News to the Poor. A New Evangelisation*, New York: Orbis.

Braidotti, R. (1994) 'What's Wrong with Gender?' in F.van Dijk-Hemmes and A. Brenner (eds) *Reflection on Theology & Gender*, Kampen: Kok Pharos.

Bright, S. (1997) *The Sexual State of the Union*, New York: Touchstone, Simon and Schuster.

—— (1998) 'Susie Bright Sexpest', Channel 4 Documentary (5/10/98).

Butler, J. (1990) *Gender Trouble. Feminism and the Subversion of Identity*, London: Routledge.

—— (1993) *Bodies that Matter. On the Discursive Limits of 'Sex'*, London: Routledge.

Cabral, A. (1973) *Return to the Sources: Selected Speeches*, New York and London: Monthly Review Press.

Califia, P. (1998) *S/M. Sensuous Magic. A Guide for Adventurous Couples*, New York: Masquerade Books.

Caputo, J.D. (1997a) *Deconstruction in a Nutshell. A Conversation with Jacques Derrida*, New York: Fordham University Press.

—— (1997b) *The Prayers and Tears of Jacques Derrida. Religion Without Religion*, Bloomington: Indiana University Press.

Caraballo, L., Charlier, N. and Garulli, L. (1998) *La Dictadura (1976–1983). Testimonios y Documentos*, Buenos Aires: EUDEBA.

Cardoso Pereira, N. (1994) 'Tempos de Remissão', *Mandrágora*, 1: 83.

Carmichael, C. (1979) *Women, Law and the Genesis Traditions*, Edinburgh: Edinburgh University Press.

Carrasco A., V.H. (1995) *Espiritualidad y Fé de los Pueblos Indígenas. Ensayos*, Ecuador: INPPI.

Carter, Heyward I. (1989) *Speaking of Christ: A Lesbian Feminist Voice*, New York: The Pilgrim Press.

Las Casas, B. (1953) *Brevísima Relación de la Destrucción de las Indias*, Buenos Aires: Mar Océano.

Castillo, D.A. (1998) *Easy Women. Sex and Gender in Modern Mexican Fiction*, Minneapolis: University of Minnesota Press.

The Catholic World Report, San Francisco, Nov. 1997.

Chertudi, S. and Newbery, S.J. (1978) *La Difunta Correa*, Buenos Aires: Huemul.

Christina, G. (1997) 'Are we having sex now or what?' in A. Soble (ed.) *The Philosophy of Sex. Contemporary Readings*, Oxford: Rowman & Littlefield Publishers.

Clark, J.M. (1989*)* *A Place to Start. Towards an Unapologetic Gay Liberation Theology*, Dallas: Monument Press.

Collings, J. (1998a) 'Closer to God', *Skin Two*, 27 (Autumn): 49–52.

Collings, J. (1998b) 'Once a Catholic', *Skin Two*, 27 (Autumn): 63–65.

CONADEP (1994) *Nunca Más. Informe de la Comisión Nacional Sobre la Desaparición de Personas*, Buenos Aires: EUDEBA.

Corinne, T. (1987) *Dreams of the Woman who Loved Sex. A Collection*, Austin, Texas: Banned Books.

Correa, R. and Subercaseaux, E. (1996) *Ego Sum*, Santiago: Planeta.

Croatto, J. S. (1973) *Liberación y Libertad. Pautas Hermeneuticas*, Buenos Aires: Mundo Nuevo.

—— (1983) 'The Gods of Oppression', in P. Richards (ed.) *The Idols of Death and the God of Life. A Theology*, New York: Orbis.

Cruden, A. (1909) *A Complete Concordance to the Holy Scriptures of the Old and New Testaments*, London: Ward, Lock and Co, Ltd.

Daly, M. (1978) *Gyn/Ecology. The Metaethics of Radical Feminism*, London: The Women's Press.

—— (1984) *Pure Lust. Elemental Feminist Theology*, London: The Women's Press.

Danto, A.C. (1975) *Sartre*, Glasgow: Fontana/Collins.

Daumer, E. (1992) 'Queer Ethics', *Hypathia*, 7, (Fall): 98.

Davis, J. and Loughlin, G. (1997) (eds) *Sex these Days. Essays on Theology, Sexuality and Society*, Sheffield: Sheffield Academic Press.

Deleuze, G. and Guattari, F. (1988) *A Thousand Plateaus. Capitalism and Schizofrenia*, London: The Athlone Press.

Derrida, J. (1972) *Marges de Philosophie*, Paris: Du Minuit.

—— (1989) *La Deconstrucción en las Fronteras de la Filosofía. La retirada de la Metáfora*, trans. P. Peñalver, Barcelona: Paidós.

—— (1998) 'Faith and knowledge: the two sources of religion at the limits of reason alone', in J. Derrida and G. Vattimo (eds) *Religion*, Cambridge: Polity Press.

Di Leonardo, M. (1991) (ed.) *Gender at the Crosswords of Knowledge: Feminist Anthropology in the PostModern Era*, Berkeley: University of California Press.

Dixon, P. (1998) 'Female sexual characteristics in Christ and Christianity'. Online. Available HTTP: http://www.postfun.com/pfp/features/98/jun/wound.html (June 1998).

Doble Jornada (1997) Marzo 7.

Dupeyron, G.R. (1992) *De Indios Imaginarios e Indios Reales en los relatos de la Conquista de México*, México: Tava.

Dussel, E. (1977) *Filosofía Etica Latinoamericana*, vol. 3, México: Edicol.

—— (1981) *La Producción Teórica de Marx. Un Comentario a los Grundrisse*, México: Siglo XXI.

—— (1985) *Filosofía de la Liberación*, Buenos Aires: La Aurora.

—— (1988) *Hacia un Marx Desconocido. Un Comentario de los Manuscritos del 61–63*, México: Iztapalapa.

—— (1993) *Las Metáforas Teológicas de Marx*, Stella (Navarra): Verbo Divino.

—— (1995) *The Invention of the Americas. Eclipse of the Other and the Myth of Modernity*, New York: Continuum.

Eagleton, T. (1992) *Literary Theory. An Introduction*, London: Basil Blackwell.

Easton, L. D. and Guddat, K. H. (1967) *Writings of the Young Marx on Philosophy and Society*, USA: Anchor Books.

Easton, S. (1994) *The Problem of Pornography. Regulation and the Right to Free Speech*, London: Routledge.

Estrada, J. (1996) *Virgen de Medianoche*, México: Patria.

Evans, J. (1996) *Feminist Theory Today. An Introduction to Second Wave Feminism*, London: Sage.

Fabella, V. (1992) 'The Development of Women's Theological Consciousness within the Ecumenical Association of Third World Theologians', Dissertation, San Francisco Theological Seminary.

Fanon, F. (1959) *Studies in Dying Colonialism*, trans. H. Chevalier, New York: Grove (1965, reissued 1970).

—— (1961) *The Wretched of the Earth*, trans. C. Farrington, New York: Grove.

Fedel, G. (1991) *Simboli e Politica*, Napoli: Morano Editori, 1991.

Finkel, S. and Gorbato, V. (1995) *Amor y Sexo en la Argentina. La Vida Erótica en los '90*, Buenos Aires: Planeta.

Foster, D.W. (1997) *Sexual Textualities. Essays on Queering Latin American Writing*, Austin: University of Texas Press.

Foucault, M. (1980) *Power/Knowledge: Selected Interviews and Other Writings, 1972–1977*, trans. C. Gordon, New York: Pantheon.

Freire, P. (1970) *Pedagogía del Oprimido*, Montevideo: Siglo XXI.

Gane, M. (1993) *Baudrillard Live. Selected Interviews*, London: Routledge.

Garber, M. (1992) *Vested Interests. Cross-Dressing and Cultural Anxiety*, London: Routledge.

Garcilaso de la Vega, I. (1996) *Commentaries of the Incas and General History of Perú*, translated and edited by H.V. Livermore, Austin and London: University of Texas Press.

Gebara, I. and Bingemer, M.C. (1989) *Mary, Mother of God, Mother of the Poor*, Maryknoll: Orbis.

Gibbs, P. (1996) *The Word in the Third World. Divine Revelation in the Theology of Jean-Marc Ela, Aloysius Pieris and Gustavo Gutiérrez*, Roma: Pontificia Universita Gregoriana.

Gollock, G. (1909) *Aunt Africa. A Family Affair*, London: CMS.

Goss, R. (1993) *Jesus Acted Up. A Gay and Lesbian Manifesto*, New York: Harper and Collins.

Gramsci, A. (1971) *Selections from the Prison Notebooks*, ed. and trans. by Q. Hoare and G. Nowell Smith, London: Lawrence and Wishart.

Graziano, F. (1992) *Divine Violence. Spectacle, Psychosexuality, & Radical Christianity in the Argentine 'Dirty War'*, Boulder: Westview Press.

—— (1997) *The Lust of Seeing. Themes of the Gaze and Sexual Rituals in the Fiction of Felisberto Hernández*, Lewisburg: Bucknell University Press.

Guy, D. J. (1991) *Sex and Danger in Buenos Aires: Prostitution, Family and Nation in Argentina*, Lincoln: University of Nebraska Press.

Hall, D. E. and Pramaggiore, M. (1996) *RePresenting Bisexualities. Subjects and Cultures of Fluid Desires*, New York: New York University Press.

Halperin, D., Winkler, J. and Zeitlin, F. (1990) (eds) *Before Sexuality. The Construction of the Erotic Experience in the Ancient Greek World*, Princeton: Princeton University Press.

Hampson, D. (1990) *Theology and Feminism*, London: Basil Blackwell.

Harvey, D. (1989) *The Condition of Postmodernity. An Inquiry into the Origins of Cultural Exchange*, London: Basil Blackwell.

Harvey, I (1986) *Derrida and the Economy of Différance*, Indiana: Indiana University Press.

Hedges, W. (1998) 'Textual Poaching', *Terms*. Online. Available HTTP: http://www.sou.edu/English/IDTC/Terms/terms.htm (29 April 1998).

Heijerman, M. (1994), 'Who would blame her? The "Strange" Woman of Proverbs 7', in F. van Dijk-Hemmes and A. Brenner (eds) *Reflection on Theology & Gender*, Kampen: Kok Pharos.

Hemming, J. (1993) *The Conquest of the Incas*, London: Macmillan.

Herdt, G. (1196) (ed.) *Third Sex, Third Gender. Beyond Sexual Dimorphism in Culture and History*, New York: Zone Books.

Hinkelammert, F. (1991) *Sacrificios Humanos y Sociedad Occidental: Lucifer y la Bestia*, Costa Rica: DEI.

Holloway, W. (1984) 'Gender, Difference and the Production of Subjectivity', in W. Holloway and J. Henriques (eds) *Changing the Subject: Psychology, Social Regulation and Subjectivity*, London: Methuen.

Humm, M. (1991) (ed.) *Border Traffic: Strategies of Contemporary Women Writers*, Manchester: Manchester University Press.

Jagose, A. (1996) *Queer Theory. An Introduction*, New York: New York University Press.

Jenkins, H. (1992) *Textual Poachers. Television Fans and Participatory Culture*, London: Routledge.

Kearney, R. (1984) *Dialogues with Contemporary Philosophical Thinkers. The Phenomenological Heritage*, Manchester: Manchester University Press.

Kee, A. (1990) *Marx and the Failure of Liberation Theology*, London: SCM.

Kiely, R. (1995) *Sociology of Development: The Impasse and Beyond*, London: UCL Press.

King, U. (1994) (ed.) *Feminist Theology from the Third World. A Reader*, London: SPCK.

Kobia, S. (1998) 'Africa is Re-Awakening', *Echoes*, 14: 7.

Kristeva, J (1984) *Desire in Language. A Semiotic Approach to Literature and Art*, Oxford: Basil Blackwell.

Laclau, E. and Mouffe, C. (1985) *Hegemony and Socialist Strategy. Towards a Radical Democratic Politics*, London: Verso.

Laclau, E. (1990) *New Reflections on the Revolution of our Time*, London: Verso.
—— (1996) 'Deconstruction, Pragmatism, Hegemony', in C. Mouffe (ed.) *Deconstruction and Pragmatism*, London: Routledge.
Lagarde, M. (1994) 'Hacia una Nueva Constituyente desde las Mujeres', *La Jornada*, August 8.
Lamas, M (1994) 'Democracia, e igualdad política y diferencia sexual', *Topodrilo 35.* Online. Available HTTP: http://www.iztapalapa.uam.mx/iztapalapa.www/topodrillo/35/td35_04.html.
Lancaster, R. (1997) 'Guto's Performance', in D. Balderston and D.J. Guy (eds) *Sex and Sexuality in Latin America*, New York: New York University Press.
Laurentín, R. (1995) *An Appeal from Mary in Argentina.The Apparitions of San Nicolás*, Great Wakering Essex: McCrimmons.
Lavrin, A. (1992) *Sexuality and Marriage in Colonial Latin America*, Lincoln and London: University of Nebraska Press.
Lawson, A. (1989) *Adultery. An Analysis of Love and Betrayal*, Oxford: Basil Blackwell.
León-Portilla, M. (1986) *Tiempo y Realidad en el Pensamiento Maya*, México: UNAM.
Liboreiro, M. C. (1992) 'La Evangelisación en la Colonia' in CEHILA (eds), *500 Años de Cristianismo en la Argentina*, Buenos Aires: Centro Nueva Tierra.
Lin Piao (1967) *Quotations from Chairman Mao Tse-Tung*, Peking: Foreign Languages Press.
Loomba, A. (1998) *Colonialism/Postcolonialism*, London: Routledge.
López-Cano, M. del P. Martínez (1995) (ed.) *Iglesia, Estado y Economía. Siglos XVI al XIX*, México: UNAM.
Lorde, A. (1994) 'Age, race, class and sex: women redefining difference', in H. Crowley and S. Himmelweit (eds) *Knowing Women. Feminism and Knowledge*, Cambridge: Polity Press.
McLellan, D. (1979) (ed.) *Marx's Grundrisse*, London: Paladin.
Marías, J. (1967) *History of Philosophy*, trans. S. Appelbaum and C. C. Strowbridge, New York: Dover.
Marini, M. (1992) *Jacques Lacan. The French Context*, New Jersey: Rutgers University Press.
Martini, M. Puchuri de (1984) *Imágenes de la Virgen en nuestro País*, Buenos Aires: L. Buschi.
Marx, K. (1939–41) *Grundrisse der Kritik de Politischen Oekonomie (Rohrntwurf)*, vol. 1–2, Moscow: Institute for Marxism-Leninism.
—— (1976) *The German Ideology*, Moscow: Progress Publishers.
Melhuus, M. and Stølen, K.A. (1996) *Machos, Mistresses, Madonnas*, New York: Verso.
Mendiola, S. (1994) 'Los Indios como Dispositivo Teológico y Fetiche', *Debate Feminista*, 5 (9): 457–60.
Mesters, C. (1960) *Rut. Comentario Bíblico Ecuménico*, Buenos Aires: La Aurora.
Mies, M. (1986) *Patriarchy and Accumulation on a World Scale: Women in the International Division of Labour*, London: Zed Press.
Mignone, E.F. (1986) *Iglesia y Dictadura. El Papel de la Iglesia a la Luz de sus Relaciones con el Régimen Militar*, Buenos Aires: EPN.
Miller, J.A. (1990) (ed.) *El Yo en la Teoría de Freud y en la Técnica Psicoanalítica: 1954–1955*, Colección el Seminario, vol. 2, Buenos Aires: Paidós.
Misfud, T. (1997) *Economía de Mercado. Interrogantes Eticos para una Acción Solidaria*, Santiago de Chile: San Pablo.

Moffatt, A. (1988) *Psicoterapia del Oprimido. Ideología y Técnica de la Psiquiatría Popular,* Buenos Aires: Humanitas.

Montes de Oca, E. (1995) *Guía Negra de Buenos Aires. Marginalisación en la Gran Ciudad,* Buenos Aires: Planeta.

Moore, H.L. (1994) *A Passion for Difference. Essays in Anthropology and Gender,* Bloomington and Indianapolis: Indiana University Press.

Morales, J.A. and McMahon, G. (1996) (eds) *Economic Policy and the Transition to Democracy. The Latin American Experience,* London: Macmillan.

Morton, D. (1996) (ed.) *The Material Queer. A Lesbigay Cultural Studies Reader,* Colorado: Westview Press.

Mouffe, C. (1992) 'Feminism, Citizenship and Radical Democratic Politics', in J. Butler and J.W Scott (eds) *Feminists Theorize the Political,* London: Routledge.

Nagel, S.S. (1994) (ed.) *Latin American Development and Public Policy,* London: St Martin's Press.

Nash, J. and Safa, H. (1976) *Sex and Class in Latin America,* New York: Praeger.

Navarro, F. (1988) *Filosofía y Marxismo. Entrevista con Louis Althusser,* México: Siglo XXI.

Navarro, M. (1981) *Evita,* Madrid: Corregidor.

Nelson, J. (1992) *The Intimate Connection. Male Sexuality, Masculine Spirituality,* London: SPCK.

Ober, F. (1883) *In the Wake of Columbus. Adventures of the Special Commissioner Sent by the World's Columbian Exposition to the West Indies,* Boston: Lotwrop.

Ortega y Gasset, J. (1969–71) *Obras Completas,* Madrid: Revista de Occidente.

Oyarzún, M.E. (1992) *Entrevista con el Gral Pinochet, Diario La Tercera de Chile* (September): 2.

Parker, R.G. (1991) *Bodies, Pleasures and Passions. Sexual Culture in Contemporary Brazil,* Boston: Beacon Press.

Pease, F. (1980) (transcriptions, prologue, notes and chronology) *Felipe Guamán Poma de Ayala. Nueva Coronica y Buen Gobierno,* Caracas: Biblioteca Ayacucho.

Pérez, L. and Castellanos U. (1994) 'No nos dejen solas. Entrevista con la Comandante Ramona', *Doble Jornada,* marzo 7.

Pérez, M. (1995) 'Situación, derechos y cultura de la mujer indígena'. Online. Available HTTP: http://creatividadfeminista.org/3–biblio/Chiapas%20%20Tomo%202/matilde2.html

Pérez, Herrero P. (1992) *América Latina y el Colonialismo Europeo (Siglos XVI-XVIII),* Madrid: Síntesis.

Perón, E. (1951) *La Razón de mi Vida,* Buenos Aires: Péuser.

Phillips, A. (1998) 'We're *cheating* our way to Heaven' *Skin, Two* 27 (Autumn): 65.

Plummer, K. (1995) *Telling Sexual Stories: Power, Change and Social Worlds,* London: Routledge.

Poe, E. A. (attributed to) (1998) 'Kissing God', *Diva* (November): 35.

Probyn, E. (1996) *Outside Belongings,* London: Routledge.

Quiroga, J. (1997) 'Homosexualities in a Tropic of Revolution', in D. Balderston and D.J. Guy (eds) *Sex and Sexuality in Latin America,* New York: New York University Press.

Raymond, J. (1991) *A Passion for Friends. Towards a Philosophy of Female Affection,* London: The Women's Press.

Rich, A. (1980) 'Compulsory heterosexuality and lesbian existence', *Signs,* 5(4): 31–60.

Ricoeur, P. (1967) *Le Volontaire et L'Involontaire*, Paris: Aubier Montagne.
—— (1974) *The Conflict of Interpretations*, Evanston: Northwestern University Press.
—— (1978) *The Rule of Metaphor. Multi-Disciplinary Studies of the Creation of Meaning in Language*, London: Routledge & Kegan Paul.
—— (1991) *From Text to Action. Essays in Hermeneutics II*, trans. K. Blamey and J. B. Thompson, London: The Athlone Press.
Rivera Pagán, L. (1995) *Entre el Oro y la Fé. El Dilema de América*, Puerto Rico: Universidad de Puerto Rico.
Rivero, S. (1996) 'salú! AMEPU al PIT-CNT', *Cotidiano Mujer, 22*.
Rose, G. (1997) *Love's Work*, London: Vintage.
Rubin, G. (1984) 'Thinking sex: notes for a radical theory of the politics of sexuality', in C. Vance (ed.) *Pleasure and Danger. Exploring Female Sexuality*, Boston: Routledge & Kegan Paul.
Said, E. (1993) *Culture and Imperialism*, London: Chatto and Windus.
Sartre, J. P. (1956) *Being and Nothingness*, trans. H. Barnes, New York: Philosophical Library.
Sarup, M. (1988) *An Introductory Guide to Post-Structuralism and Post-Modernism*, Worcester: Harvester Wheatsheaf.
Sauval, M. (1998) 'Ciencia, Psicoanálisis y Posmodernismo. Acerca del libro "Impostures Intellectuelles" de Sokal y Bricmont', *Acheronta*. Online. Available HTTP: http://www.acheronta.org/acheronta6/ciencia.html
Schüssler, Fiorenza E. (1993) *Discipleship of Equals*, London: SCM.
Skin Two (1998) Issue 27, London: Tim Woodward Publishing Ltd.
Sedgwick, E. Kosovsky (1990) *Epistemology of the Closet*, Berkeley: University of California Press.
Segundo, J.L. (1948) *Existencialismo, Filosofía y Poesía. Ensayo de Síntesis*, Buenos Aires: Espasa-Calpe.
—— (1982) *El Hombre de Hoy ante Jesus de Nazareth. Fé e Ideología*, Madrid: Cristiandad.
—— (1973) *Our Idea of God*, trans. J. Drury, New York: Orbis.
—— (1988) *El Dogma que Libera*, Santander: Sal Terrae.
Setel, D.T. (1985) 'Prophets and pornography: female sexual imagery in Hosea', in L. Russell (ed.) *Feminist Interpretation of the Bible*, Philadelphia: Westminster Press.
Simon, R. (1982) *Gramsci's Political Thought. An Introduction*, London: Lawrence and Wishart.
Smith, A.M. (1998) *Laclau and Mouffe*, London: Routledge.
Soble, A. (1997) *The Philosophy of Sex. Contemporary Readings*, Oxford: Rowman & Littlefield.
Sobrino, J. and Ellacuría, I. (1993a) (eds) *Mysterium Liberationis: Fundamental Concepts of Liberation Theology*, New York: Orbis.
—— (1993b) *Systematic Theology. Perspectives in Liberation Theology*, London: SCM.
Spiegelberg, H. (1989) 'The phenomenology of the look', *Journal of the British Society for Phenomenology*, 20(2): 107–23.
Stuart, E. (1995) *Just Good Friends. Towards a Lesbian and Gay Theology of Relationships*, London: Mowbray.
—— (1997) *Religion is a Queer Thing*, Sheffield: Sheffield University Press.
Suleiman, S.R. (1985) 'Writing and motherhood', in S. N. Garner, C. Kahane and M. Sprengnether (eds) *The (M)other Tongue*, Ithaca, New York: Cornell University Press.

Tamale Institute of Cross-Cultural Studies (1997) 'Culture and Development Seminar', *Newletter*, 20 (May).

Tamayo, J.J. (1994) *Presente y Futuro de la Teología de la Liberación*, Madrid: San Pablo.

Taylor, M. (1987) *Erring: A Post/Modern A/theology*, Chicago: University of Chicago Press.

Thatcher, A. (1978) *The Onthology of Paul Tillich*, New York: Oxford University Press.

Theunissen, M. (1984) *The Other: Studies in Social Anthropology on Husserl, Heidegger, Sartre and Buber*, Cambridge, Mass: MIT Press.

Tisdale, S. (1994) *Talk Dirty to Me. An Intimate Philosophy of Sex*, New York: Anchor Press.

Todorov, T. (1987) *La Conquista de América: El Problema del Otro*, México: Siglo XXI.

Trias, E. (1998) 'Thinking religion: the symbol and the sacred', in J. Derrida and G. Vattimo (eds) *Religion*, Cambridge: Polity Press.

Tribble, P. (1978) *God and the Rhetoric of Sexuality*, Philadelphia, PA: Fortress Press.

Van der Meer, T. (1996) 'Sodomy and the pursuit of a third sex in the early modern period', in G. Herdt (ed.) *Third Sex, Third Gender. Beyond Sexual Dimorphism in Culture and History*, New York: Zone Books.

Vázquez, M.A. (1998) *The Brazilian Popular Church and the Crisis of Modernity*, Cambridge: Cambridge University Press.

Verbitsky, H. (1987) *La Posguerra Sucia. Un Análisis de la Transición*, Buenos Aires: Legasa.

Vika, G. (1998) 'Don't stand on my story. A critical reflection on land and reconciliation in South Africa: its implication for the future of development,' unpublished MTh Dissertation, New College, The University of Edinburgh.

Vitale, L. (1986) *Historia del la Deuda Externa Latinoamericana y Entretelones del Endeudamiento Argentino*, Buenos Aires: Planeta.

Wamue, G. (1996) 'Gender, violence and exploitation: the widow's dilemma', in G. Wamue and M. Getui (eds) *Violence Against Women. Reflections by Kenyan Women Theologians*, Nairobi: Acton.

Waylen, G. (1996) *Gender in Third World Politics*, Buckingham: Open University Press.

Weeks, J. (1995) *Invented Moralities. Sexual Values in an Age of Uncertainty*, New York: Columbia University Press.

Weinberg, T. S. (1995) (ed.) *S & M. Studies in Dominance & Submission*, New York: Prometheus.

Westbrook, R. (1991) *Property and the Family in Biblical Law*, Sheffield: Sheffield University Press.

Weston, K. (1996) *Render me, Gender me. Lesbians Talk Sex, Class, Color, Nation, Studmuffins...* , New York: Columbia University Press.

White, A. (1960) *A History of Warfare of Science with Theology in Christendom*, vol. 2, New York: Dover.

Williams, R. (1977) *Marxism and Literature*, Oxford: Oxford University Press.

Wilson, N. (1995) *Our Tribe: Queer Folks, God, Jesus and the Bible*, San Francisco: Harper.

Young, K., Wolkowitz, C. and McCullagh, R. (1981) (eds) *Of Marriage and the Market: Women's Subordination in International Perspective*, London: CSE Books.

Zapata, M. (1997) 'Filosofía de la Liberación y Liberación de la Mujer. La Relación de Varones y Mujeres en la Filosofía Etica de Enrique Dussel', *Debate Feminista*, 16: 69–97.

Index

CPSIA information can be obtained
at www.ICGtesting.com
Printed in the USA
LVOW01s1804290317
528917LV00002B/141/P